Psychoanalytic Psychotherapy
in Institutional Settings

The EFPP Clinical Monograph Series

Editor-in-Chief: *John Tsiantis*

Associate Editors: *Brian Martindale* (Adult Section)
Didier Houzel (Child & Adolescent Section)
Alessandro Bruni (Group Section)

OTHER MONOGRAPHS IN THE SERIES

Psychoanalytic Psychotherapy in Institutional Settings

edited by
Julia Pestalozzi
SENIOR EDITOR

Serge Frisch
R. D. Hinshelwood
Didier Houzel

Foreword by
R. D. Hinshelwood

published by
KARNAC BOOKS

for

The European Federation
for Psychoanalytic Psychotherapy
in the Public Health Services

First published in 1998 by
H. Karnac (Books) Ltd.
58 Gloucester Road
London SW7 4QY

British Library Cataloguing in Publication Data

A C.I.P. record for this book is available from the British Library.

ISBN 1-85575-198-4

Edited, designed, and produced by Communication Crafts

Printed in Great Britain by BPCC Wheatons Ltd, Exeter

10 9 8 7 6 5 4 3 2 1

ACKNOWLEDGEMENTS

Editing a book means relating to a great number of people and learning about their thinking and their work. It is also an occasion for much gratitude. First of all I would like to extend warm thanks to all the contributing authors, who were not only very creative and industrious: they were also very kind and amazingly tolerant towards their editor's idiosyncrasies.

That editorial work remained a pleasure for most of the time is also, and to a large extent, due to the understanding and very active support I received both from the Editor-in-Chief of the EFPP Monograph Series, John Tsiantis, and from the co-editors, Serge Frisch, R. D. Hinshelwood, and Didier Houzel.

Translating the articles into English was a task for the authors. I should personally like to express my gratitude to Daphne Briggs for her unusual sensitivity, her professional input, and for all the trouble she took.

I would like to reserve especial and cordial thanks for Philippa Martindale. She has been immensely helpful and efficient in improving the text and the reference section, and in coordinating links between the authors, the editors, and the publishers, to whom, and in particular to Cesare Sacerdoti, I am much indebted for help and encouragement, as are all the editors of the EFPP Monograph series. Gratitude is also due to Eric King for his meticulous final copyediting.

I should also like to thank my husband, Karl Pestalozzi, who, kind and patient as ever, has heard more about a monograph than anyone could ever have wished for.

Julia Pestalozzi
Basle, February 1998

ABOUT THE AUTHORS

THEODOR CAHN (Switzerland), MD, specializes in psychiatry and psychotherapy. In the 1970s he was deeply influenced by the Italian Democratic Psychiatry Movement. Since 1979 he has been director of the State Mental Hospital of Liestal, near Basel. As well as being active in the Swiss EFPP, his main interest lies in the integration of psychoanalysis and social psychiatry within the frame of institutions.

REINMAR DU BOIS (Germany) is a child and adolescent psychiatrist. He has been Professor of Psychiatry and Medical Director of the Adolescent Psychiatric Department, Olgahospital Stuttgart, since 1995. He researches in the long-term in-patient treatment of severely disturbed adolescents, body experience in schizophrenia, psychotherapy of adolescent delinquents, sociology of childhood, and intrafamilial violence. His numerous publications include *Children's Anxieties, Young Schizophrenics between Everyday Life and Hospital Treatment*, and *Body Experience and Emotional Development*, and he is the editor of *The Scope of Interdisciplinary Co-operation in Child and Adolescent Schizophrenia*.

SERGE FRISCH (Luxembourg), MD, is a psychiatrist and a psychoanalyst. He is the Chairman of the EFPP. He is also the Founding Member of the Groupe D'Etude et de Recherche Clinique en Psychanalyse D'Enfant et D'Adulte (GERCPEA) in Luxembourg. He undertakes individual supervision in private practice as well as group supervision of institutions. He has published on various topics such as suicide, psychic crisis reactions, and the connections between psychotherapy and psychoanalysis.

LISELOTTE GRÜNBAUM (Denmark), MSc, is a senior psychologist, psychotherapist, and supervisor. She has many years' experience of clinical work and psychotherapy with children, adolescents, parents, and families, particularly with the implementation of out-patient psychotherapy with children in socially disadvantaged and traumatized families. She is a psychotherapist at the Research Centre for Torture Victims, Department for Children and Families, and is Chairwoman of the Danish Association of Child and Adolescent Psychanalyic Psychotherapy, as well as the Danish delegate of the EFPP (Child section). Her publications include those concerning the above topics and the treatment of the children of schizophrenic mothers.

MICHAEL GÜNTER (Germany) is a child and adolescent psychiatrist and psychoanalyst (DPV/IPA). He is Consultant at the Department of Child and Adolescent Psychiatry and Psychotherapy, Tübingen University. His research is in the long-term in-patient treatment of severely disturbed adolescents, art therapy, forensic adolescent psychiatry, and emotional adaptation of children under bone marrow transplantation. His numerous publications include the monograph *The History of Art Therapy in Psychiatric Hospitals*, and he is editor of *Offenders and Victims: Actual Aspects of Forensic Psychiatry in Childhood and Adolescence*.

ROBERT HALE (United Kingdom) is a psychoanalyst and Medical Director of the Portman Clinic and a Consultant Psychotherapist at the Tavistock Clinic. During psychiatric training his research interest was in the pharmacological and dynamic treatment of suicidal states. At the Portman Clinic, his interests have included the study of paedophilia and alleged ritual abuse, whilst at the Tavistock Clinic he runs a service for doctors in need of psychological help.

R. D. HINSHELWOOD (United Kingdom) is a psychiatrist and psycho-analyst. His interest in the dynamics of institutions arose from work in therapeutic communities (Marlborough Day Hospital, and The Cassel Hospital) and the application of psychoanalytic ideas to understanding the deleterious effects of institutional life on vulnerable people institutionalized in mental hospitals. His publication *What Happens in Groups* is on this topic. He has also published *A Dictionary of Kleinian Thought*, *Clinical Klein*, and *Therapy or Coercion*. He has recently taken up a post as Professor of Psychoanalysis at the Centre for Psychoanalytic Studies, University of Essex.

JULIA PESTALOZZI (Switzerland) qualified in clinical psychology in Budapest, in medicine in London, and specialized in psychiatry and psychotherapy for children and adolescents in Switzerland. She lives in Basel and works as a psychoanalyst, psychoanalytic psychotherapist, and supervisor in private practice. Her main interest lies in the field of psychoanalytic psychotherapy of psychoses, particularly of adolescents. She discussed her theoretical framework in *Psychotische Uebertragung als Chance* [Psychotic Transference as a Chance]. She is the Swiss delegate of the EFPP (Adult section).

RENÉ ROUSSILLON (France) is Professor of Clinical Psychology and Director of the Department of Clinical Psychology of the University of Lyon 2. He is also Director of the Research Group on the Representational Process and Symbolization. He is a full member of the IPA and *membre titulaire* of the Paris Psychoanalytic Society.

VALERIE SINASON (United Kingdom) is a Consultant Child Psychotherapist at the Tavistock Clinic and a research psychotherapist at St George's Hospital Medical School. She is currently completing a Department of Health–funded research project on patients alleging ritual abuse, based at the Portman Clinic. She is a poet and writer and has published several books, including *Mental Handicap and the Human Condition*, and edited *Treating Survivors of Satanist Abuse*.

WILHELM SKOGSTAD (United Kingdom) is a psychiatrist and psychotherapist who trained in Germany and more recently in Britain at the Tavistock Clinic, the Cassel Hospital, and the Institute of Psycho-Analysis in London. He has worked in a variety of medical, psychiatric, and psychotherapeutic institutions in Germany and the United Kingdom, among them various in-patient psychotherapy settings. He has a particular interest in institutional dynamics. He has worked at the Cassel Hospital since 1993 and is the Consultant Psychotherapist on the Adult Unit of the Cassel hospital.

ULRICH STREECK (Germany), MD, MA, is a psychiatrist, psychoanalyst, and sociologist. He is Professor and Medical Director of the Tiefenbrunn Clinic and Hospital for Psychotherapy, Psychiatry, and Psychosomatic Medicine of Lower Saxony in Germany. He is Past President of DGPT, the German psychoanalytic umbrella organization. He has conducted qualitative psychotherapy research on psychotherapeutic dialogues, group psychotherapy, and in-patient psychotherapy and is the editor of several books on clinical psychoanalysis and qualitative research.

M. J. VANSINA-COBBAERT (Belgium) has a PhD in psychology. She is a full member in the Belgian Psychoanalytic Society and in the International Psychoanalytic Association. She is a staff member at the Psychoanalytic Department of the St-Joseph University Centre in Kortenberg, Belgium, and a psychoanalyst in private practice. She is the author of a book and several articles in Dutch, French, and English in the fields of psychoanalysis, group dynamics, and organization development.

R. VERMOTE (Belgium), MD, is a member of the Belgium Psychoanalytic Association and the Flemish Association for Psychoanalytic Psychotherapy. He is a staff member at the psychoanalytic department of the St-Joseph University Centre in Kortenberg, Belgium, and a psychoanalyst in private practice.

MARTA VIGORELLI (Italy) is a member of the Italian Association for Psychoanalytical Psychotherapy (SIPP) and works as a fellow and member of the Board of Examinations in the University of Milan "Università degli studi". She is a psychotherapist and has extensive experience as supervisor in psychiatric institutions. She is the editor of *Institutione tra inerzia e cambiamento*, a collection of papers on the psychodynamic approach to work in the public sector.

CONTENTS

R. D. Hinshelwood

Patients who have to be admitted into institutions for treatment are the most difficult. This is to be expected. They have found insufficient help outside, and the world at large has usually had enough of them. This is not the usual beginning for a hopeful contract and consent for treatment. Indeed, the initial step may be one of deep suspicion and reluctance—and on both sides. Thus, psychotherapy conducted within an institution is rather special. Perhaps its specialness is the only enticing quality. Certainly, something is needed to explain the enthusiasm that is so evident in this book, in which the contributors have written generously and confidently about the difficulties and the challenge of the work, and their own solutions to the special problems.

Perhaps this unnatural enthusiasm spreads to editing this volume. Writing a foreword to and helping Julia Pestalozzi to edit this new monograph, which comes from sources across the cultures of Europe, feels like playing God. However, if I were God, I would not only ban trifling things like forewords, but I would seriously consider what I had done in bringing about a creation—

human beings—so skilled at forming institutions yet so unskilful at running them.

Somehow or other the human race is beset by institutions. They are an alien species competing with man to inhabit the globe—and who knows who will win the competition. The race is on. Our only weapon is to try to understand the beast. Our one advantage is that, for sure, *they* will never understand us.

The grip that institutions have on us can be traced from the early days of pastoralist societies, in which kinship systems and ceremonials placed everyone rigidly in place. Later, city-states and empires were dominated by the (usually blood-thirsty) power of religion and the churches. In the present day, our lacework of multinational organizations is entrapping the planet. How can we free ourselves from such a grip?

There is an idea that we can unpick the secret of institutions by particular concentration on healthcare institutions. Perhaps it is just because the latter, in which the most anxious people are congregated together, show us best the strongest pathological grip on the inmates. Over and over again we have to re-learn that a practice within an institution has to incorporate a practice of the institution itself.

Because those who come in need to an institution's door are the more disturbed, it is they who have the greatest impact on the people surrounding them, including the psychotherapy (or psychiatric) institution itself. Just because we, the staff within the institution, are experienced in this work, this does not mean that we are not all affected. We are. The disturbance is highly contagious, and, as we become affected, so the institution becomes distorted in one way or another. Frequently our highly charged work suffers from the creation of social defence systems, which arise, unconsciously, to support our defences against too much contagion from our patients.

This is a kind of institutional "countertransference" to the disturbance contained within the walls. Though it is not strictly appropriate to use such a term about an institution, countertransference is a useful analogy, since there definitely are institutional reactions. They seem to create distance from the contagious disturbances, and it is essential that we are aware of how our work is distorted by these reactions. We cannot have enough thoughts and writing about how things "ought to be". Only by constantly referring to these exhortations for proper work can we be helped to maintain our insight into how disturbed we have become. In my experience at the Cassel Hospital, it is the constant questioning that has protected the liveliness and responsiveness of a venerable old institution—and even that energy has been intermittent over its long life.

What are these people who are more than society can cope with? On the whole, they receive diagnoses by professionals as severe personality disorders (borderline or narcissistic), or psychotic. But, in the relationship terms that psychoanalytic psychotherapists are interested in, they either have problems of engaging and sustaining relationships, including therapeutic ones (the personality disorders), or they have profound difficulties in sustaining meaning in relationships and the purpose of symbols (the psychotics). However, it is not that they do not have relationships. It is that they use relationships with others in quite unusual ways—invariably, to encroach upon others psychologically, so that they endanger the balance of mind of both. Frequently, this mode of relating involves violent physical behaviour or severe self-harming. But even if they use words and ordinary communications, almost always they have a quite extreme impact. Instead of ordinary communication, a kind of acting-upon the mind of others takes place—a kind of "psychic" action, as it were, which invariably has a violent effect on the receiver of these actions—and that is what we have to contain in our institutions.

Psychoanalysis does not have a very good theory of what action is, and therefore it has trouble accounting for action without simply labelling it acting-out—and that is pathological. The point is that action is pathological in a psychoanalytic setting, in the consulting-room. But clearly some forms of action are highly necessary to keep the world going. When it comes to working with people in institutions, a lot more has to happen than just the verbal free-association of a psychoanalytic setting. We need a better theory of what action is—and what it is not.

This is similar to the problem that psychoanalysis has had with symbols. In the first place, symbols were all regarded as pathological (or more or less so), because the theory started with Freud's interpretation of dreams: symbols are simply distortions and concealment of truth. This is not a good starting point, as symbols are highly useful as well and are, in fact, the basis of all culture and the success of the human race.

Now, it is not just that these two problems—of action and of symbols—are alike. They are in fact related. We are interested in those occurrences when action takes place *because* symbols fail. This separates one class of action from all others, and it points towards the process of symbol-formation and those occurrences when it fails.

We can clarify this by saying that there is a need for a distinction, which psychoanalysis has not been good at, between action *upon* others and symbolic communication *with* them. We have recovered somewhat from those faulty early beginnings, and there are now some serviceable psychoanalytic theories of symbols which can form the basis for an adequate distinction: I am thinking of Lacan and of the work of Bion and Segal. In this book, Roussillon is claiming, rightly I think, that the home of symbols *is* the institution—therefore we need the institution in order to help with problems when the development and use of symbols is faulty.

All this is a complicated way of saying that our institutions are places where ordinary communication fails, and that we, as staff, have a dual function—to police the acting (physical and psychic), and also to take in, without too much flinching, the emotional impact of those actions. At moments, we can certainly feel these functions come together in us—we can then set and defend limits, whilst also containing distress. But, so often, these functions come apart, creating a conflict between harsh discipline versus sentimental sympathy.

We need to be continually vigilant and keep our heads clear for thought as well as emotion. This is no minor task, and we have to be ready for it. In my view, there is no better way to prepare ourselves than to be exposed to clear-headed reflection about these issues. That is where a thoughtful book such as this becomes essential. The contributions presented here are, in my view, not just treatises by people wanting to share obscure issues with each other: they form an essential clinical support to keep us clear-headed and our functions integrated.

INTRODUCTION

Julia Pestalozzi

> "The psychotic will only be freed when the healthy is liberated
> from his own tyrant. For thousands of years attempts have
> been made to free him, but in vain. What is essential is not
> freedom from chains but moral liberation from fear of the
> latent, terrible stigma of madness."

These words were written by István Hollós, co-founder (with Sándor Ferenczi) and vice-president of the Hungarian Psychoanalytical Society and perhaps the first psychoanalyst who used psychoanalysis to understand psychoses (Hollós, 1914) and to succeed in removing the locks and fences from a mental hospital before World War I, in the name of psychoanalysis.

Look at the forerunners of the "Yellow House": sometimes the madhouse stood outside the cities, together with houses for the plague, or syphilitics, and houses for fallen maidens, the executioner, and the slaughterer. Later on, towers were built, then barracks—and cloister-like buildings, then pavilions and increasingly modern and humane sanatoria. But everywhere there still remained the fences, the isolation, and, as the main

> instrument in doctors' hands—the key. My friend! Herein lies
> the Fall of the "Yellow House"! [Hollós, 1925]*

But he also knew that psychiatric institutions are our own means of defence against the "madness" within us and are at the same time "places for our wishes: places where one can live without responsibility. The House of Horrors is also the House of Longings: Calvary is also Nirvana . . . *we cure ourselves there*." By this he meant society at large, and psychiatric personnel in particular. Already in the 1910s he was convinced that "liberation" of the mentally ill from the chains of their stigmatization will only become possible if society arrives at a psychoanalytic understanding of its own madness, if nurses are taught that there is meaning in psychotic talk, and if caregivers analyse *their* Unconscious—which he always wrote in capital letters—and integrate the "mad" parts of themselves. In his book of 1925, which is a collection of thoughts on psychoanalysis, institutions, and society, full of sadness but also full of hope regarding a future psychoanalytic understanding of the world that might even liberate mankind from war, he voiced the thought that "there was a man who took the first decisive step in this liberation, who understood the mad . . . [namely] Freud". Hollós's book became a best-seller at the time, but Freud's response was more than disappointing. In a letter to Hollós he wrote: "I did not like those patients. . . . They make me angry and I find myself irritated to experience them so distant from myself and from all that is human. This is an astonishing intolerance which brands me as a poor psychiatrist. . . . Could my attitude result from . . . my hostility towards the id?" (see Dupont, 1988, p. 250; Haynal, 1988, p. 59).

**Búcsúm a Sárga Háztól* [My Farewell to the "Yellow House"] was written after Hollós had had to resign as director of a clinic in accordance with early racial legislation by the right-wing Hungarian government. Twenty years later, in 1944, Hollós and his wife came close to being executed by the Nazis. After standing for many hours "naked in snow and ice on the embankment of the Danube, one of the sites of mass-execution, where the victims—shot dead or half dead—were indiscriminately thrown into the river, by pure chance the slaughter stopped just before it was their turn to be killed" (Lévy, 1957). A letter written subsequently to his first analyst and later friend, Paul Federn, is an essay on the defensive functions of the ego during such an experience (Hollós, 1946, in E. Federn, 1974).

Institutional psychotherapy still deals with the outcasts from society—the mad, the bad, and the sad, one might say—people who cannot sufficiently contain "madness" and "badness" in themselves and who cannot, as Roussillon puts it in Chapter 3, use "ordinary social institutions as supportive frameworks for their efforts to symbolize". And sadness? In the first instance, it is the caretakers who have to bear this. Again and again they must restore the depressive position in the face of attacks, splitting, and denigration from inside and outside the institutions, *at the interface*, with powerful projections from patients on the one hand and from a society on the other which still wishes and perhaps needs to deposit and stigmatize its mad parts in institutional settings. It also means dealing permanently with the mad and the bad in ourselves—getting in touch with and giving meaning to our own "psychotic core" and the psychotic and perverse elements that are unavoidably inherent in our well-meant institutions, since the latter are the eggshells of fragmentations which separate "inside" from "outside". How can we "put Humpty Dumpty together again"? In our own minds, obviously, first of all; and subsequently by sadly acknowledging the limits of such an omnipotent fantasy. How, then, can we at least devise institutions with a frame that will damage and retraumatize their users as little as possible?

The first volume of the EFPP Monograph Series was entitled, *Transference and Countertransference in Psychoanalytic Psychotherapy with Children and Adolescents*. Having had the enormous pleasure of reading and re-reading the contributions by the authors of the present volume, and following them through the labyrinthine paths of their various institutions, I thought that this book might equally have been called, "Transference and Countertransference in Institutional Settings", as this seems to be the Ariadne's thread. The great variety of all the contributions should help in finding a way through this labyrinth at the level of psychoanalytic thinking in the 1990s, in very different institutions and in different cultural and historical settings.

The asylum or "madhouse" of former times is the large mental hospital today, with an admissions system that usually leaves no choice either for patients or for the institution. This is a ubiquitous type of mass institution, found in every part of Europe except perhaps in Italy, following its radical reform of the 1970s. Under these conditions, psychoanalytic psychotherapy—in the sense normally understood when addressing a patient who is able to enter into an agreement—is more of a hope than a practical reality. The author of the first chapter, Theodor Cahn, is a psychoanalyst and head of one such public mental hospital—a man who knows the value of therapeutic regression but must also defend society at large against "madness" by virtue of his appointed position on the side of law and order. In reading his contribution I imagined him and his team as a sort of semipermeable membrane separating and absorbing the violent despair of their patients on the one hand, while on the other hand absorbing the coercion of society—which is not interested in the meaning of madness but has to defend itself against it and stands for health in a very medical sense of the word. There may perhaps be no better place to think about the power of evacuating projections (from both sides) than by doing this job, which at first sight seems to be paradoxical, an extreme variant of the "impossible profession". It ceases, however, to be so impossible if therapist and team begin to reflect on the paradox and see themselves as active agents whose task is to metabolize forces from outside and inside, with all the opportunities that this presents and all the dangers of failing to metabolize or proving incapable of what one might describe as institutional reverie. Cahn describes this project in detail and shows where hope is concealed in seemingly hopeless situations.

The project is very different in Italy, twenty years after the law that brought about a truly radical shift from the asylum system to a system of local responsibility generally referred to as "community therapy". The Italian mental health system is now organized into a network of about 800 Mental Health Centres. It is no longer possible to admit new patients to the old mental hospitals, which nevertheless still house about 1,800 patients who cannot be discharged (Furlan, 1997). New patients are treated with different sorts of "tailor-made" provision on a home and community basis, according to four different models as previously defined by Janssen: the *bifocal* model, with emphasis on a dual therapeutic relationship; the *small integrated-group model*, based on individual intervention involving the interaction of several professional figures and models, including, for instance, psychotherapeutic, pharmacological, and rehabilitative; the *community model*, based on the tradition of the "therapeutic community"; and the *network model*, with theoretical origins that can be traced back to Foulkes, but adapted to a modern nationwide organization unique to Italy. Marta Vigorelli (Chapter 2) shows how psychoanalytic thinking, especially regarding the psychoanalytic psychotherapy of the psychoses, has made an impact on all these models (and vice versa), and how experience of transference and countertransference issues within these models has become part of psychoanalytic culture. The ability to *integrate different models* of psychoanalytic thinking on psychoses is juxtaposed with that of providing a holding, facilitating environment for the maturation and *integration of psychotic patients*: this is a fascinating proposal for further thinking about how professionals cathect theories—and patients.

After these first two chapters, whose theories emerge from and reflect upon some very concrete realities of psychiatric life, Chapter 3 seems to come from another planet—though, in fact, just from France. While reading René Roussillon's contribution, I became very conscious of the way in which a French manner of thinking about the very same things that we encounter again and again in this book—fragmentation, split transference to the team, countertransference issues, and so forth—sheds a different light on paths of thought that we tread all too readily with a happy feeling of consensus. The French schools' passionate interest in symbolizing enriches his approach to institutions: in this chapter he develops a theory that it is the very setting of institutions that symbolizes symbolization. This raises the fascinating question of what sort of "response" by caregivers to patients' institutional transference is most apt to promote users' capacity to form symbols. Use of countertransference to understand and reconstruct what is "waiting for ownership" is discussed in its institutional dimension.

In the subsequent chapters we meet institutional settings that are special in various ways, either because their methods express a policy that is unique to those institutions—such as psychosocial nursing at the Cassel Hospital (Chapter 4), a modern classic of the therapeutic community, and Kortenberg (Chapter 5), with its policy of group therapy—or because they offer psychotherapeutic help to very special users: delinquents, psychotic adolescents, extremely disturbed children, or children who have survived torture.

In the fourth chapter, R. D. Hinshelwood and Wilhelm Skogstad describe the Cassel Hospital, founded by Tom Main and directed until recently by Hinshelwood. It is a unique institution in that it combines individual psychoanalytic psychotherapy with the concept of the therapeutic community at a highly sophisticated level, which results in the Cassel's distinctive practice of psycho-social nursing. The basic, psychoanalytically inspired idea that a whole range of what are often split transferences tend to develop to members of staff, other patients, or the setting as a whole, and that only integrative mental work by staff members can enable patients to work on integration, is common to much thinking about the integrative and community models of psychiatric care, and we meet these ideas repeatedly in this book. Yet the Cassel is a place where such ideas are taken seriously in every detail of institutional life and thinking. This is what Main (1983) called "the culture of enquiry". Psychosocial nursing is a manner of "being with" the patient in a non-interpretative but psychoanalytically inspired way, using and stimulating the healthy parts of the self (a Bionian idea) while working in a practical day-to-day manner with the dysfunctional parts that are usually dispersed all over the institution. This chapter describes how such an orchestration of individual therapy, the work of the "therapeutic couple", and many other figures in the community's life becomes a therapeutic reality.

While Hinshelwood and Skogstad state explicitly that "in-patient psychotherapy is not just psychotherapy in an in-patient setting" and refer to the actual hospital as a "stage" onto which figures of patients' internal worlds can be projected and where they can be played out, understood by staff, integrated through their communication, and reintegrated by patients, R. Vermote and M. J. Vansina-Cobbaert from Belgium make the opposite proposition in Chapter 5. Likewise in tune with Bion's theoretical ideas, these authors stress that, in their view, "work in an in-patient setting is not very different from what would be done in an out-patient setting". In their institution they have tried to build a setting, or protective frame, within which psychoanalytic group therapy can be practised effectively in a manner not very different from out-patient provision. Essential to their work is close attention both to the therapeutic frame—particularly important with borderline patients—and to disruptions of symbolization by these patients as a consequence of their severely disturbed, fragmented, and partially projected object-relations. Thoughts are formed out of an ability to tolerate mental pain, and symbolization—or *mentalization*, as the authors describe it—creates a psychic skin of the sort that Anzieu (1974) described. The objective of the treatment offered by these authors is to increase patients' ability to mentalize psychic pain, and for this to happen a modicum of "basic trust" must be developed. They describe, with telling examples, how in the process of *psychoanalytic group therapy* within the institution such a process of mentalization can take place in patients who would probably have been untreatable outside an in-patient setting and might have derived less benefit from individual therapy.

Again, it is interesting to see how important a role is given to symbolization in the work of francophone colleagues. The same is true of the frame, which is so central to the thinking of authors like Anzieu, Racamier (1970: "the frame is essential"), or (the Argentinian) Bleger (1967), who considered it a "non-process" in the sense that it is made up of "*constants within whose bounds* a process takes place" (p. 466) and that "The frame refers to a strategy rather than to a technique" (p. 459).

Bleger thought that a patient's representation of the "frame" rested on "his most primitive fusion with the mother's body, and that the psychoanalyst's frame must help to re-establish the original symbiosis in order to be able to change it", but that the "de-symbiotization of the analyst–patient relationship is only reached with the systematic analysis of the frame at the right moment. And here we are likely to find the strongest resistance because it is not a repressed thing but something split and never differentiated. . . . In these cases we do not interpret what is repressed; we give rise to the secondary process" (p. 465). This is in some ways very different from and in others very related to Roussillon's idea of the way in which the (institutional) frame symbolizes symbolization. I have myself been impressed more than once by the symbolic equation that psychotic patients make between the therapeutic frame as we wish to provide and maintain it and the frame of the analyst's phantasied body, as experienced in "parasitic transferences" (Rosenfeld, 1971, p. 125), delusions of the analyst's pregnancy, and so forth. Neurotic analysands also experience the setting—the room, the couch, and temporal rhythms—as a maternal cavity or, vice versa, as a place dominated by the "nom du père" and, with it, the symbols of symbolization. Hollós wrote, in the early days of psychoanalysis, "Whatever *institution* the psychiatric patient goes into, he will be searching for a mother, irrespective or just because of his hatred, conflicts, etc. with his real mother" (Hollós, 1925, p. 116).

If we visualize the patient's version of the frame as being the mother's body, then we may understand more clearly what is going on in the institution for the very disturbed children that Valerie Sinason describes in Chapter 6. In the tones of a poet (which Valerie is) but with the knowledge of a psychoanalytic child psychotherapist, she gives an impressive description of "the way the nightmare lives of three boys percolate through the structures and boundaries of the Unit". Most children in her Unit have in fact suffered massive physical and/or sexual abuse. Containing institutions with mainly female staff will be cathected by children, many of whom have been desperately identified with their mothers' infanticidal wishes, or damaged by *de facto* sexual abuse, precisely as a mother's devouring, aggressively or sexually abusing, incestuous body, and the children, themselves imbued with disowned death wishes, will attack the very frame of people's bodies, and any other living thing in the institution. Triangulation, reverie, and space for reflection on countertransference issues are scarce but desperately needed supplies that are under permanent threat from violence and disgust. Reading the many clinical passages in this dramatic chronicle of a day in the life of such an institution, I thought that in this instance "containment" meant having the poetic creativity (a form of Winnicottian "survival") to formulate the "sad" in the face of a trans-generational patrimony of the "really bad". Sinason's moving contribution is the story of therapeutic survival and the never-ending reparation of the "ability to repair".

It is perhaps no accident that the other chapter in this book with a movingly poetic quality also comes from a world where *prima vista* "badness" predominates. The Portman Clinic "treats people who 'have carried out criminal acts or consider themselves to be suffering from sexual deviation'". Robert Hale is Clinical Director of this out-patient clinic, with its long tradition stretching back to Edward Glover and a certain psychoanalytic optimism in the

1930s. In Chapter 7, he describes, through a patient's history, the double-faceted nature of delinquency: the delinquent as offender and as victim, and the delinquent stuck between his badness and his sadness and between the law system and the health system. The institution is similarly stuck between these systems, while caregivers face opposing dangers of being punitive or moralizing (thereby identifying with the patient's projected superego) and being naively therapeutic, or of being too distant from or too close to the patient, thereby colluding with one or other of the frightening alternatives of Glasser's (1979) "core complex". Hale expresses this succinctly: "it is the lot of the psychopath that he will bring out the worst in an institution". How to deal with this, and how to think, and promote thinking, instead of acting out, are central concerns of this short and psychoanalytically ethical paper, which highlights the ethical dimension of familiar technical terms like neutrality and abstinence.

As psychoanalysts and psychoanalytic psychotherapists we may understand the intricate dialectic of the position of offenders and victims in all of us and also understand how Hale's institution specializes in containing the "badness" that society does not want and that the criminal is unable to contain, but as citizens we tend to make clear distinctions between offenders and victims. There is an institution in Denmark, however, which specializes in treating the *victims of history*—of man-made disasters—and this is the Rehabilitation and Research Centre for Torture Victims (RCT). Victims of governmental torture are victims in a painfully obvious sense, and their children—who are involved through having actually being hurt or having witnessed their parents' torture, or have mainly suffered from the extreme difficulties in being parented at times of and following torture—arouse feelings in us that are difficult to bear. Liselotte Grünbaum (Chapter 8) is a psychologist and psychoanalytic psychotherapist on an RCT team who treat these children and their families. They face children who have suffered inconceivable mental pain, and interactions in families that remind us of the consequences of the Holocaust. They face families that often break down after reaching safety, unconsciously repeating towards their children and other family members all the uncontainable "badness" that they themselves had suffered. Treating children individually and in a family context is absolutely indispensable here, and it requires very special institutional adaptations to this unique, crisis-prone reality. It also requires extraordinary capacities for dealing individually and as an institutional team with the countertransference problems that arise in the face of such suffering. Grünbaum takes a view, both in her theoretical discourse and in her case presentation, that is admirably psychoanalytic and at the same time soundly realistic.

Chapter 9, the final clinical paper in this volume, comes from Germany. Based on a memorable paper given at the International Symposium for the Psychotherapy of Schizophrenia in London in October 1997, it was considered too important for the theme of this book not to be included. Michael Günter and Reinmar du Bois describe an in-patient setting for psychotic adolescents. Their ideas are based on modern psychoanalytic concepts of the dynamics of adolescence and on a seriously taken and therefore practised belief in the usefulness of therapeutic regression. The authors have made equal space for severe psychotic regressions to be sustained and "answered" by the whole team and for patients to have as "normal" and "everyday" an adolescent life as possible. It is their experience that even profound psychotic regressions, when contained in a psychoanalytically inspired and supervised milieu—very different from the regressive world of the usual psychiatric wards— tend to be self-limiting conditions and even of positive prognostic significance. The authors say that "the patients use everyday life as their stage", and they understand this all-important *"everyday life"* on the one hand as a facet of real life, to be supported by the team, the routines of the agenda, and if necessary by psychopharmaca, and on the other hand as a screen for projection, "an outwardly turned representation of inner problems". Actions and attitudes of the different members of the team and their context within the team—indeed, the very construction of the team itself—is always considered as being at once both real and transferential. Günter and du Bois describe how their practical concepts of institutional settings for adolescents have developed and changed with the historical and ideological changes in Germany over the past twenty-five years. In many details of the way in which they deal with familiar everyday problems, such as smoking, the reader may visualize the frame of their setting as a fine-meshed envelope, interlinked at every point by the threads of psychoanalytic thought. This, we assume, is what is known at the Cassel Hospital as "the culture of enquiry".

Chapter 10, by Ulrich Streeck, systematically reviews important concepts in the history of psychoanalytic psychotherapy in institutional settings, and his article recapitulates many of the recurrent themes in this book. Streeck is a very experienced clinician who has been running a clinic for psychiatry, psychosomatics, and psychotherapy for many years. His theoretical orientation—for instance, using Piaget's concepts to describe typical interactions by severely disturbed patients, or models of short and focal therapies—differs in some respects from that in most of the other chapters in this book in that it makes a clear dichotomy between analysable neurotic conflicts, which in fact seldom turn up in inpatient settings, and the clinical consequences of the "basic fault", including "disorders of the self and the internalized pathological object-relations". These lead to faulty regulation of impulses and affects, and to difficulties in adapting to the social environment. The therapeutic aim is to focus precisely on these problems and (by using the information from split transference) to relate to the patient in a way that helps him* to compensate for "the basic developmental fault". Once again, judicious, psychoanalytically conceptualized, operational use of the frame is a central theme, and the chapter would have been a fitting conclusion were it not for a special "parting shot".

The parting shot is Serge Frisch's chapter, in which the mirror is suddenly turned upon ourselves, and our own institutions—upon the institutions where we were trained, and where we teach—which are the larger envelopes of our professional identity. Indeed, as psychoanalysts and psychoanalytic psychotherapists we are, and have been since our training began, parts of institutional settings no matter where we work. The institutes and associations of psychoanalysis have a long and very painful history, in which successes and failures in negotiating power have played an important part. Lack of reflection on the psychodynamics of power play may have contributed—as Kernberg (1992) suggests—to the present crisis at the interface of the psychoanalytic movement and

---

*For simplicity, in general discussions we have used feminine pronouns for therapists and masculine pronouns for patients.

the rest of the world. What conclusions can be drawn for the organizations for psychoanalytic psychotherapy? How should a new framework be constructed, a new biface envelope that will be firm and supportive but not strangling, devouring, and inimical to fresh thought? How should it relate to the outside world and to the exigencies of modern political and economic reality, which entails dealing with or pseudo-abstaining from power? What can psychoanalysis gain from psychoanalytic psychotherapy, both theoretically and at the institutional level? We are indeed an institutional setting, and it will depend to a great extent upon ourselves how we structure the frame of our future professional lives. This will also have direct consequences for the frames and settings that we will help to construct for our patients.

* * *

While reading through the wealth of lively material in this book and the thoughtful impetus of endeavour that all its authors manifest, one tends to forget that this is a time when psychodynamic psychotherapy is rapidly losing ground to all sorts of other seemingly cheaper and less time-consuming approaches. As psychoanalytic psychotherapists, we are convinced that institutions pervaded by psychoanalytic thought can offer to severely disturbed patients a unique potential for human growth and maturation. We are also convinced that the ethics inherent in an *ostinato* in which the symmetries and asymmetries of movements of transference and countertransference are continually considered serves to humanize institutional life and restores a portion of patients' dignity, even in moments when our understanding or intentions fail. This book should be a testimony to such thoughts and intentions, and our hope is that it will stimulate colleagues to join us in this effort.

Psychoanalytic Psychotherapy
in Institutional Settings

Beyond the treatment contract: psychoanalytic work in the public mental hospital

Theodor Cahn

The object of this chapter is to contribute some ideas and experience on the possible significance of psychoanalysis in the context of a psychiatric hospital having a general, public remit: what specific conditions for psychotherapeutic processes arise from the structures of such institutions? I should like to consider this problem from the point of view of a kind of applied psychoanalysis, as a *"psychanalyste sans divan"* ("psychoanalyst without a couch": Racamier, 1970). At issue here are the principles of in-patient psychotherapy in a general psychiatric framework rather than a particular psychoanalytic setting or a technique. The question relates to a more fundamental, less differentiated level.

* * *

When a patient is admitted to a public psychiatric hospital, those involved usually have no choice: there is no contract between the patient and the team at the accepting institution (referred to hereafter as a "non-selective hospital", or NSH). The aim of psychotherapy in the NSH is precisely to bring about (or to re-establish) this choice and capacity to contract—a primitive version of

Freud's principle: "Where id was, ego shall be." In terms of the rule that psychotherapy must begin with an agreement, this statement sounds paradoxical. This paradox constitutes grounds for retreating to the conventional view that, with isolated exceptions, psychotherapy is impossible in the NSH. To overcome the paradox, it is necessary to postulate a broadened concept of psychotherapy. However, the idea that there might be such a thing as a psychoanalytically based in-patient psychotherapy beyond the treatment contract and that this might be capable of integration into the day-to-day practice of the NSH seems to be more a hope—a concrete utopia—than a demonstrable fact. My experience as the head of a public mental hospital, with a catchment of some 250,000 inhabitants, providing general psychiatric services in Switzerland indicates that such an approach is feasible. That is the basis of my hope.

Objective conditions in the psychiatric hospital

The *objective conditions* encountered by patients denote a "secondary world" of the institution and hence an external reality *sui generis*, which on the one hand exerts great pressure to conform and on the other hand is capable of absorbing certain quite specific forms of defence and transference.

1. Every institution is substantially moulded by its *task*, which must therefore be examined first. In Switzerland, the public authority responsible for psychiatric hospitals defines them as "medically run institutions": that is, all other activities, such as psychotherapy or nursing, are deemed to be subordinate to the medical requirement. The hospital is, so to speak, merely a general container, or extensive infrastructure, for medical treatment. Accordingly, such an institution is expected to operate with the objective rationality that characterizes medicine today. Tensions inevitably arise between psychotherapy (and, *a fortiori*, psychoanalysis)—which allows space for and gives a voice to the subjective, the irrational, and the ambivalent—on the one hand, and the principle of medical hierarchy on the other.

Indeed, the institutional power of the medical establishment is even stronger in psychiatric than in somatic hospitals: whereas a patient undergoing somatic treatment can usually enter into a therapeutic contract himself, this is usually not the case on admission to an acute psychiatric ward, when agencies often have to stand in for the patient commissioning the hospital: on average in Switzerland (Borghi, 1991), about a quarter of admissions to public psychiatric hospitals are compulsory. Moreover, although the status of the remaining patients is officially informal, most of them are not admitted by a decision of their own based on insight: many are bowing to manifest pressure, while others are too regressed to do anything but submit passively or are too confused to understand their situation. A strikingly large number of patients come to the hospital plainly because they "simply cannot manage any longer". When confronted by these phenomena of generalized regression, psychiatry is thus assigned a law-and-order function that is partly explicit and partly implicit and is superimposed on its therapeutic mission. It would be wrong to deny this.

2.   Manifestations of *violence* and destructiveness are frequently bound up with the regression. A great deal of violence is thus inevitably introduced into the NSH and hence into the relational field of the institution (Cahn, 1995). The hospital is required, first of all, to contain and control this violence: a policing function. It cannot stand apart from acted-out violence, as is and must be taken for granted in any psychotherapy unit. For this purpose, the NSH provides locked rooms and intensive surveillance, coupled where necessary with physical *coercion*. It is designed for patients with violent tendencies, thereby making a negative selection. For the other, better-adapted patients, the NSH nevertheless remains a place of coercion and potential violence, and the latter becomes part of their experience even if they do not themselves manifestly practise or sustain it.

3. The institution must accept all patients referred to it unconditionally and at short notice. These patients are very *different* in terms of age, diagnosis, social situation, cultural origin, indications for treatment, pathological course, and so on. The length of stay varies accordingly. With the coming and going of an enormous

diversity of patients, the equilibrium of group life is under constant threat.

4. The foregoing clearly shows that for most patients admitted to an NSH, as well as for the staff who treat them, there is no choice of whether to work with somebody or with whom; nor in most cases is there any mutual agreement on treatment. The procedure is determined solely by the official commitment of the institution and by the professional rules of the helpers (Matakas, 1988). The NSH consequently partakes of the logic of the "total institution", which subordinates the entire lives of the inmates to the abstract purpose of the institution and controls all conditions of life around the clock (Goffmann, 1961). People enter the institution at someone else's instigation and have no choice but to conform, in the same way as in the army or in a prison. This element of structural violence operates independently of the therapeutic orientation, attitude, or critical insight of the responsible staff.

Subjective experience of these conditions

1. *Patient experience.* I concentrate here on the concepts of regression, devaluation, and helplessness. Most admissions resulting from a breakdown are dramatic culminations of a regressive trend. Regardless of the structural level of the personality, the regression is generalized and far-reaching: the mature defence and the preservation of the boundaries of the self have collapsed. Admission to the world of "psychiatry" seems to confirm this collapse to the patient: the acting out has had the effect that the patient meets again his paranoid or masochistic fantasies, his punitive, archaic superego, his passive expectations, and so on as external reality. They are completely externalized in the reactions of the institutional setting. It is a fact that he has been the passive object of other people's actions, has been brought, under pressure or against his will—at any rate not as an adult contractual partner—to a place, usually under lock and key, where physical coercion prevails, and has been plunged into a society of manifestly disturbed people not

of his choosing and beyond his control (Matakas, 1988). He is locked up and almost totally looked after.

This process clearly illustrates the concept of institutional defence: it assumes that transferences—or, more precisely, transference elements—are deployed towards the institution. The institution absorbs these and, as mentioned above, creates de facto situations that correspond to the various projections. In this way the institution functions in the service of collective and individual defence (Erdheim, 1982; Leuschner, 1985; Mentzos, 1990). It is this very defence that constitutes a further injunction for the patient to regress: "If I have been admitted in the hospital as a mad person, then I can behave like a child here in the funny farm!" (It is also possible to see this patient–institution interaction as a form of secondary gain from illness.)

At the same time, the entire process of "admission" signifies an appreciable threat to the social person, who is marginalized, humiliated, and devalued at all levels. The psychiatric hospital is "the pits"; one cannot sink any lower. To be sent there is still as powerful a stigma as it was in the past. Catastrophic self-expectations are reflected concretely in the external circumstances. Against the overwhelming institutional power, the patient feels that only the weapons of regression remain to him: helplessness, clingingness, and attempts at seduction. Patients may also try to cast off the multi-layered narcissistic injury in a variety of ways by externalization or re-externalization, so that the staff come in for a great deal of devaluation, and the other patients are also involved. This often gives rise among a group of patients to an aggressive climate of devaluation and a hierarchy of mutual degradation. The "moral" quality of "the pits" reinforces resistance and impedes progressive processes. This can be reduced to the simple formula that patients frequently experience the institution and its representatives as "bad". We should therefore not one-sidedly ascribe the negative appreciation of which we are so often the subject in the hospital to primitive defence mechanisms on the part of patients.

2. The *experience of the staff* is, of course, drawn very much into these processes. I focus again on devaluation, because it is precisely this feeling that quickly communicates itself to the teams. It no

doubt includes a variety of countertransference aspects, such as reactions to projective identifications, to depressive parts of the patients, or to narcissistic draining. The staff likewise experience echoes of the real, "bad" significance of the institution for the patients, as well as being exposed to latent or overt discrimination against the psychiatric hospital as the "dustbin" of society: our colleagues "out there" who work with out-patients and simply practise "therapy" or even "analysis" often adopt a highly critical stance towards the public hospital, and its public reputation remains at least latently precarious, notwithstanding superficial improvements.

The possibility of positively cathecting one's own work and the place where it is done—an essential prerequisite for a therapeutic attitude—is persistently undermined by these objective circumstances. It is essential for us to counter these negative factors by being able to tell patients and their families that here, in our own hospital, the patients are in the right place, and that we can offer them valid and competent help. In view of this negative initial situation, however, it is difficult for us to attain such a conviction, the precondition for which is a realistic appraisal of the therapeutic possibilities.

Specific requirements for a therapeutic approach
at the psychiatric hospital

1.   The overriding objective of treatment at the hospital is *the return of the patient to his accustomed social environment* or, if necessary, to an appropriate substitute environment in a decentralized unit, with adequate capacity for psychic functioning and improved contextual conditions, usually coupled with ongoing treatment and care. This objective follows unequivocally from the hospital's official task. For these reasons, an in-depth therapeutic process will preferably take place in an out-patient setting.

The individual objective of in-patient treatment is therefore formulated primarily on the reality level and is measured by social parameters. The immediate precondition for discharge is neither freedom from symptoms nor internal development achieved by psychotherapy, but adaptability, so that the patient can cope independently with his everyday life—or is at least prepared to cooperate to some extent in accepting the necessary help, which, after all, cannot be forced upon him in the outside world. A consensus on discharge and what is to follow it should therefore exist between the patient, his family, and those involved in his treatment and care. In view of the initial situation mentioned above, the achievement of such a consensus can by no means be taken for granted. Without a certain degree of "capacity to contract", progress in relatively unprotected social environments outside the hospital is not possible. The principal variable in this case is the ego function, which is responsible for keeping agreements. This calls for a level of functioning with adequate coherence of self and object images. Not uncommonly, a therapeutic (internal) process begun during the in-patient phase is an essential prerequisite for the achievement of this objective, but this is never an end in itself in the context of the NSH.

2.   It follows from this objective that the staff must enter into *direct contact with third parties* and work together with them—that is, members of the patient's family, specialists, and other agencies. These contacts are components of the standard setting of the hospital, enjoying equal status with psychotherapeutically orientated provision.

3.   Allowance must be made for the *inhomogeneity* of the *patient* group mentioned earlier: to cater for different patients and requirements in this way, a number of different methodological approaches and combinations of approaches are called for.

The *team*, too, is not homogeneous but multidisciplinary in its composition: nursing staff and social workers perform important functions in their own right alongside physicians and psychologists and contribute their own methods, which must be integrated. This adaptation of psychotherapy to the requirements of general psychiatry will inevitably give rise to problems: a diffuse pragmatism and eclecticism—which now seems to be in fashion—is never very far away. Another difficulty is that (at least in Switzerland) staff turnover at public mental hospitals is quite high, and an appreciable proportion of the staff are still in training.

The consequence of these factors, coupled with the pressure accruing from the patients' inner chaos, is a marked descent towards a loss of structure in therapeutic work. The responsible staff must attend to this problem on a priority basis: before they can deal with individual therapeutic matters, they must preserve the structures of the ward-setting and ensure that these do not break down.

Proto-psychotherapeutic processes

As we have seen, admission to a NSH involves no choice, and this lack of capacity to choose must be regarded precisely as an essential symptom of the patient's regressive pathology. Furthermore, it is a symptom that may undergo secondary reinforcement in the institution. Consequently, the question of the *indications* for psychotherapy is bound to arise in unconventional form. Normally, decision-making on psychotherapy precedes process. As it happens, this also applies when a patient is admitted to a psychotherapy unit; this is an important methodological consideration, because, for obvious reasons, the NSH would if possible wish to adhere to the approaches developed in these specialized institutions—although substantial modifications are necessary in view of the differences in the initial situation. But in the case of a regressed psychiatric patient suffering from, for example, delusions, it is at first neither possible nor reasonable to enter into an argument about whether psychotherapy is indicated.

This means that a specific process is necessary before it is possible to discuss psychotherapy as such with a typical NSH patient himself. However, I should like to define this very process from the outset as psychotherapeutic, although perhaps it would be better and more correct to describe it as "proto-psychotherapeutic". If, in this difficult situation, methodical psychotherapy with a defined setting is not applicable, one must lower one's sights somewhat, without feeling devalued or therapeutically inadequate.

In the NSH situation, psychotherapy appears at first not as a particular setting but "latently", as a potential—an open possibility held out by the team and presented to patients as a prospect within a defined framework. Whereas the hospital must initially simply guarantee vital protection, and while actual treatment often commences with the administration of drugs, spaces or settings are provided in the day-to-day life of the ward that invite the patient to engage and reflect—for example, in a group, at the art therapy bench, or in discussion of practical matters with the doctor and assigned primary nurse. A number of partners are usually then available to interact with. Patients may venture forward, withdraw again, refuse to react, make a scene, put their interlocutor to the test, and so on. In favourable cases, although by no means always, this may lead to coherence and relationship—step by step, or in a to-and-fro process, by the assembly and structuring of individual elements, or by rapid "crystallization". Consistency and relationship are often evident at first only to the therapeutic partners through their empathy, because preverbal, usually symbiotic elements predominate at this still highly regressive stage. On the basis of this experience, it may be possible in a next step to determine that psychotherapy in a methodologically defined setting is indicated. This will coincide with the phase when longer-term agreements become possible, which is often synonymous with the patient's discharge. Psychotherapy—by analytic or other methods—towards which the patient has been guided during his hospitalization will then begin in an out-patient setting.

The requirements of practical work seem to contradict the rule of abstinence in every respect. It is necessary to intervene *with action* at all times. The necessary interventions concern vital interests of the individual or the preservation of the external structures of the community. Yet it is essential to avoid blindly re-acting or counteracting the patient's acting out: a psychotherapeutically orientated NSH must be characterised precisely by avoidance of any medical or therapeutic "actionism"—that is, of problem-solving as an end in itself. Abstinence thus means concentrating on a critical perception of one's own actions and of one's own needs towards the patient. It also means permanent reflection about the impact of the institution on the patients and therapists concerned, and about the defensive organization of the institution.

A characteristic of the in-patient situation is that *transferences* are divided among a number of persons, with informal contacts and open groups playing a significant part. Attention also needs to be paid to the specific aspects of the object-relations of severely disturbed patients, who predominate in the NSH. Because of the combination of these two factors, the formation of continuous relational processes and coherent transference development must be deemed the exception rather than the rule in this "proto-psychotherapeutic" phase. It is much more likely that unintegrated, psychotically tinged transference elements will appear here and there, and discontinuously. Whereas these scattered transference factors are likely to be, to some extent, held together de facto by the external structures of the ward during a brief hospitalization, they cannot readily be conceived and integrated promptly by the therapists.

Beyond the personal relationship, it seems reasonable in our situation to extend the concept of the transference to the institution as an impersonal entity, as mentioned above. According to Matakas (1988), fragments of early relations, usually with clear qualities of omnipotence/impotence, are transferred onto the institution. Their personal, object-related character is defended against (disavowed), in accordance with the anonymous nature of the institution. The persons exposed to this form of transference are perceived merely as occupants of a particular role. This pattern is more intensified the more the institution presents itself as a predominant power.

The real reasons for deprivation, distrust, hurt, rage, resignation, and so on demand full attention—especially because discharge from the hospital is the priority. In particular, the often fundamentally disastrous life experiences and the highly constricted perspectives of many psychiatric patients are real. Precisely because the psychotic defence is directed on a grandiose scale against these real limitations, therapists must also concern themselves with practical matters affecting the patient. If the therapist adopts a differentiated and neutral attitude towards these problems, aggression can be defused to some extent and a kind of joint control of reality arrived at. This gives rise to a seedbed, however initially fragile, in which a degree of trust gradually arises, together with the rudiments of a working relationship. It will then eventually be possible to proceed to an agreed therapy, in which the transference processes will become more structured and more clearly identifiable.

*Clinical example**

Mr K, a middle-aged bachelor with a scowl on his face, has been psychotic and incapacitated for years. His diagnosis as a paranoid schizophrenic is not in doubt: he is tormented by painful hallucinations and delusions. He has wide-ranging experience of in-patient psychiatry, having been admitted to a number of hospitals, and has always quickly withdrawn from out-patient treatment. He considers himself to be not ill but the victim of comprehensive persecution by his family. He has been engaged in litigation with them for years over the inheritance of the parental house, from which his siblings would like to exclude him—and they are really treating him unfairly. Mr K is capable of asserting his rights in due form out of a situation of seemingly total psychotic refusal. Recourse to the courts has manifestly become an important aspect of his way of life; he can thereby "materialize" his enemies legally, in a kind of institutional transference.

He was compulsorily admitted to our hospital after barricading himself in the disputed house and terrorizing his neighbours by throwing stones at their windows and uttering delusional threats. Following his admission, the hospital was confronted with a petition from the neighbours and an application by his family's lawyers for his permanent detention under lock and key. The patient, in turn using his own lawyer, appealed against his hospitalization to the court. However, he was manifestly psychotic and hostile and took his medication only under pressure; it was as if he transformed his environment and the hospital into real persecutors. This was quite a typical situation with maximum pressure and no room to manoeuvre, but only coercion. The only therapeutic prospect here lay in an attempt to negotiate with the patient on his status; for this purpose, it was also necessary to respect his paranoid views. Negotiation is a preliminary to a possible agreement, something that is fought for in the phase of "proto-psychotherapy". It is by no means yet a question of establishing a defined psychotherapy setting.

---

*I am indebted to Dr. Hanspeter Stutz for this account.

The senior physician in charge of the ward, a trained analyst, undertook the treatment himself; the situation, although it involved the placing of a great deal of real power in one person's hands, was clear. Mr K was given two interviews a week. The doctor was here trying to mediate between realities, informing the patient of his adversaries' reactions like a go-between. He was also in direct negotiation with the neighbours, to whom he in turn explained the reality of the patient, showing them that he was less dangerous than they thought. In the process, he adopted a fairly confrontational attitude towards both sides, with clear, well-defined decisions. On condition that he took his medication, he granted Mr K a short period of leave to stay in his house, making sure that the neighbours were informed. This worked satisfactorily a few times. However, the patient absconded just when a court hearing was due. The proceedings were therefore suspended without a judgment. The adversarial contact with the external agency may have performed an integrating function for the patient, who consequently sabotaged its conclusion. Mr K disappeared in the Alps for five weeks. When he was found, he appeared less psychotic and more open. However, after the court confirmed his compulsory hospitalization on the grounds that it was not clear whether he presented a danger, the psychotic manifestations were exacerbated, the refusal appeared complete, and communication was practically broken off. So the doctor's attempt to introduce himself as a defined object into the rigid paranoid institutional transference had initially failed, and he ultimately had to commence injection treatment, for the first time involving physical coercion; persecution and delusions of persecution now coincided in the medical institution too.

Because the doctor steadfastly persisted in his attempts to talk to the patient, the latter slowly became more accessible again, and a degree of communication proved possible. The neuroleptic drugs no doubt also had some effect, and this subject was now raised: Mr K described the negative side-effects of the neuroleptics and was listened to. He now accepted a relatively low dose of a different medication (clozapine). The doctor had the impression that a degree of trust was arising, no doubt because he did not allow himself to be "taken over" by the patient's neighbours and family and remained neutral with regard to the lawsuit over the inheritance, while, however, declaring himself to be competent in the matter of the compulsory hospitalization: the sessions with the patient consisted mainly of negotiations on the reasons for his admission and on the conditions for a discharge. Over a period of time, the patient spontaneously began to talk about his earlier experiences of psychiatry, which had so impressed their stamp on him. This contribution of material marked a turning point in the therapeutic relationship. Even in the groups, in which the patient had previously remained completely withdrawn, he cautiously thawed out. He now entered into agreements and kept them reliably. As a result, we were able to obtain permission for him to be discharged from the hospital. The patient now wished to continue seeing, on an out-patient basis, the doctor who had looked after him at the hospital. Mr K appeared regularly for a few months, but the contact took the form of a psychiatric follow-up treatment rather than psychotherapy. He then moved to another region.

The objective of a formal discharge from the hospital was achieved. Substantial, competent psychotherapeutic efforts had been necessary for this to be feasible by mutual consent and even with a modicum of trust, even though virtually nothing but action and negotiation and hardly any psychoanalytic talking had been possible between doctor and patient. However, this gave rise to a degree of relationship, which for a while revealed in the patient a different, object-directed potential, outside his closed paranoid world.

*Working levels and the psychotherapeutic function
in the mental hospital*

On the basis of the ideas developed so far, this section deals rather more concretely with therapeutic functions in the institutional setting of the hospital. I follow the sequence of the hierarchical steps—or rather, concentric circles around the patient—from the governing body of the hospital down to the level of individual treatment.

1. *The institution and its governing body.*   In accordance with the principles of a therapeutic community (M. Jones, 1968), the entire institution is regarded as a therapeutic system or environment. The hospital, as an institution operating as a single entity, must endeavour to create and keep open spaces in which therapeutic processes and progressive developments can take place, subject to risks that can to some degree be calculated. Psychoanalysis affords us a more differentiated picture of such processes. It shows us clearly that they cannot unfold without major crises, especially in the case of patients whose capacity for psychic integration is overtaxed for structural or situational reasons. Libidinal and aggressive conflicts, ambivalence, and other manifestations of the unconscious will arise in the patient–staff relationship, on both sides, in the form of action. As the front line, the medical director and the senior staff must champion and promote such a conception of the process. When the inevitable difficulties and crises inherent in the process arise, these individuals must be capable of containing them with as specific an understanding as possible and, if necessary, of setting limits, without conveying the impression of looking first of all for shortcomings or incompetence.

The governing body of the hospital should play a mediating role between its patients and the public and must therefore occasionally tolerate tensions and distance between itself and the authorities to which it is responsible. If a public psychiatric institution should identify completely with the political or economic power and aspires to thoroughgoing control and linear efficiency, this would lead to totalitarian pressure within which no space for therapeutic activity would remain. On the other hand, the hospital must be able to deploy convincingly its competence for the necessary protection and containment of at-risk patients, because there is nothing better than public psychiatry for these purposes.

2. *Ward structures.*   When a regressed patient in a crisis has to enter a mental hospital, the environment of the acute ward initially constitutes a clearly defined space within which he can live: the

boundary is concrete, tightly drawn and firm, the door at first usually locked. The space inside and the space outside are completely separated from each other physically. By virtue of his admission, the patient has been given an entitlement to this security, but has lost the competence to cross the boundary between these spaces autonomously. This situation was described at the beginning of this chapter as signifying latent devaluation or structural violence. However, let us now demonstrate the therapeutic resources inherent in it.

A therapeutic potential necessarily develops on and in the concrete structures of the ward: this confined, enclosed space is opened up and extended for each patient in an individual process, step by step, by way of predefined regimes that lay down the stages of freedom of movement. *Can the patient leave the intensive-care ward—will he remain in the open part of the ward as agreed? Can he be trusted to return from leave?* In addition to these spatial boundaries, the daily and weekly schedule lays down a time-based organization for the ward, as a basis for the same processes of structuring: *does the patient get up by himself and present himself punctually at mealtimes? Can he now go to a workshop, and how long should be remain there?*

An appreciable risk is, of course, always inherent in the power gradient between staff and patients and also in the tendency of any institution to delegate personal responsibility. For example, these matters can easily be dealt with in the form of a banal, anonymous, alienated, and, as it were, official routine—in which case, abuse of the power to confine a patient will not be far away. The therapeutic quality depends crucially on the attitude of the team, and inherent in it is surely the most important contribution of the psychoanalytic approach in a public mental hospital: the acting out, ambivalence, and aggression against the "framework of the ward" and regarding the "extension of this framework" must be seen as necessary parts of the therapeutic process of development and not as disturbances or instances of maladjustment, let alone punished as such. These resistances in fact offer important opportunities for meeting the patients, for initiating verbal and emotional interaction, and for securing mutual understanding.

What is being negotiated is autonomy: if doors are opened, something else must ensure that the "frame" is preserved and that the treatment continues. For this purpose, it must be possible to make valid agreements, as a result of which patients and those who treat them become partners. To this end, the ward lays down a graduated system of levels with a specific nomenclature, which are entered on a board in specified colours against the patient's name. ("Grounds" means, for example, that the patient can roam freely in the unfenced part of the hospital grounds. An agreement is made with him that he will remain within this area.) By means of such agreements, symbolic boundaries thus gradually replace material ones. This begins within a limited radius and for short, easily conceived periods of time. Each stage provides a field for practising the "capacity to contract". There will be major differences in the course of different patients' "careers" in this respect, and inevitable crises in which patients relapse into regression; a careful, individualized approach is therefore necessary. Whatever the vicissitudes, a psychoanalytic approach will be necessary to ensure that the team elaborates and upholds the principle that what is involved are the patient's attempts to come to terms with his problems through trial and practice in the therapeutic environment and not primarily the adaptation of patients to the institution.

This process begins immediately with the patient's admission. It is only secondarily that, depending on the patient's progress and capacity, individual therapy settings proper are introduced into this day-to-day organization (moreover, these settings also operate in the form of temporal structures, appointments, and intervals). If the negotiation of the structures and boundaries that define daily life in the hospital are of such central importance, the nursing staff—who, after all, accompany the patients in the routine life of the ward—must undertake a significant proportion of the therapeutic work. For this purpose, the nurses need the institutional and professional competence to participate responsibly in the process of relating. This capability must be established and cultured on a long-term basis by appropriate further training and supervision.

3. *Groups.* The group aspect of in-patient therapy is important, the ward itself constituting a living and working environment for a large, heterogeneous group (Kibel, 1987). In other words, like all institutions (or parts of institutions), the "hospital/ward system"

must be understood in terms of group dynamics (Kernberg, 1980). For this reason, formal group occasions afford the best opportunity for reflecting on the life of the group, making it transparent, and working on it. A particularly appropriate occasion in this connection is the ward meeting, which is a standard feature of a therapeutic community. As far as possible, all patients and the entire team should take part in the meeting. In this way, it will represent the entire ward, with all its subgroups and subsystems, and constitute a public forum for the space represented by the ward. As such, the ward meeting in an NSH forms an interface between the institution, the patients, and the ward team.

Each session begins with a discussion of everyday organizational matters, special events (e.g. violent incidents) and problems with the "framework" of the ward; these make up the life of the group. The patients are then free to bring up subjects of their own, although the group leaders must quite often provide structural help. The central topics, whether manifest or latent, will always be the patients' enforced presence in the hospital and the conditions and consequences associated with this. It is then possible to address the problem-complex of power, helplessness, and dependence, as well as devaluation and the associated destructive aggression. Public discussion is essential to avoid the spread of despotism, the danger of which is not a mere paranoid spectre in the institution. That is why the ward must have a public forum where patient rights and responsibilities can be discussed on the same basis as the responsibilies of the institution, the therapists, and the nursing staff. In this way, problems can be processed at a higher level, understood, and shared. This provides a foundation for efforts to promote the capacity-to-contract in patients.

The following is the account of a ward meeting in a women's acute unit.

The atmosphere at the beginning is very disturbed: an excitable patient of shapeless appearance, Mrs Z, appears, puts on a big show, and is asked to calm down; she then storms out, mouthing insults. Members of the team are told that two other patients have stayed in bed and that it has not been possible to induce them to attend the compulsory meeting. The patients are asked who would like to assume certain "duties" in the housekeeping of the ward, for which they take turns. It proves difficult, and needs persuasion to find anyone to assume such tasks. There follow a jumble of questions to staff, involving personal wishes and requests for extensions of leave. The psychologist in charge of the meeting has trouble establishing a coherent theme. As a result, certain questions that deserve an answer go unheard. After a few seconds' silence, another patient, Mrs N, wants to leave; detained at the door, she declares: "I cannot stand it, there is no progress, everyone is talking rubbish here!" She is persuaded to return to her place. A male nurse now intervenes: he has heard a number of other complaints and encourages another patient to have her say, and she complains that her cigarettes and other property are being stolen. Other patients animatedly concur. Mrs Z, who briefly "attended" the group at the beginning, is manifestly the butt of all criticism. As a counterweight to this scapegoat dynamic, the group leader seeks to define the aggression as a group problem: whether or not it was just the problem with Mrs Z, he says that he has noticed that there is a lot of tension anyway, with people encroaching on each other's territories. However, this intervention goes unheard and the complaints about Mrs Z continue. It is only when the senior physician asks by way of interpretation whether there was a feeling that the team was leaving the problem of keeping order too much to the patients themselves that a clear echo is heard from Mrs N: "The staff are not there, or else they just stand by and watch. I would have been put in seclusion long ago if I behaved like Mrs Z!" The ward sister then explains how the staff see the situation complained of and how they handle it, and she mentions the problems presented by overcrowding. This relieves the tension somewhat towards the end of the meeting.

The foregoing is a typical illustration of group life on the ward: coercion and degradation, on the one hand, and aggression and chaos, on the other, tend to reinforce each other. The public forum of the meeting now reflects the irritation of this chaotic situation. The team, for its part, needs to make an effort not to lapse into a predefined role characterized by defensiveness and impotence, which could best be described as that of "guardians of a witches' cauldron". At the end of the meeting, the problematic situation has found appropriate description in words, but no more. However, this creation of a "public language" seems to me to be a decisive foundation for elaboration of the word in the individual therapeutic process, which can then serve as a word given in an agreement.

4. *Individual work.*   Thus, we must regard every therapeutic and other care-related intervention tailored to an individual patient. Psychotherapy shares the platform with pharmacotherapy, social-psychiatric management, psychoeducational procedures, and so forth, and occasionally little if any space may be left to it. In the in-patient situation, whether a therapeutic relationship of any depth can be established is largely a question of length of stay. However, as we have seen, in the NSH situation discharge is the priority objective. Time consequently has a negative selective effect, because it is usually those patients with particularly severe and chronic disturbances, suffering from social disintegration, who remain as inmates of the NSH for longer periods—and these are precisely the patients who seem furthest from being able to tolerate a conventional individual setting. The achievement of a process in an exclusive dyadic relationship, in the isolated therapeutic space of verbal reflection, is feasible with them only in exceptional cases, even after relatively long-term therapeutic contacts.

For this reason, an approach aimed at securing a close connection between, or even interweaving of, individual interviews and concrete life in the therapeutic environment has proved its worth. The therapists, as doctors or psychologists in the ward team, are also involved in the practical care of their patients and coordinate the treatment plan. All patients are assigned a primary nurse to accompany them on a day-to-day basis. This primary nurse is always involved in the interviews with the patient, either on each occasion or at defined intervals. The nurse introduces the concerns of daily behaviour, and possesses a therapeutic understanding of this particular patient, which he or she can carry into the ward and represent to the team. More limited psychotherapeutic settings without the primary nurse, in which the therapist refrains from direct interventions in the patient's present life, become rare, confined to situations where they are particularly indicated. However, the "triadic setting" is delicate, because it is not a simple matter to fill and handle the triangulated role positions, so that specific attention on the part of the therapist is called for in this connection.

5. *"Integration."* Psychotherapy, nursing, social management, pharmacotherapy, art therapy, and so on are not separate boxes in a therapeutic supermarket; nor are they administered as sub-institutions, each by a given profession. Instead, these forms of treatment represent different methodological poles within the same field—that of the ward environment. The distribution of forces among these poles will differ according to the individual patient. In the process, the treatment approaches, the development of the individual relationship and of the group and institutional conditions will interact dynamically.

However, a psychoanalytic "meta-methodology" to underlie this conception as a "theory of integrative technique" in a NSH seems to be still either undeveloped or in need of updating. The question of the interference between the institution and therapy was tackled paradigmatically by the pioneers of the therapeutic community (Main, 1946, 1977) a generation ago. Particular attention was devoted by the French school of *psychothérapie institutionnelle* (Mannoni, 1970; Racamier, 1970) to the situation of general psychiatric institutions. Since then, psychoanalysis has taken little interest in these issues: the psychoanalytic literature on in-patient psychotherapy is concerned explicitly or implicitly with the situation of specialized—that is, selective—institutions. This also applies to the work of Kernberg (1976, 1984) and Janssen (1987). The complex problem of integrating methods tends rather to be left to a crude eclecticism, cloaked in empty formulae of holism or "bio-psycho-social access", or given over to conceptions of cognitive-behavioural therapy, which nowadays offer disorder-centred, "multimodal" treatment programmes. Gabbard (1990) adopts the disorder-centred approach in his textbook *Psychodynamic Psychiatry* and deals systematically, on the basis of the DSM-III-R nosology, with the combination of psychoanalytic forms of access and other methods (namely, behavioural therapy, pharmacotherapy, and marital counselling). However, he tends to base his position more on empirical findings or hospital experience than on a consistent psychoanalytic argument. Again—as seems typical of this disorder-related approach—the institutional context is virtually disregarded.

Importance of reflection

If psychotherapy is not to be confined to an insular existence in the institution, well-established structures of joint, interdisciplinary reflection also covering the emotional issues—that is, the counter-transference—are called for, relating not only to the individual patients and groups but also to team dynamics and the institutional structures. The foundation of this wide-ranging reflection must, in my view, be a psychoanalytic approach, which, while being faithful to its guidelines, does not enjoy a monopoly. However, psychoanalysis is particularly well suited to making tensions tolerable and fruitful. The settings for this process of reflection are well known: supervisions, team case conferences, and in-service training.

It seems particularly important, just in the context of the NSH, for spaces for this reflection to be thoroughly protected and sustained in the institution because (or even though):

- psychotherapy cannot, in practice, usually be applied in settings isolated from the rest of the patient's existence in a pure form;
- pharmacological and social interventions often necessarily take priority in our daily work;
- by their severe regressions and their besetting external realities, the patients press us extraordinarily to join in their acting out and to re-act;
- pressure of time frequently precludes extended consideration.

These conditions give rise in the hospital to a powerful tendency to withdraw cathexis from therapeutic understanding until the latter degenerates into an insignificant accessory. Obviously, where reflection is not taken seriously enough and forfeits its importance in the institution, psychotherapy too will sooner or later fall by the wayside. Only the culture of a permanently shared reflection may guarantee a therapeutic attitude as competence maintained by a group or by an institution.

We can return to the question raised at the beginning of the chapter: how is it possible at all for an institutional psychotherapy to exist in the NSH, which is a bad place where psychotic experience does not find a voice and regressive pathology affords no transitional space, where no substantive symbols appear to exist, and where the concretism of the material (physical coercion, chemical substances, and locked doors) holds sway? This goal can be achieved by way of the therapeutic attitude of the teams, which supply the patients with auxiliary ego functions based on thorough deliberation—providing, as it were, institutional mediation between internal and external reality. In this way, they create the transitional space of communicable symbols, words, and concepts while standing in for the patients, and sketch out an image of understanding. This image serves as the foundation of a therapy whose prerequisites we substantially elaborate in advance, without the presence of the patients, but in their name. Benedetti et al. (1979) describe a similar approach to the individual psychotherapy of schizophrenics. The process corresponds to the thesis mentioned earlier, according to which psychotherapy in the NSH initially appears only as a potential, arising virtually, as an "evenly suspended" psychodynamic consideration, first communicated in the team, and into which the patient can, but need not, himself enter. (The process certainly has a significant preverbal component; certain of its elements may be seen as analogous to Bion's concept of "reverie".) It is liable to disturbance, can easily miscarry and often demands great patience. A patient's "entry" into it is often revealed indirectly, by modest indications. These may be vacillating attempts to accept a commitment.

A female patient of dysplastic appearance, with learning disabilities and a psychotic structure, can discharge her tension only by a stereotyped, self-injuring type of acting out: at the slightest frustration she cuts herself violently with the first sharp object she can find. By this acting out, the patient has developed the ability to create a powerful impact on the team and on the entire institution, thereby disseminating intense feelings of impotence. She was the subject of case conferences, but all attempts at reflection seemed to go round in circles, while the regression intensified and grew in malignance. The image finally occurred to me that this patient was sucking in any energy directed towards her, so that it disappeared for ever "as if in an astronomer's black hole". Although this was hardly a hopeful idea, it did allow the problem to be seen in graphic terms and thereby manifestly contained to some extent; at any rate, the potential for reflection was no longer completely destroyed. This led to a slight but perceptible alleviation. The patient, who had previously been unable to persist in any activity and totally depended on immediate discharge of tension, was suddenly able to declare, "I can stand occupational therapy only for one hour!", and then actually engaged in it for an hour, after which she withdrew. This modest progress nevertheless corresponds to an agreement offered and kept by the patient and may therefore signify an initial step towards a psychotherapy.

Conclusion

The prime function of a hospital providing public psychiatric services is to accept severely regressed patients at all times and to supply them, at first unconditionally and physically, with containment and boundaries, simply because the hospital is already there. One cannot relieve the institution from this responsibility; there is no alternative. Psychotherapy begins—only in our heads, so to speak virtually—and is then absorbed by patients usually in small, seemingly fleeting doses. In this way there arise the nuclei of a therapeutic process. Modest as these may seem, they contain within themselves the prospects for, and the characteristic quality of, psychotherapy in the non-selective mental hospital.

CHAPTER TWO

Integrated theoretical/clinical and organizational models for the institutional treatment of psychosis

Marta Vigorelli

Freud, speaking about the psychotic forms that he called "narcissistic neuroses", makes the following statement in the twenty-sixth of his *Introductory Lectures on Psychoanalysis* (1916-1917):

> The narcissistic neuroses can scarcely be attacked with the technique that has served us with the transference neuroses . . . and what always happens with them is that, after proceeding for a short distance, we come up against a wall that brings us to a stop. . . . At the most, we are able to cast an inquisitive glance over the top of the wall and spy out what is going on on the other side of it. Our technical methods must accordingly be replaced by others; and we do not know yet whether we shall succeed in finding a substitute. [p. 423]

Since that day, many generations of psychoanalysts have accepted the Freudian challenge, a challenge of such complexity that it involves the whole field of modern epistemology which, in this area, takes on the form of a particularly contradictory task—one that leads us to oscillate between, on the one hand, the passion of exploring the unknown, as we grasp the key to understanding the pathology (in the illusion of eliminating it), and, on the other, the desire to widen this unknown space by going beyond the wall of psychotic defences and by attempting to share states both primordial and unthinkable. The contradiction becomes more bearable if we view it as a challenge to accept and cure severe suffering, thereby aiming at a better way of living out our human condition.

The impact with pathological forms previously considered outside the theoretical/clinical field, particularly the psychoses, has engaged psychoanalysis in many areas—theoretical, technical, and institutional. Interest in the origins and genesis of psychosis has stimulated research into early stages of development. The resulting models of how the mind functions are increasingly rigorous and serve to build up theories on these areas and on primitive states of subjectivity (Aparo, Casonato, & Vigorelli, 1989, pp. 28–31). These psychoanalytic theories are rich and varied, but we can summarize the various viewpoints under three main headings.

1. There is the school of thought that considers that psychotic disturbances differ mainly in *quantitative* terms from the neuroses. These theories hold that the mechanisms operating in the psychotic patient are the same as in any other, but more intense and severe. Primary persecutory anxieties and schizoid mechanisms are stronger, and symptoms are explained by the predominant use of projective identification. This approach—shared by Abraham and the Kleinians (Klein, Bion, Rosenfeld)[1]—is based on the assumption that the more severe the mental disturbance, the earlier are its origins. With some differences in emphasis, these authors all see psychosis as marked by the classic early, inborn intrapsychic conflicts but more intense, founded on aggressivity and inner sadism, with greater regression leading to disturbances of thought and of the organization of the ego. This view sees the mind as a container of recognizable internal objects and addresses the "parts of the self" that must be identified in the analytic relationship.

This "unitary" theoretical approach (London, 1973) employs much of the "classic" therapeutic technique—the couch, analysis and interpretation of defences, transference and countertransference, and so forth—without any special modifications for psychosis. The psychoanalyst has to start by containing the projections, thereby gradually reducing splitting, using the "non-psychotic" part of the patient's personality for leverage. All measures needed to deal with episodes of crisis during the therapy—admission to hospital, psychopharmaca, contacts with relatives, and so on—constitute a sort of fence, to protect the core of the treatment, which is the psychoanalytic relation.

2.   The second school of thought sees the difference between neurosis and psychosis as a *qualitative* question, on the grounds that the structural disturbances of psychotic pathologies are produced by a *deficit* dating back to the early stages of infantile development, leading subsequently to an inadequacy of certain important psychological functions. Fenichel (1935), Hartmann (1953), Jacobson (1954), Federn (1952), Greenson and Wexler (1969), and Wexler (1971) all agree that psychosis and neurosis differ substantially, because only the former involves the loss or decathexis of object-representations.[2] This "specific" theoretical approach requires a change in the classic technique: treatment aims at rebuilding the lost structures and enabling the patient to acquire a stable sense of the self, more than at interpreting conflicts and defences. Bearing in mind the patient's deficiencies—genetic and functional—the therapist prefers a protected environment and tries to keep a positive transference, achieving a therapeutic alliance through supportive, restraining measures.

3.   The third approach—which is closest to our own clinical and theoretical work—takes account of the *qualitative and quantitative* differences between neurosis and psychosis, as much as of the *deficits and conflicts* underlying these states. American authors draw on the experience of Mahler, Fromm-Reichmann, Searles, Kohut, and the interpersonal theories of Grotstein, Giovacchini, and Pao. In Europe, the theorists are Winnicott, Tustin, Racamier, and Zapparoli.

We have to thank Pao and the far-reaching research done at the Chestnut Lodge Clinic for a systematic overview of this question. Psychosis is considered as a *"multideterminate" phenomenon*, emerging in a vulnerable self from a complex network of biogenetic, phantasmatic, relational, familial, and environmental factors. Pao's proposed diagnostic-prognostic formulation—involving three subtypes of schizophrenia, depending on the severity of the deficit—

views the factors related to *self cohesion* in relation to the patient's *individual history*, and to the intrapsychic and relational dynamics followed throughout that patient's development (Pao, 1979).

This approach, too, involves modifications to the classic technique, since treatment must be adapted to the psychotic patient's needs. For instance, it may be fundamental for him to be simultaneously close to and far from the object, in a "dilemma" between need and fear (Burnham, Gibson, & Gladstone, 1969). The therapist must therefore be in tune both with the basic faults, and with the conflicts. To begin with, he will preferentially try to help restore the cohesion of the self, by being empathically present, employing non-verbal messages and an adaptable setting face to face with the patient. Once the relationship has been structured, he can then flexibly tackle analysis of the defences and transference, in order to help the patient face up to his conflicts and modify his distorted representation of the self and of the object (Arrigoni Scortecci, 1988, pp. 624–629).

The complexity of severe pathology calls for integrated theories

Recent studies of the psychoanalytic treatment of psychosis in Italy today, conducted within the SIPP [Italian Association for Psychoanalytical Psychotherapy] and by a SPI [Italian Psychoanalytical Association] Study Committee for severe pathologies, illustrate the growing impact of this type of research which has led to an expansion of the techniques—groups are used, as are integrated therapies, family or community therapies, combinations of psycho- and pharmacotherapy, and so on. It has, however, also led to self-examination and debate among psychoanalysts about the real potential for understanding and treatment. *Severe mental illness* causes problems for the stability, continuity, and sharing of the analytic setting and therefore compels us to change our techniques— especially the ductility and modulation of the setting. More than any other clinical field, it stimulates a continual confrontation with neighbouring disciplines, particularly the neuropsychological, cognitivistic, systemic approaches, and developmental psychology.

The limits of using any single reference method are amply underlined by the complexity of the aspects and problems these disturbances involve, affecting not just one individual but his whole family and social grouping.

In line with the latest reflections in Italian psychoanalysis, I would like to propose that the complexity created by the issue—psychosis and severe pathology—calls for a widening of our analytic functions, and for attempts to integrate the numerous theoretical psychoanalytic models representing the multifaceted phenomenology of mental life.

My definition of integration between models—instinctual, structural, based on unconscious fantasy, on object-relation, on self psychology—implies ". . . introjection of every model, affectively transformed by the therapist so that the model itself becomes a sort of internal object, shorn, in other words, of its ritualistic and ideologized aspects and enriched by an individual perspective" (Correale & Rinaldi, 1997, p. 5).

I believe that this is the challenge psychosis holds out for our research. On the one hand, we therapists have to develop an internal setting and affective–cognitive–phantasmatic quality as a real person, in continual contact with strong, often explosive, basic emotions. On the other, we have to work to blend the different theoretical elements, in terms going beyond mere addition or an eclectic vision:

> The self as a structure and function at the same time, the fluidity or rigidity of object relations, the boundaries between intrapsychic, intrasubjective and relational, the relation between empathy and countertransference—these are all examples of basic psychoanalytical elements, particularly suitable for working at integration and confrontation. . . . In other words, it seems to us useful not to put self psychology and psychology of object relations against each other, or the theories of conflict and deficit, but on the contrary, there is a need to focus precisely on how these spheres constantly interact, and how the object relations partly adapt to and partly deeply influence the state of the self which, in turn, partly influences and partly is influenced by the vicissitudes of object relations.
>
> Against this background, the different models acquire specific placings, each casting light on its own zone of the psychic world: the fate of instincts; balance in the inner world; how closed or open are the boundaries; how concrete or symbol-

ized is thought; how far symbolization can proceed in relation to the degree of trauma—leading to the question of the relations between psychoanalysis and expressive or supportive psychotherapies, etc. [Correale & Rinaldi, 1997, pp. 4–5]

This viewpoint leads to important consequences. On the clinical level, it tends to combine insight, knowledge, curiosity, and interpretation on the one hand, with an attitude that stresses the depth of the relation—a space for a holding environment—the emotional contact, empathy, the possibility of testing new emotions, and a response modulated to the patient's affective needs. On the practical/organization level, it tends to overcome the opposition between pharmacological and psychotherapeutic approaches, between therapy and rehabilitation, between individual and group (particularly family) dimensions, and between private dual settings and institutional settings.

Psychoanalysis
and institutional intervention models

Historically speaking, surmounting the wall mentioned by Freud in the quotation at the beginning of this chapter has thus led to a significant invasion of psychoanalytic thinking in psychiatric institutions, both public and private. This has been a remarkable encounter between psychoanalysis and society and has led therapists to work "outside the session" face-to-face with dramatic suffering, in contact with a range of different professionals, a variety of theoretical/clinical tendencies, and organizational restrictions that are not always coherent or adequate. However, the institutional context is increasingly considered indispensable in dealing with pathologies that need extensive spaces, personnel, and treatment tools, which form a complex field with specific organizers that themselves must be continuously regulated (Vigorelli, 1994).

A pioneering psychoanalytic experience was led by Bion in England, with small groups and a rich range of interventions involving groups, couples, and families at the Tavistock Institute of Human Relations, where a worthwhile model of integration between psychoanalytic technique and systemic orientation has been built up (see "The network model", below).

In Italy, too, we have witnessed the gradual entry of an increasing number of psychoanalysts and psychoanalytically orientated psychotherapists, often heading services specialized in the institutional care and therapy of psychotic patients. The 1970s and 1980s saw a systematic investigation of the theories and techniques of group psychotherapy (Bruni, 1985; Corrao, 1982; Neri, 1991, 1995), a reflection concerning the primitive dynamics of the institutional field (Correale, 1991), while a research activity in this field has been carried out by some universities (Genova, Bologna, Florence, Rome, Palermo), and particularly by Dario De Martis and Fausto Petrella in Pavia.

Relations between psychoanalysis and the psychiatric institutions, initially very strained, gradually improved as numerous interesting experiences were reported in Europe, the United States, and South America, most of which differed widely in their methodology and organizational approach. I shall pick out a few important models of psychotherapeutic organization in institutions where priority was given to treatment of psychoses and severe pathologies.

The psychoanalytic approach seems to have been based on four main theoretical/clinical models, which are still in current use:

1. The bifocal model lays emphasis on the dual therapeutic relationship, with some technical modifications of the classic setting, specific for psychosis, in a highly protected institutional context.

2. The small integrated-group model is based on individual intervention involving several professional figures whose work is coordinated in response to the patient's different needs: psychotherapeutic, pharmacological, care, and rehabilitation.

3. The community model proposes a group of staff taking care of a group of patients, involving their families too in an everyday-type psychotherapeutic environment.

4. The network model comprises the first three models within a series of coordinated structures in the same geographical area, where the patient can follow his own progressive path through

the various stages of the illness and treatment—acute, subacute, and chronic—and can draw on local resources to fit into the social context.

Two interesting questions arise: do these four models express four clear-cut concepts of psychosis? To what extent do the models reflect the different attitudes in the various parts of the world where they were thought up?

I personally feel that there is no real match between place of origin, theoretical concept, and organizational model (although a separate investigation would be warranted to answer this point reliably). I do, however, feel that there is a theoretical difference between the first model and the others, in the sense that it shifts the main emphasis from the setting and the relation to which the patient must adapt to a concept of a "facilitating environment"—that is, the small group, community, or network of structures—that can flexibly adapt and articulate itself according to the various needs of the patient.

This shift is in line with the growing conviction that psychoanalytic treatment and analytically orientated psychotherapy are not enough on their own to achieve significant gains in the psychotic patient. They can, however, be used effectively as part of a continuum of interventions involving shared everyday experiences. This serves not only to contain the primitive, chaotic phantasmatic world or re-acquire lost affective-cognitive functions but also to live new emotions, which can to some extent help repair the deep wounds to the structure of the self (spatial-temporal, corporeal, cohesive structures stabilizing the sense of self: Correale, 1997, pp. 29–39).

The sequence of organizational models outlined here is progressive in its complexity and interaction with other viewpoints, which I feel reflects the need for integration expressed on a theoretical level earlier in this chapter.

The bifocal model

The first organizational model to be analysed here lays emphasis on the dual therapeutic relationship, with some technical changes specific to psychoses, situated in a highly protected institutional context. It started in the Chestnut Lodge private clinic, near Washington, at a time when insurance companies in the United States financed long-term psychoanalytic therapy. For fifty-odd years it has served as a fertile laboratory for care and research by Fromm-Reichmann, Sullivan, Searles, Burnham, Gladstone, Pao, and Feinsilver.

Patients admitted are psychotics or borderline cases or present with severe character disturbances, and they are kept under initial observation for diagnosis—mainly without drugs. They all lend themselves to intensive psychoanalytic psychotherapy (four sessions, spatiotemporal regularity, confidential dialogue, abstinence). For a fairly long initial period, patients remain housed in the clinic; they subsequently move out of the clinic into small apartments and find employment, coming to the hospital for individual psychotherapy.

They are not obliged to stay as in-patients, but the clinic serves as a stable container for: (1) intensive psychoanalytic treatment, modified in order to resolve conflicts; (2) a protected lifestyle, where functional deficiencies and developmental arrests can be overcome; (3) help to family members. Every intervention, however, is aimed primarily at initiating, maintaining, and ensuring the therapeutic process, with a view to structural change of the personality.

The leading role is played by the therapist, backed by a second figure, the administrator, whose task is to manage all the other aspects of the patient's life—drugs, rehabilitation, contacts with the family. To guarantee the coordination of the two roles, there are discussions, meetings, and team supervisions.

These two main figures are part of an organization headed by a director of psychotherapy and a clinical director. If disagreement arises about a clinical assessment, the matter is referred to a council made up of senior therapists, and the final decision in particularly difficult cases is made by the head of the clinic. Hardly applicable outside a protected environment and prolonged hospitalization, this model assumes that the patient needs intensive psychoanalytic therapy—involving the possibility of a working alliance and at least a minimal call for help—and that the two therapists have complementary ideas aimed at integrating the split aspects that the patient—on account of the very nature of his ailment—tends to project into the two persons in charge. If they are not aware of the projections in play, the therapists' own conflictuality may aggravate the symptoms considerably, with serious iatrogenic consequences.

The small integrated-group model

This model involves several professional figures who employ an integrated method in response to the patient's different needs: psychotherapeutic, pharmacological, care, and rehabilitation. In Zapparoli's nearly thirty-year-old elaboration, still widely adopted in Italian institutions, this model is not viewed merely as the sum of several combined interventions, but as a dynamic process of emotive-cognitive integration of intrapsychic and relational functions aimed at answering the needs of the patient and his family, assessed after thorough diagnostic observation. The model can be applied in public or private institutions. In the latter case, the psychotherapist or psychiatrist who receives the request directly from the patient, or from his relatives, calls on a nurse or educator and social assistant to form a small group, planning an individual therapeutic project and coordinating the various roles. A team comprising several professional figures means that the intensity of the psychotic transference can be spread over more than one person, at the same time overcoming the concept of the omniscient therapist, who alone could not deal with all the patient's complex requirements. We start out from the psychotic patient's need "to receive at multiple levels stimuli toward integration, in order to counteract the disintegrating force manifested by the peculiar resistance to change common in this pathology" (Zapparoli et al., 1988, p. 19). This is what distinguishes the integrated model from the "organicistic", bio-psycho-social one: not ideologically favouring any one approach, but starting from an understanding of the needs expressed by patients, by listening as openly and fully as possible.

The small integrated-group model is effective when there is a constant interactive exchange between its members, transforming individual opinions about the patient into an overall representation, whilst working simultaneously on different levels of integration: the relationship between the individual and his environment and that pertaining to the different intrapsychic structures or functions of the personality.

This multiple approach, with its different observation points, forms a sort of preliminary scaffolding for the various separate parts that the psychotic patient cannot integrate within his self. He may project a personage from his own inner group onto each team member, or use the group as a whole to activate fragments of his self. He may therefore deposit a body aspect in one of the staff, a cognitive part in another, an instinctual part in yet another, and so on, plotting out a very rough map of his internal world.

In their group meetings, therefore, the staff can re-assemble the patient's split parts, creatively thinking them over. Each fragment can gain from the passage from one mind to another, and from the meeting of various viewpoints.

The group work can be considered the preparation for a central, stable, lasting relation, implying a spontaneous affective investment by the patient. This type of relation need not always be with the therapist: a nurse or teacher can serve as the continuous supporting presence. The resulting hierarchy, with different importance attributed to the various functions, is not based on the application of a scheme established outside, as in the previous model, but results from the gradual progress of the work. In this sense, the group serves as a "sort of protective system for a nascent relation in which the patient can feel that a very important part of himself is guarded and developed" (Correale, 1991, p. 134).

The community model

The community model proposes an overall psychotherapeutic milieu—the group of staff and group of patients in the context of everyday life—divided into its different moments and paths. Although it started as an ideologically orientated movement, outside the psychoanalytic culture, many psychoanalysts have used the therapeutic community as a special sort of research laboratory, their experience subsequently becoming part of psychoanalytic history. I am thinking particularly of the communities of Cassel Hospital in Great Britain, founded by Tom Main[3] in the 1950s; of Les Cèdres in Switzerland in the 1970s;[4] of Lieu de Vie in Villeurbanne, where Marcel Sassolas worked; and, above all, of Velotte in Besançon, set up in 1968 and headed by Racamier.

Although starting out in very different contexts, with specific clinical and organizational methods, these communities display interesting analogies: first, all the relationships and everyday activities within the community have therapeutic purpose, and all the members—physicians, nurses, administrators, families—take part in the management of the community. Another factor is that patients are activated and given responsibility, in a climate of acceptance and spontaneous communication. Finally, group periods of self-reflection, coordination, and decisions about therapeutic projects open to the whole community or to the group of staff are assigned ritual importance. They alternate with periods aimed at individual patients or the small group.

How can we define in general terms the specific therapeutic factors of the community method for treating psychosis? Above all, there is the flexibility and attention to the sense of cohesion, the *ésprit de corps*, in a tightly shared emotive climate. This is what makes the community setting so stimulating and change-orientated. The therapeutic community can be considered the site of a process that serves virtually as a "nursery" in its early stages, gradually developing into a training field for life and for planning a new future (Caltagirone & Smargiassi, 1997).

Unlike the first manifestations of the community movement, which considered themselves a revolutionary force in contrast to the culture of the prison-like asylum, the more recent therapeutic communities open to psychotic patients—in Italy recognized by the Psychiatric Reform Act—view themselves not so much as exemplary events, but rather as experiences available within a wide range of possibilities: communities for "adolescents", for "young psychotic adults", for "chronic psychotics", and so on. The layouts and organizational and clinical procedures all differ according to the severity of the patients' illness, and their different needs for protection (protected communities, residential therapeutic centres, halfway houses, etc.).

In contrast to the first and second models, the community model exploits to the full the specific therapeutic factors and potential of the group, meaning not only the staff but the overall interactions between the staff and the residents and their families. This simultaneous mix of relations means that each member of the group can usefully make the self-observation from experiencing, how his own inner contents resound in the minds of the others. This possibility of making his own affective experiences reflect in other people gives the psychotic patient an extraordinary opportunity to recapture aspects of himself that he could not tolerate before. The sense of the group as a whole, the energy holding it together, is like a limiting membrane, a skin, that the patient gradually absorbs, internalizes, acquiring a sense of his own boundaries.

The community group also offers everyone involved an occasion for externalizing and presenting "on stage" their own stories, dreams, and memories, reviving old relational models that have been lived but never thought out. The therapeutic group can help turn them into lived representations, which become symbolized.

At an even more primitive level, life in a therapeutic community is aimed at strengthening the self, meant as a multiplicity of functions and as structure. The self as a structure develops through the repetition of psychophysical states that give the subject the feeling of a compact existence. At the same time he feels the vital flux that gives a sense of continuity. The functions of the self focus on the organization and integration of perceptions and events, on animating life, and relate to space, time, and affects. The first structuring experiences take place in a presymbolic phase, which is where the therapeutic factors of the community take root. The community, with its repetition of shared moments, can serve as a place where a more cohesive self emerges, gradually acquiring a three-dimensional inner reality (Correale, 1995a, 1996).

The network model

Another model of an institutional setting where psychoanalysis has been widely used for the treatment of psychoses involves therapeutic interventions divided up and differentiated throughout a territorial network. A community network perspective[5] provides a dimension that pervades the totality of institutional life, creating a shared cultural and affective richness, supported by a strong sense of belonging, that can powerfully affect the growth and development of the whole context in which it originates. Paradigmatic examples are the experiences of the XIII Arrondissement in Paris (Paumelle, 1970), Antonio Andreoli in Geneva, and Nicolas De Coulon in Montreux, to mention only those I have had the opportunity of seeing at first hand.

The implementation of this setting (still only partially completed) has marked a decisive turning-point in Italy, too, compared to the segregation of the mental asylum. (We are referring to the historic transformation of the psychiatric organization in Italy, which is the shift from the asylum system to the territorial system, embodied in Law No. 180, 1978.) This has been facilitated by clinical work of reintegration and rehabilitation of psychotic patients, which has revealed ever more clearly how the individual pathology is a function of a wider pathology involving an entire group, with the whole network of intersubjective relationships created among its members.

Attempts at understanding are therefore orientated at a system that comprises the patient, his family, his environment, and the social structure of the community. In this perspective, the focus can be set either on the patient, as one point in the network, correlated with others, or on the pathology, which can be viewed as something diffused, affecting the entire network, in which the patient presents a symptomatic urgency (Petrella, 1978).

Aspects that are traditionally perceived and filed in separate "cubby-holes" are thus connected in a dynamic weave; the hard task of mediation is work done by the local team, which has thus to clarify its identity, its culture, and its therapeutic strategies. Every group ends up oscillating between a tendency to defensive isolation from its outside context, or to dispersion that translates itself in a loss of specificity. These are typical difficulties that every group has to overcome if it is to become truly integrated with the community. This requires periods of construction and close evaluation, adopting a comprehensive, internal and external, individual and group-orientated perspective. The field of operations of the team itself is structured as a network, wherein the different perspectives are highlighted and connected, by developing dialectic exchange and, occasionally, by reflecting, from time to time on significance and meaning.

This mobile, dynamic view can be extended from the individual workgroup to the more complex network on which the various therapeutic spaces are laid out, according to the different stages of the pathological itinerary. An inter-system map emerges, with numerous operating centres, each relatively autonomous but all regularly exchanging input and output. The model inspiring this structure dates back to the 1950s at the Tavistock Institute of Human Relations and the Grubb Institute in London. These combined the systemic approach with the psychoanalytic theories of Bion, Jaques, Miller, Rice, and Turquet about groups and defence mechanisms specific to institutions. The dynamic interaction between the individual, the group, and the institution is investigated, starting by looking at the aims, the circulation of information inside, and the permeability of boundaries to the outside environment. The institution, considered as a whole made up of tasks, hierarchies, instruments, structures, and people, is viewed within a play of social forces that, to variable extents and in different periods, influence the life-experiences and the imagery of the individuals and of the group as a whole. It follows that the approach taken to treatment is likely to be strongly affected by expectations and social pressures, which are passed on in concentric circles to the management, to the administration, to the staff, to the dynamics of the group, and to the defence systems adopted (Rice, 1976).

The therapeutic process and organization of institutional settings

Our own experience leads us to believe that, during his therapeutic journey, the psychotic patient may need two or more interlocutors and structures, each separate but complementary and closely interdependent. The path need not be linear but may swing between regressive-fusional moments when the environment must be predominantly containing, and more mature periods that can be enjoyed in more open and stimulating surroundings.

This does not detract from the importance of the mediation provided by the correlations between the therapeutic couple (using a psychotherapeutic technique specific for psychosis), the small integrated group working with the patient, the residential and daytime community structures, and the network team as a whole. However, this is what makes therapeutic continuity possible, an assumption of the responsibility for the therapeutic process taken by a therapist and a therapeutic team, even when different operations and teams are used during the various stages of the therapeutic process. In the Italian National Health System, the network of these services reports to the Mental Health Department, headed by a chief psychiatrist, who coordinates the different operative centres in close collaboration with the general administration of the Local Health Care Unit (USSL).

In psychotics, the process of differentiation and integration is often damaged at different levels; plans for these patients must therefore take this into account, and all interventions must be appropriately scaled, and gradually extended over time, using progressively different structures.

Along the continuum of concept pairs that mark the starting conditions of the patient—fragmentation/cohesion, deficit/conflict, denial/awareness of illness, dependence/emancipation, and so forth—an intermediate range of intrapsychic and relational possibilities emerges. These require specific methods and specific places for housing and treatment and range from full-scale protection and containment to more independent facilities, leading gradually towards social rehabilitation and a better level of subjective living.

- *The basic structure:* Usually an out-patient facility serves for the initial functions, which are reception and an understanding of the demands of the external social milieu. These mostly concern those patients who contact the service not through normal channels, but by proxy of others (family, an institution, neighbours, etc.) because they themselves are unable to apply for help, or are in a state of serious fragmentation. This is the place where a diagnosis is made—a space for listening and decoding the requests and the specific needs both of the patient and his family. The aim is to work out a therapeutic plan, which means responsibility is taken either for psychotherapy (individual, group, family, etc.) or for the small integrated-group approach, home care, psychopharmaca, and social assistance. The patient may have to be sent to a more specific structure for treatment and rehabilitation.

- *Places for treatment:* This heading comprises two criteria. First there are the structures that serve as a protective system in situations of temporary or prolonged acute crisis, of breakdown, collapse, or destructuration of the psychic organization, or when the dual relationship becomes too problematic to be able to contain the patient's self- and hetero-destructive tendencies. For acute states, there is the hospital ward or the crisis centre and high-protection communities, with no time limits, designed to protect and support the chronic psychotic patient's remaining resources (Lanzara, 1994). These are places where the patient is considered as "being with us" (Sassolas, 1987), with a strong bond of dependence on account of the extreme vulnerability of the self.

- *Places for living:* A second group of structures deals with the patient who is relatively capable of "being with himself", dealing with the institutional space more like his own territory, and maintaining his relationship with the group. These are intermediate structures and function either on a daily basis (day-hospitals, rehabilitation workshops, structured activities, etc.), or on a residential basis (residential centres for therapy and rehabilitation, therapeutic communities, halfway houses, etc.). They offer a community lifestyle, where individual projects can be worked on for discharge, with the ultimate aim of rehabilitation in the outside world.

* * *

At whatever point of the institutional network the patient finds himself, it is essential to be able to refer to a setting—meaning a sensorial and affective space with temporal rhythms, rules, and limits, together with the possibility of leaving and returning. "The frame is essential", Racamier stresses, "with reference to the temporal, spatial and often corporeal confusion in which psychotics live, which they may transmit to those around them. It represents a mental mooring place for patients who have a broken psyche" (p. 23).

This brokenness, or discontinuity, takes us back to that fundamental lack of "being" in people who have been significantly dropped in a series of environmental failures (Winnicott, 1965, 1989). To these patients, one responds with a concrete function of "holding", but with a "holding" that can contain such dynamically complementary elements as continuity and discontinuity. Therapy working only on the continuity level risks chronicization, whereas if it is discontinuous—for instance, if the structures close for weekends and holidays—it generates in the patients the effect of alternating between crises and improvement, with subsequent relapses, along the model of the revolving door.

At least one structure in the institutional network must stay open all the time, even if no patient is there; this provides a means of maintaining continuity despite discontinuity. Even when all the patients go home for short or long periods, they know that there is a place where there is always someone to meet them, which never completely shuts down. This enables them to leave with the certainty that they can come back should they need it, hence gradually internalizing the notion of continuity of existence. The same applies with regard to the medical staff, which, though discontinuous and alternating, are always only a telephone call away.

Whereas in the classic dual setting everything must be focused and linked up in a single space, patients with such scant internal resources for putting up with waiting or for containing their excitement or aggressiveness need differentiated and progressive means for shaping images and emotions. Divided up in a logical order, these places and intervals work like "settling basins" through which primitive aspects gradually become more fluid and mobile, and easier to work through.

At the same time, a workgroup is entrusted with the fundamental task of containing the psychotic structure: ". . . jelling, aggregating, constructing units starting from fragments and details. This habit of integration, possible only in groups, gradually becomes a source of fresh thinking, bringing with it an emotive and cognitive richness that is new for each individual" (Correale, 1995, p. 22). The therapeutic frame does not consist solely of spaces, rules, and functions, but—above all—of people. The therapeutic team—comprising psychiatrists, psychotherapists, nurses, educators, social workers, rehabilitation specialists, supervisors, and so forth—and the various operative units work together on the elaboration, synthesis, and restoration of the meaning of what is happening in the institutional network. Regular, scheduled encounters are therefore indispensable for the coordination and vital circulation of information and affects, as much as a spirit of unbroken collegiality and a climate of listening to all the different and differing viewpoints, so as to overcome the misunderstandings, deadlocks, and hostilities that any approach to the complex plots of psychotic pathology often brings about.

* * *

To conclude this overview, I would like to make a few points about the position of the psychoanalytic psychotherapist when acting as a leader in the therapeutic institutions network. Regardless of whether she works within the institutional context with psychotherapeutic and organizational responsibilities or is an external consultant acting as supervisor, trainer, or adviser for an institutional group, the complexity of the various levels of the game obliges her to take a global perspective so as to recognize the recurrent defence mechanisms, the different levels of conflict, and those group dynamics that often tend to paralyse the process of confrontation, circulation, and exchange. It is a tiring job, requiring a willingness to deal with primitive, unstructured emotive states and identify the needs and specific features of the individuals and of their shared potential.

Orientating clinical strategies in institutions implies a sort of amplification of the group, based on the ability to put the new-found awareness into circulation, bringing out each team member's personal resources and stimulating their curiosity and their satisfaction in working together. This is what inspires the images of the orchestra, used by Racamier on many occasions (1970, 1978, 1992), as an arrangement for cultural and affective exchange based on different talents and skills within an organism that has to be made to live and grow.

In the creation of this environment, the emotive qualities of the atmosphere, the oneiric animation, and patience while waiting constitute the elements of choice for diluting the intensity of totalizing transferences and the threats of primitive defences.

NOTES

1. Some North American authors, such as Arlow and Brenner, moved in this direction in the late 1960s, stimulating an interesting debate on the conflict theory as opposed to the deficit theory. At the XXVIth International Congress in Rome in 1969, they presented a paper entitled "The Psychopathology of the Psychoses: A Proposed Revision" (Arlow & Brenner, 1969), in which they upheld the idea of a continuum between neurosis and psychosis, explained by a single theory taken from Freud's *Inhibitions, Symptoms and Anxiety* (1926d [1925]). According to this theory an intrinsically weak ego plays a pivotal role in the psychopathology of the psychoses, and the formation of the symptom can be understood in terms of conflict–anxiety–defence, being so strong as to provoke the experience of an inner catastrophe.

2. These authors rest their case on Freud's theory in "Psychoanalytic Notes on an Autobiographical Account of a Case of Paranoia" (1911c [1910]), which explains symptom formation in two steps. In the first there is libidinal decathexis of the object, expressed by the experience of inner catastrophe, and hypercathexis of the ego, in the form of megalomania or hypochondria. The second step involves an attempt at cure by object-recathexis, this being expressed by schizophrenic symptoms such as delirium, hallucination, and thought disturbances.

3. Tom Main's book *The Ailment and Other Psychoanalytic Essays* (1989) shows clearly and in depth the theoretical and organizational origins of this pioneering institution, which has managed to grow, keeping its own precise identity despite strong outside pressures. It is worth reading R. D. Hinshelwood's paper, "Cultural Pressure on the Therapeutic Community: Internal and External Factors" (1996).

4. We are referring to Woodbury's attempt to turn the closed section of Les Cèdres, in the Geneva Rives de Prangins clinic, into a therapeutic community.

5. The theoretical roots of the concept of a network—meaning not just the sum of various relations, but a whole with the features of all the parts—can be traced back to S. H. Foulkes, on the topic of the group (in analysis) and the idea of mental illness, referring to the whole plexus of relations between several people, more than just the function of an individual's personality (Foulkes, 1946, 1964, 1975).

CHAPTER THREE

The role of institutional settings in symbolization

René Roussillon

I would like to present a series of reflections about care-giving institutions and their therapeutic functioning, and to link them with the issue of therapeutic work in institutions, especially by psychotherapists, and the particular way that therapeutic space is constructed within such settings. These reflections arise from my position as a psychoanalyst, which has led me to define psychoanalytically orientated psychotherapeutic work as the task of symbolizing a subject's experience and his place within the representational process. The effort to symbolize strikes me as being the most profitable means of bringing about a real, subjective appropriation both of historical and current experience and of the instinctual investment that has been or is now being made in them.

The reflections are based upon three types of clinical experience that have furnished the material that prompted them.

For more than twenty years, as well as working as a psychoanalyst in private practice I have practised psychoanalytic psychotherapy at a day hospital in one of the adult psychiatric sectors in the Lyon region. There, in collaboration with teams of social workers, my particular concern has been with patients or "users" of the day hospital and consultation centre who are described as "psychotic" or "borderline", and who form the majority of the patients seeking help.

Apart from this direct experience of the issue, I have also developed extensive activity as a supervisor—or, rather, research supervisor—of psychotherapies in institutions with a varied population, though mainly made up of people presenting disturbances of identity and narcissism (autistic, psychotic, and children and adults with an antisocial tendency, as Winnicott, 1956, defined it). I emphasize research supervision because part of this work has consisted precisely in trying to construct "tailor-made" psychotherapy arrangements for one or other type of disturbance or psychopathology, and it takes place at the research centre where I work in the University of Lyon 2 (CRPPC).

Finally, as the third strand of clinical experience underlying my reflections, we have developed—again, within the research centre at Lyon 2 (directed by Professor P. Fustier)—a practice that intervenes in caregiving institutions "in crisis", something that has enabled us to take an overall view of the problems encountered by those institutions that, apart from re-education projects, set themselves "therapeutic" aims.

There are three themes to which I would like to pay particular attention here. The first concerns the concept of transference, a central theme when thinking of psychotherapeutic functions, and especially the notion of *transference to the setting or institutional provision*. From this perspective, there arises the question—itself essential to our theme—of institutional countertransference to its "users", of disturbances of narcissism and identity.

Naturally, the second point to be addressed concerns clinical treatment of narcissistic/identity disturbances in "users" of caregiving institutions, and the characteristic intersubjective difficulties that this type of disturbance provokes in institutional relationships, especially those with "therapeutic" aims.

Finally, this should leave us well placed to broach the question of the "echoing", "reflexive", or even "mirroring" function of institutional arrangements for psychic care; this is in addition to the question, dialectically linked to the last, of their "symbol-generating" function, or the symbol-generating productivity of a certain type of institutional "response" to what is acted out in caregiving relationships.

"Institutional" transference: particulars of the problem

The notion of a transference specific to a caregiving setting strikes me as being absolutely essential when thinking about processes that develop within institutions for "psychic" care. This was present in Freud's thinking in 1912 when he described the development of transferential processes in caregiving relationships in general before specifying the particular form that such a transference tends to take in psychoanalytic treatment (1912b, p. 99). In 1914 he characterized the latter as "analysable" transference neurosis, not "simple" transference (1914g, p. 147). It lies behind the analysis he offered in 1921 of "organized" groups, in which he stressed that one part of the mind links up with the "institutionalized" group organization—for example, by superimposing ego-ideal and leader upon one another—a notion that was subsequently developed much further (e.g. by Bion, 1959; Bleger, 1970; Jaques, 1953; Roussillon, 1995).

The notion of transference to the setting or institution is an attempt to define the particular investment in the setting itself and the specificity of those aspects of the subject's history that are replayed in it. The idea is that a specific psychic problem tends to be displaced onto the setting rather than onto anything else, and this is related to the setting's particular psychic function: *it symbolizes symbol-forming activity*. By the same token, there is a tendency to displace, repeat, and replay around it issues connected with the activity of symbolization. Therefore, I stress most emphatically the issues connected with symbols in general and symbolization itself, not simply issues connected with any one particular symbol or specific fantasy. This hypothesis therefore implies that whatever is chosen to be "transferred" onto institutional settings belongs to the history of the subject's relationship with the activity of symbolization; the history of its successes and, above all, its setbacks and vicissitudes; and the history of the particularities of its construction as well as of its deconstructions and traumas. *If a setting symbolizes symbolization, this means that it also potentially embodies the conditions or preconditions for symbolization to occur, since it represents or carries symbolization, or even gets called upon to stand in for it.*

What are often, perhaps awkwardly, referred to as "attacks on the setting" could then better be understood as active traces of the history of the way in which a user's symbolizing activity has historically been "attacked" by life circumstances or in certain modes of relationship.

I mentioned above that the institutional setting might be called upon to provide the framework of conditions for the act of representation or symbolization. "Transference" of this kind depends upon these preconditions, or rather on a certain number of facilitating conditions. The conditions that favour its development exclude any demand that users should submit passively to caregivers or to the institutional use of terror or despair. These conditions are, unfortunately, not always met, although they do occur often enough to promote the possibility of using institutional settings as ones that can generate symbolization.

When favourable conditions do coincide, transference both to the whole institution and to its individual sectors can develop, so that traumas that had affected the subject's history might be replayed, repeated differently, and thus have a new and integrative outcome. This is the way that caregiving institutions can have an overall therapeutic function. In all events, whether transference to the setting is utilized by caregivers or not and whether it is facilitated or not, it does in fact creep into both relations with the setting as a whole and the relationships within it.

Experience shows that one can usually identify two phases in the installation and development of transference to caregiving institutions.

In the first phase, the central issue is to establish whether what is pent up within a potential user can be taken in by the caregiving place, and whether what is "astray" or unallocated in the subject (discussed below)—in other words, what has not thus far found a fitting symbolic form—can be "adopted" by the institution. This first phase uses the institution as a primary, palliative, linking system, so that cathecting the setting is partially confused with "dumping" things into it, and hence the subject's psychopathology and the institution become unified and lack proper internal links.

This is a period when "belonging" to the institution is very much at issue and when the investment that underlies transference to the setting is being made. At this level, one could describe the "caring" function of the institution as an "attractor" and "collector" of wandering and excluded parts. This first period sees the installation of transference to the institution and is a precondition for it. Bion (1959), Jaques (1953), and Fornari (1971), following Freud, have described the ways in which institutions bind and structure the fundamental anxieties of identity; institutions thus function along lines that I have suggested may be described as "metadefences" (Roussillon, 1978).

In the second phase, once this initial "attachment" and belonging has been firmly enough established, and from the basis of the primary bonding that it affords, the history of the trauma—those psychic zones specific to a particular patient's efforts to symbolize—can be replayed. All that had been united and split up in the course of cathecting the setting can now start making a return. It does so in terms of the subject's relationships that provide opportunities for "attacking"—or, rather, "tackling"—arrangements, and thus testing out the ability of the institution to symbolize aspects of his history that could not previously be symbolized. This replaying might primarily involve relations with the setting itself, but in fact it may affect, in consequence or directly, relationships that develop with caregiving staff or other members of the institution. This phase is not always reached, and, where that is the case, we must question the authentic therapeutic function of the institution that is otherwise reduced to nothing more than organizing everyday life. In this phase, caregiving institutions aim for subjective integration of aspects of users' history that they could not previously symbolize. They transfer, in action, heated questions about their exclusion and its historical particularities, and also transfer what had been excluded from previous integrative work.

If we grant the existence of the sort of transference that is being described, then we must also consider how institutions appear to be products of the countertransference of their caregiving staff. We can understand their reactions as organized responses to the replay of such excluded, unsymbolized, or poorly symbolized material. Caregiving institutions could be regarded as a product of staff countertransference in two senses of the word: on the one hand, receiving transference (which also means potentially refusing it); on the other, dealing with all that it involves, its intrapsychic and intersubjective investments. Another way of formulating this is to stress that the institution's countertransferential function is a function of the "transformation" of what is going on in its users' transference. Ideally, such countertransference can serve to make "treatable" whatever is seeking replay within it. Making it treatable means helping it to be taken up symbolically, extracting its meaning, and allowing that meaning to be integrated. Before taking up in more detail the question of this institutional treatment of what is unsymbolized in its users, we need to specify the "means" of treatment that institutional settings generally offer and have at their disposal.

Caregiving institutions usually offer three types of structure for receiving and treating what seeks linkage and symbolization, and three models for symbolization.

The first could be described as a "general container", which encompasses the whole structure of the institution, its differential organization of tasks, and the means and objectives of each function by which life and everyday living are organized (meals, bedtimes, activities, etc.). It thereby secures the cohesion and coherence of functioning that are supportive of the self-preservative and ego instincts, while collectively managing the repetition compulsion in an organized way through daily routines and the fundamental rhythms of life. These foundations lend structure to time, delayed response, and the hierarchical differentiation of the symbolizing function. As a whole, it meets the intensity of the transference and the psyche with an organized, "diffractive" structure that offers divisions in relationships and a range of different "objects" upon which various aspects of psychic raw material can play, and different functions by which different ego functions can be defined or made known. In other words, in institutions not everything is played out in a single "place" or with a single person, but what the ego needs and has at stake is diffracted through the whole setting or at least through "more than one" place or person. This moderates what is going on with each of them. Transference is at once diffracted and held within a "contained", organized, and coherent whole.

A second way in which an institution produces symbolization involves the "artistic" or craft activities that it provides. By this I mean arrangements set up for users that have no functions other than to produce representational objects, as, for example, in groups for drawing, photography, pottery, mask-making, storytelling, drama, and so forth. These groups or "activities" are centred on symbolic "production" mediated by "play objects" ["*objeu*" in the original—*J.P.*] that give them definite shape: *they offer users an opportunity for new experiences of symbolization* so long as they are not handled in an unduly "technical" way and they leave patients enough freedom to exercise creativity. They can be supportive of a certain sort of primary symbolization as one internal-world element or other is given "thing-representation". Here what is on offer is a medium that can accept an internal psychic "thing" that has never hitherto been given shape. In other words, it is a chance to transfer it into the selected "medium" and thus to find a mode of symbolic connectedness. The subject can now try out and develop new possibilities for expression in representational form.

The third structure for symbolization in caregiving institutions takes us back very centrally to our thinking about psychotherapeutic spaces, which I call *analytic provision*. Most straightforwardly, these are the time-spaces devoted to so-called psychotherapy proper. Issues about the way that these fit in with the rest of institutional life are discussed at the end of the chapter. Time-spaces are based on transference analysis as a "medium" for symbol-formation and involve reconstruction and reinterpretation of the active core of the users' traumas in the area of identity and narcissism. Psychotherapeutic work is based not only on what is transferred into the analytic space but also what is coming—or trying to come—into play in the person's current life. Formulating things in this way highlights once more that such work cannot really be isolated either in theory or in practice from what happens elsewhere in the host institution. One of the key issues for psychotherapies in institutions is therefore what type of linkage they arrange between the therapy and the institution and how they get that linkage to work.

From this analysis of the different symbol-generating functions in the institutional domain, it emerges that problems remain both

with the coherence of each of these different levels and how they fit
the effects of this diffracted transference together. The latter tends,
in fact, to split along the lines of differences already existing within
the institution as a whole. Split transference is absolutely specific to
psychotherapy in institutions, which makes it necessary to take all
its different levels and components into account when trying to
understand the therapeutic process. Splitting also necessitates collective working-through of what is acted or played out at different
points in institutional life.

Users' narcissistic/identity problematic

To deepen our analysis of the current issue and tackle the problem
of symbolizing unassimilated aspects of a person's history, we
must now return to specific aspects of clinical work with users of
caregiving institutions.

An initial remark will immediately state the problem in all its
intensity: if users of a caregiving institution stand in need of a
particular institution, this is precisely because of their inability to
"use" ordinary social institutions as supportive frameworks for
their efforts to symbolize. This defines what we could describe as
social "non-adaptation". Such an incapacity could be put down to
different types of psychopathology and different types of psychic
suffering, but in every case it includes an element of narcissistic/
identity suffering bound up with deficient or disturbed self-
representation.

Self-representation is a reflexive act that could be summed up
briefly as having three different but possibly interrelated levels: as
being able to "feel" sufficiently, to "see" oneself sufficiently clearly
and with a friendly enough eye, and to "hear" oneself sufficiently
and accurately enough. All these are needed to make psychic self-
regulation of relations with internal ideals a possibility. Reflexivity
is the subject's capacity to reflect self-information back to himself
and to himself in relation to others, in the light of which he can then
regulate his psychic and relational life.

Disturbances or deficiencies in reflexivity occur when the subject does not feel or feels inadequately, when he cannot "see"

himself or does so poorly, or when he cannot "hear" himself or does so poorly. These three effects are caused by a lack of representation or subjective assimilation in a different area of psychic life. While what the subject cannot hear, or hears poorly, in himself suggests repression, what he cannot "see" or "feel" in himself should rather be thought of along lines suggested by Freud (1927e, 1940e [1938]) and then Ferenczi (1928) in terms of ego splitting. The effects of this type of splitting on relations with the self and others are at the root of a whole series of disturbances and dysfunctions.

Metapsychologically speaking, it should be stressed that what is split off from the ego cannot be integrated during psychic functioning governed by the pleasure–unpleasure principle. It is subject to the repetition compulsion, which threatens a disorganizing return of all that the mind is unable to symbolize and integrate into chains of representations. The mind may react in different ways to the threat of such a "return of the split-off", perhaps by attempting to freeze or immobilize whatever is seeking return, and thereby "neutralizing" it. Alternatively, when that process is too costly and threatens too much disorganization, the mind may try to evacuate or externalize what cannot be bound internally. Then it seeks to "control" it outside, and thereby to preserve it through relating to another person who now has part of the subject's self "on deposit" (Bleger, 1970).

The subject therefore makes the other person experience those aspects of himself that he cannot represent to himself. This means that when he cannot "feel" something of his own he makes others feel it, and when he cannot "see" something in himself he makes others see it—he shows it to them, and they must then cope with the relational effects of his failure in self-ownership. What cannot be represented and owned in the mind will therefore be "acted out" in and through relationships with others, in the hope that it will thereby be bound and later, possibly, symbolized.

Formulated another way, we will find that an "object-use" level has crept into the "object-relations" level. Other people will react to the "use" that is being made of them. They will react to what is going on in this way within the relationship and is doing them violence. They will often react with symmetrical violence, withdrawal, or exclusion. It is, indeed, this reaction to the effects of a lack of reflexivity that is at the root of the processes of exclusion from ordinary social institutions that makes placement in a caregiving institution necessary.

One direct consequence of this state of affairs is that the subject cannot be thought about if account is taken only of himself. He can only become intelligible if other people's "response" to what he is doing to them is also taken account of. Part of his internal psychic "identity" regulation depends upon his objects' response and what they actually "reflect" back. Part of himself cannot be thought about except by integrating the effects of the negative "mirror" his environment provides. It is a negative "mirror" in so far as what comes back of himself is precisely those aspects that he cannot himself "perceive" and integrate into his subjectivity, and which he has "sent out" and lodged in other people without knowing why. This keeps the repetition compulsion going, and periodically reactivates the subject's trauma, together with the trail of self-destruction and violence that accompanies it.

In these cases, individual psychology must be regarded as "social" psychology, as Freud stressed (1921c, p. 197). Anyone trying to think through such processes must therefore relinquish the illusion of an individual mind and of seeing it as an undivided whole. This also opens up the possibility of an "institutional" or group psychology that would not be reduced to a mere sharing of fantasies but included the existence of joint processes or communities of psychic process (denigratory pacts, communal denial, shared splitting, joint debarment, etc.). It is time now to consider problems of the therapeutic domain within mental care institutions.

The "echoing" or reflexive function
of caregiving institutions

This "last lap" of our reflections returns to the issue of transference in places that care for disorders of identity and narcissism, and which are therefore affected by the processes just described.

Transference must no longer be thought of simply as a mode of psychic displacement that leaves protagonists in their own places and is content with treating their functions and actions as metaphor. Instead, it must be thought of as a seriously disrupting process that inverts identities and functions in psychic interactions. What is transferred must be understood as having been actively evacuated. This reverses the passivity of the trauma into an active process dealing with something that failed to find symbolic form in the mind, and has thus remained "traumatic".

What is transferred is unconsciously split off. It is neither repressed nor represented: it is acted out in relationships.

Specific features of "working-through in the countertransference" can be considered in this light, bearing in mind the processes involved.

The first thing required of caregiving staff will be to be able to "contain and tolerate" what is being evacuated and deposited with them in therapeutic or educational relationships. This is what Winnicott (1965) called "surviving", which means being able to take in what the other person evacuates without retaliating against what often resembles psychic violence, and without withdrawing from interaction and breaking the intersubjective link that has been made. These two first requirements are not, however, sufficient when thinking about the fundamental aspects of caregiving relationships, though they do form the basis on which authentically therapeutic work can start. The third characteristic requirement is how to achieve symbolization of what is difficult to represent both within the self and in relationships with other people. It is necessary to "invent" a "tailor-made" response to what is thus being held back from play, and to bring it as play into interactions.

For instance, to take an example from Racamier (1970), in one psychiatric service a patient "sabotaged" everything undertaken either by himself or by caregivers.

The nursing staff began to despair because of the repetition of this behaviour and the futility of their efforts. The patient was offered a little piggy bank into which he was to put an "echo" of every success he had and every effort he made to change and take on board the cost of his own psychic needs. This little "anti-me" pig, representing the subject's anti-force, was to receive payment for each and every psychic shift. It was placed in the cupboard in the service's pharmacy. This arrangement "signified" to the patient that each and every one of his efforts was matched by a corresponding anti-effort that had to be acknowledged and settled up. The arrangement would be abandoned when the patient was ready to engage in play with the anti-ego force that it embodied. One day the patient asked for a glass for himself and at the same time asked for a glass of water for "anti-me". The "special" arrangement made for this particular patient had allowed his destructiveness to find a status in his relations with himself and with other people, so that it was no longer acted out in relationships but could be represented. It acquired an intersubjective status and thus opened the gateway for possible play.

Another example allows us to explore the question of reconstructing trauma.

In an institution for psychotic and anti-social children, one particular room is "reserved" for the reconstruction of traumatic infantile history. Whenever a teacher, engaged in a difficult relationship with a child, understands something that the child is replaying from his early disturbed relationships with his first environment, he asks that child to go to a certain room in the institution, "the memory room". There he communicates to the child his current understanding of the part of the child's history that has been active in their relationship. This provision also allows for the gradual creation of a specific place in which reconstruction and symbolization of the transference can occur. It permits "spatial" differentiation between what is actually current in a relationship and what is "reminiscent" within it. This initiates a topographical differentiation of a psychotherapeutic space "for symbolization", a process of which it is itself symbolic.

We could multiply examples of such creativeness in the response of caregiving staff, which would be of some interest but would take us far away from our present task. What is essential for the moment is to stress the importance of creating a space within which a history that is being acted out can be transformed into a play-representation that embodies intersubjective symbolization.

In essence, caregivers will be made to relive in relation to their patients the affects and experiences that are or have been unbearable for those patients: disappointment, impotent rage, distress, shame in existing, despair, and so on. Their task is to transform these affects into "good" opportunities for patients to represent to themselves what was historically suffered and had given rise to the splitting. That replay is now in an inverted form (making the other person experience something he has not himself been able to experience, and has caused him to withdraw and split himself). Using countertransference, carers can understand what is waiting to find subjective ownership, and they can promote a creative re-experiencing that seems necessary if the symbolizing function of caregiving institutions is to be mobilized.

Diffraction of the transference, already mentioned, is a necessary precondition if transference is to be metabolized by practitioners in caregiving institutions. It diminishes the level of intensity of affects, renders them tolerable, and makes possible their metabolism. But this implies a collective working-through of what is diffracted in this way through everyone, or at least more than one caregiver. If the transference is split, countertransferential working-through must, of necessity, be collective. A psychotherapist's concern to protect therapeutic space by shrouding in secrecy what goes on there is illusory and is an attempt to protect therapeutic space from negative transference or certain negative aspects of the transference.

The setting that actually yields understanding is the institution as a whole, and what is played out specifically in psychotherapeutic space can often only be fully understood with reference to what is going on elsewhere and with other people; otherwise, split transference is "answered" by split countertransference, with an attendant loss of meaning for the user. In the therapeutic domain of an institution, one cannot understand what is going on in the transference in one place without taking into account what is going on elsewhere in the institution: in this way, a "thirdness" ["*tiercéité*"] emerges in group and institutional spaces. ["Thirdness" is a concept coined by the American philosopher and linguist Charles Sanders Peirce (1839–1914) to refer to the triadic relationship between a symbol, an object, and an interpreting thought: the semiotic triangle.—*J.P.*]

One essential consequence of this state of affairs in institutions is that consensus must necessarily be arrived at and certain time-spaces be deployed specifically to provide for the purpose. My discussion concludes that, in institutional life, time must be devoted to collective working-through of the intersubjective effects of transference and its splitting. By the same token, one of the conditions that will make possible such intersubjective working-through is to agree this definition of the therapeutic aim. It must be collectively accepted, and its fundamental implications must be recognized. The activity of different caregivers is inevitably interdependent in a caregiving institution, and the concrete organization of group life must take account of the effects of this interdependency and integrate them into its design and workings. It is by this means and this alone that we can address those aspects of "narcissistic" transference that inevitably creep into all relationships caring for pathologies of identity and narcissism. Only then will they stand a chance of disentanglement and being thought about instead of giving rise to too many institutional reaction-formations.

CHAPTER FOUR

The hospital in the mind: in-patient psychotherapy at the Cassel Hospital

R. D. Hinshelwood & Wilhelm Skogstad

David Bell (1997), a former consultant of the Cassel Hospital, called in-patient psychotherapy the "art of the impossible" and compared it to walking a tightrope whilst having both feet on the ground: we try in this chapter to give some idea of how this art is attempted at the Cassel Hospital. We first describe the setting of the Cassel and then focus on the role that the hospital takes in the mind of the patient and the ways that its different aspects are played out across the institution and how they may be integrated within the team and in psychotherapy.

Janssen (1993), a leading practitioner and theoretician of in-patient psychotherapy in Germany, pointed out that in-patient psychotherapy was initially practised in a way that the therapeutic relationship was set completely apart from all the other things happening on a ward—in effect, "out-patient therapy in an in-patient setting". In its separateness this proved to be unsatisfactory, and even analysts who carried out formal analysis with

This is a revised version of a paper given at the Symposium on In-Patient Psychotherapy in Dortmund, Germany on 28 June 1997, held in honour of Paul L. Janssen's 60th birthday.

patients on psychiatric wards, such as Rosenfeld and Searles, emphasized the need for regular meetings with the nursing staff (Bell, 1997; Searles, 1959). However, these meetings were intended mainly to increase the nurses' understanding and tolerance of the patient, and not as a two-way process.

Further development of in-patient treatment with the aim not just to allow psychotherapy to be carried out in an in-patient setting but to give the setting itself therapeutic potential led to different models that Janssen (1987, 1993) described as bipolar and integrated. In the bipolar setting there is a strict divide between a therapeutic space in which psychotherapy and potentially other therapies take place, and a social space in which patients are nursed and gather for social activities. Interchange between these spheres is, at the most, partial. Transference is only taken up in relation to the therapist(s), and transference splitting is sought to be avoided. Further development led to a more integrated setting, as described by Janssen (1987). In this integrated model, all levels of treatment are seen and structured as a whole in which patients develop multiple transferences that can involve all the various figures in the hospital. These multiple transferences are allowed to take their course while the team of therapists and nurses try to piece the different transferences together to form an integrated whole.

The setting of the Cassel Hospital

The setting of the Cassel Hospital has characteristics of both the bipolar and the integrated model but also additional characteristics, which are probably unique. The Cassel is structured in two different spaces: on the one hand, the space of psychotherapy where individual psychoanalytic psychotherapy is carried out (on some of the units of the hospital, also group psychotherapy); and on the other hand, the therapeutic community in which a specific form of nursing practice, called "psychosocial nursing", takes place. The formal psychotherapy is the place where the inner world is thought about and transferences of the individual to the therapist—but also to the nurse or to other parts or the whole of the institution—are interpreted to the patient. The area of psychosocial nursing is based on psychoanalytic thinking, but understanding is put to the patient not in interpretations but much more in thoughtful words and actions (Griffiths & Leach, 1997; Hinshelwood & Griffiths, 1996).

Together, the setting is seen as a whole in which various transferences occur in all areas. The therapist and primary nurse are often the main transference figures, and great emphasis is put on this "therapeutic couple". More distant figures—like the community doctor, the senior nurse and consultant of the unit, and the clinical director—may become transference objects, as do fellow patients. Also, the hospital as a whole can become the object of a powerful transference (Denford & Griffiths, 1993). The patient finds in the hospital and in the people within it an arena to project and "stage" his whole inner world and builds up a "hospital in the mind" which reflects his own inner world.

To understand fully the inner world of the patient, one must try to bring together the various split-off transferences. The place where this complex linking function needs to take place is, first of all, in and between the minds of the staff. Only then can the patient begin to introject a more integrated view of himself. To facilitate this process, staff at the Cassel work together in an intensive way: patients are discussed in conjunction with the staff's countertransference in daily team meetings, regular reviews of patients, informal chats between nurse and therapist, and regular nurse–therapist supervision. In the latter, a supervisory couple discuss a patient with the "therapeutic couple", the therapist and primary nurse, in order to understand and integrate the different aspects of transference and countertransference around these main transference figures (James, 1987; Tischler, 1987).

Psychoanalytic psychotherapy is carried out twice weekly within an ordinary fifty-minute setting, face-to-face rather than on the couch, usually by a trained psychotherapist. This space is separate, fairly protected, and to some degree, although limited, confidential. The patients have a nurse allocated to them as the "primary nurse", who is usually responsible for about five individual patients. The working together of nurse and therapist is made explicit by a joint meeting with the patient at the onset of treatment when the patient is given their session times but is also clearly visible to the patients who see their workers go to, or come out of, team meetings. In the therapeutic community, patients work with other nurses as well. There is also a community doctor who, together with the primary nurse, is responsible for the physical health and its psychosomatic dimension.

What makes the Cassel special, however, are two aspects that have grown out of a specific development in Britain that psychiatrists such as Main, Bion, and Foulkes started in the army during the Second World War (Main, 1946, 1983). This development has led to a particular emphasis in psychoanalytic thinking on institutional dynamics and to the formation of "therapeutic communities" (Main, 1983) with their increased participation and responsibility of patients. These two aspects are:

- "Psychosocial nursing", with its particular emphasis on the healthy, adult aspects of the patient and the responsibility of the patients, as well as on the mutual support between them.

- The "culture of enquiry" (Main, 1983) as a process of thinking about the dynamics of the whole culture of the hospital (as represented by patients and staff), with the ongoing aim of sustaining a therapeutic culture.

Psychosocial nursing
and the culture of enquiry

Psychosocial nursing has been developed at the Cassel Hospital over the last half a century (Barnes, 1968; Chapman, 1984; Flynn, 1993; Griffiths & Leach, 1997; Hinshelwood & Griffiths, 1996; Irwin, 1995; Kennedy, Heymans, & Tischler, 1986; McCaffrey, 1994) and is quite different from traditional nursing or what Janssen (1993) has described as "tending and providing nurture". This way of working is based on psychoanalytic thinking but translated into the realm of everyday reality and action: "The role of the nurse is to interact and to 'be with' patients in an everyday way. The role of the nurse is not occupational therapy, it is not to occupy the patient in between treatments. Nor is it to care for patients in need of care. Although the nurse may in part do these things" (Hinshelwood & Griffiths, 1996).

Patients are part of a community of adults, adolescents, and children while also belonging to one of three different units: adult, adolescent, family. The whole group of patients of the hospital, "the community", meets three times a week; the patients of each individual unit, called "the firm", meet four times a week, with nurses participating in the meetings. The community forms a living and working environment in which patients take on responsibilities that—and this is essential—are real responsibilities and not just contrived ones. Patients take part in cleaning and maintaining specific areas of the hospital and in managing a household budget for these areas. They are responsible for planning and cooking breakfast, tea, and supper. They help babysit the children of the Family Unit. Patients are also elected as managers of certain workgroups (e.g. breakfast manager) or recreational activities and into posts of greater responsibility such as chairpersons of the firm or of the community. Chairpersons, apart from actually chairing firm and community meetings, have an important role in thinking about disturbance in individual patients or the whole group.

In all these jobs, patients work closely with nurses whose task it is to work "alongside" the patient rather than for them, and to help them think about the difficulties they encounter and forms of support they may need. This nursing work is based on the conviction that patients have a sane and functioning side that can be mobilized and that more often than not they can go on functioning while confronting their dysfunctional and disturbing sides. This itself can give a sense of achievement to patients who have given up functioning outside. Of course, patients, with their deep regressive wishes—which have been increased by hospital admission and have frequently been fostered in a long psychiatric admission prior to the Cassel—often react with deep resentment to the expectation that they should function as responsible adults.

This practical arena also becomes the stage on which patients experience and enact many of their conflicts, which can then be worked on in this arena as well as in psychotherapy; the sharing of real responsibility brings up issues of concern, guilt, and reparation, so vital in the ability to form and sustain relationships.

Phantasies of omnipotence and total independence—or, on the other hand, of complete failure and absolute dependence—are brought into the open. Patients can be helped to carry responsibility with support and face the feelings connected with confronting these phantasies. For some patients, this setting brings up a particular pathology: they use it, as Bell (1997) puts it, to "bolster the 'as-if' aspects of their personality" and "become expert managers whilst projecting their overwhelming needs into other patients who they control", and for them this becomes a particularly important aspect to challenge.

Patients normally go to their own homes over the weekends, and hard work is done with nurses about handling this experience. This brings up, from the start, the issue of separation, which is so crucial in a time-limited therapy and such an important area of disturbance in most patients with severe personality disorder. On the other hand, joining the community makes problems of engagement, so important with these patients who have a long history of failed relationships, a prime focus.

In all of this, the nurses have the difficult and stressful task of challenging and confronting the patients in addition to containing the patients', as well as their own, anxiety, love, and fury. So, nurses themselves need much support, which they get within the team and nurse meetings and in their individual supervision. This support comes particularly from an understanding in these settings of transference and countertransference issues and of the mutual enactments they get drawn into.

In this culture of living together and sharing responsibilities, fellow patients acquire a great importance, and this side is particularly emphasized at the Cassel. Patients find themselves in a network of interdependence in practical and emotional matters, and this confronts them with their need for others as well as their effect on others. Patients both receive help and experience themselves as able to give help to others. We would like to illustrate this aspect with a clinical example.

The patient was a woman with a severe narcissistic pathology who idealized her independence and felt deep contempt for her needy self and any wish for help in herself. Her therapist's attempts to be helpful and understanding were treated with scorn. Any session where she allowed herself to feel under-stood was immediately followed by angry outbursts in the community and, in the next session, by a stubborn silence and an air of cold triumph. In her sessions she often heard a voice telling her not to speak to the therapist. The narcissistic part of herself also convinced her that the therapist was not interested in her and wouldn't mind if she killed herself.

When she became severely suicidal, over a few days a rota of patients was organized who looked after her and made sure she didn't make an attempt on her life. In this contact with patients, she was now able to experience them as helpful and caring and to feel that their wish to see her alive was genuine and that she really needed their help.

While her destructive narcissistic organization did not allow her, for much of the time, to feel dependent and in need of help from her therapist, in this crisis (and obviously after consider-able work in her individual therapy) she *was* able to experience this in relation to other patients. This led to an important shift in her treatment.

The other aspect that is crucial for the functioning of the Cassel is the emphasis on thinking about the dynamics of the whole insti-tution. Examining "the conscious and unconscious use each [is] making of each other" (Main, 1983) is seen as essential to sustain a truly "therapeutic institution" (Main, 1946). Parallel processes be-tween the patient community and the staff team are a well-known phenomenon (e.g. Stanton & Schwartz, 1954), and the Cassel staff take this seriously by attempting to understand the resonances between the patient and staff groups. This "culture of enquiry", as Main (1983) called it, is difficult to sustain against the constant pressure of mutual projections and the always present tendency to turn creative thoughts into ritualized practice (Main, 1967). It needs the on-going effort of all staff to prevent this culture of enquiry from being closed off (Griffiths & Hinshelwood, 1995; Levinson, 1996; Norton, 1992). This effort pervades all meetings at the Cassel, so that patients and incidents are not just thought about individually but also in the context of unconscious group dynamics within the patients and between staff and patients. An essential part of this process is a once-weekly large group meeting of all the clinical staff, in which institutional dynamics are a main focus.

Recently, there was massive acting-out and self-harming and a worrying lack of cooperation in the patients' group. This was brought into the large group meeting as a deep concern. It was happening at a time of strong tensions in the staff group around changes in the senior management that were causing great anxiety and anger in staff. The link between the two was made by a senior nurse in the meeting, and then these tensions and conflicts were brought into the open and the group meeting became quite difficult and heated. After this large group meeting, the acting-out receded again and more cohesion returned to the patients' group.

The functioning of the whole hospital is closely interlinked with the "hospital in the mind" that is active in both the members of the staff and the patients.

The "hospital in the mind" of the patient

The patient's inner world is populated by various internal objects. These internal objects are projected into different parts of the hospital. By way of reintrojection, the patient creates in his mind a hospital that he inhabits, which may be quite different from the actual hospital. However, this "hospital in the mind" has a powerful influence on the patient's functioning within the hospital as well as on the people around him. The multiple transferences that the patient develops to different members of staff (or patients) come to contain different split-off aspects of his internal world, which are then spread out over the hospital, and its different aspects are played out on the stage of the actual hospital. The members of the team need to try to bring together the different transferences that they represent. Often these different aspects, even though spread out over the hospital, come directly into the individual psychotherapy and can be seen and, if understood, integrated there.

Of particular importance in the in-patient setting is that the different transference figures have—and are seen by the patients to have—actual relationships with each other. These actual relationships between members of staff may be directly influenced by the projections of the patient's internal objects and the relationships that these internal objects have with each other. The phantasy that the patient has of the relationship between members of staff is particularly significant and can itself be an important focus of psychotherapy in an in-patient setting. At the Cassel Hospital, for example, the therapeutic couple of nurse and therapist may come to represent the oedipal couple, whose relationship the patient may have severely distorted phantasies and strong hateful feelings about—or, with severe personality disorders, they may represent the splits in the patient's mind.

The preoccupation with the links between transference objects often comes up around the issue of confidentiality of the psychotherapy sessions, when patients wonder what the therapist tells the nurses, but also what the therapist is told by the nurses. In the setting of the Cassel, with its two different spaces, a therapist may not bring up in a session material that has been told to him by a member of staff outside of the session. Instead, such material from outside is often used in a different way by the therapist to increase his understanding of the patient's inner world and to enable him to be more sensitive to aspects he has missed so far, without addressing the piece of outside reality directly. For example, if the therapist hears from the nurse about the contempt their patient exhibits towards her, this may enable him to find the hidden or split-off contempt for himself in the transference.

This boundary between the nursing side and the individual psychotherapy has to be dealt with flexibly, however. For example, if something serious (self-harm, for instance) has happened and is not brought up in the session by the patient, the therapist would often collude with a denying part of the patient if he did not take it up himself and did not address the meaning of the patient's failure to bring this to his therapy. By not taking this issue up, the therapist might also confirm a phantasy of the patient that his objects barely communicate with each other or have no link at all. Important phantasies about the relationships may thus remain unexplored.

A certain degree of confidentiality of the individual psycho-therapy is seen as important to enable trust and provide a protected space. It is also part of the containing function of the therapist to hold within himself most of his disturbing counter-transference feelings, rather than burdening the nurses unduly with them. Unlike in an out-patient setting, such confidentiality and holding within the therapy has to be limited in an in-patient setting. Only with sufficient communication between the therapists and the nurses can integration take place, and a therapist has to be wary if he feels a pressure from the patient or within himself to keep certain things secret.

Some patients are intensely curious to find out what has been communicated between nurse and therapist. They may have the phantasy that everything about them is passed on and feel omnipotently in control of this relationship which is only about them. More often, they feel excluded from an intense and excited inter-course, which arouses their hatred and envy and which they wish to attack. The worry about confidentiality can sometimes be the external expression of the patient's internal need to keep certain things away from an enquiring part of his own mind, and this is then often reflected by an open or subtle pressure on the therapist to keep certain things confidential. By keeping thoughts or actions confidential, the patient may wish to prevent them from being properly explored and thought about or even taken seriously.

The pressure to keep things confidential can, on the other hand, also represent a wish to keep the oedipal couple apart whose link is felt to be unbearable. Some patients seem to ignore that there is any link between the therapeutic couple. They behave as if they had an individual therapist and, completely separate, a nurse, who had nothing to do with each other. This kind of denial of the oedipal configuration has been described for the analytic situation by Britton (1989). Such a patient can experience it as a catastrophe if he suddenly becomes aware of the active link between nurse and therapist.

These thoughts are illustrated in two brief vignettes from a female patient.

This patient's mother had tried unsuccessfully to abort her and was quite cruel and physically abusive to her in her childhood.

As a child and adolescent, the patient was sexually abused by her stepfather who used to ejaculate on her abdomen. She often harmed herself by cutting, particularly her abdomen, and had attempted suicide a number of times. She felt extremely persecuted by any criticism and managed quickly to arouse in other people an attitude of rejection. In her therapy, she was initially very intrusive, much more interested in exploring her therapist's mind and life than in finding out about herself.

Two weeks prior to her discharge and transition to out-patient treatment, she starts her therapy session by saying that there are only two weeks left. She says that she is now caring for other patients again, which she has not done for a while, and calls this her façade. She then speaks appreciatively of her therapist, but as if therapy has already ended. The therapist takes up the appreciation and how difficult it is to end the relationship to her (the therapist). The patient then talks about the firm meeting in the hospital and the psychotherapy group that she will attend after her discharge and dismisses them as difficult, unhelpful and a place where people are just got at. The session has a superficial chatty mood. In the following two days after this session, the patient becomes more difficult in the community, sulks and is aggressive, and eventually cuts herself.

The patient attempted successfully in the session to create a harmonious relationship with the therapist, and she did this characteristically through splitting defences. With the end of her in-patient treatment approaching, she felt some appreciation of her therapist but was beset by fears about the separation and feelings of abandonment, rage, and persecution. These troublesome feelings were then felt in relation to the nurses, the firm, and the future psychotherapy group. They were actively prevented from being part of the relationship with the therapist. She also split off the needy part of herself, which was seen as being within other patients who she then looked after.

In this massive export of experiences and parts of herself, the therapeutic relationship became superficial and already a matter of the past and the patient appeared as a façade. The hospital had become a spread-out version of the patient's mind. Different aspects were located in various different groups and people in the hospital. The reality the patient then lived in was the reality of the "hospital in her mind". Even though the internal relationships and various aspects of the self were spread out over the hospital, they were nevertheless all brought into the therapy session as part of the patient's material. The therapist had the opportunity to see and understand not only the transference to herself but the hospital that the patient had created in her mind, and could then help her to integrate the different aspects of herself.

In this case, the split-off aspects were not sufficiently contained within the therapy, and the patient became more disturbed for a few days. Later, however, these splits could be brought together in our minds in supervision, and the integration in the workers' minds helped the patient.

* * *

Another vignette of the same patient earlier in her treatment shows again how the staff can gather together the patient's splits: in a session after the therapist's Christmas break, the patient complains bitterly about her nurse. She says that she has no time for her and is hardly ever there, that she doesn't see her individually and was even away for some days. The therapist thinks to herself: "She is right, I can understand her anger, the nurses are really hardly available." She tries to point out to the patient the reality of the limitations and the difficulties that she has in accepting them, but in her mind she clearly sides with the patient in her anger and disappointment.

With such material, one might interpret the anger towards the nurse as a split-off aspect of the relationship with the therapist—that is, that the patient is angry because the therapist has abandoned and neglected her during the Christmas break. Such an approach may help her experience more ambivalent feelings towards the therapist but leaves out what is happening in relation to the nurse. One might instead interpret that she feels neglected by both the therapist and the nurse and angry with both but chooses to direct the anger and disappointment towards the nurse, because she is afraid that these feelings would destroy the good therapist in her mind and the good relationship to her in the session.

However, there is another important aspect of such material in an in-patient setting which concerns the relationship between the therapist and the nurse. This vignette was in fact told by the therapist in nurse–therapist supervision. The therapist felt that she had a good contact with the patient, while the nurse reported what a terrible time she was given by the patient. The nurse felt angry with the patient and guilty for not giving her enough and envied the therapist, who seemed to get on so well with this difficult patient. The therapist, in turn, was resentful of the nurse for being "so neglectful ".

In nurse–therapist supervision, we were able to bring the different sides together. We could see that both nurse and therapist had caring as well as neglectful aspects in their relationship to the patient, which she, however, had split into two separate relationships. Through projective identification this split in her mind had an impact on the minds of her workers. The nurse was carrying the hated and neglectful aspects while the therapist carried the idealized and caring ones. This understanding helped both workers to feel more balanced about themselves, each other, and their patient.

But we could also see that the patient had invited the therapist successfully to join in with her anger and hatred towards the nurse. This way, she had achieved a situation in which she and the therapist were closely linked with each other, while the link between the therapist and the nurse was severed. The patient had attacked this link between nurse and therapist because she could not bear feeling excluded from their relationship. In a similar vein, it was intolerable for her to be excluded from the private lives and holidays of her therapist and nurse, and their breaks had increased her unbearable feeling of exclusion. This enactment also had a significance in the light of her history: exclusion had meant something cruel, being locked in a room, and intimate closeness had been mixed up with a breakdown of boundaries and abuse.

We can see that the patient showed not only multiple transferences to different separate people, but that in her mind the relationship between the transference objects was of equal importance. Again, this whole scenario in the mind of the patient—in this case, with an overclose relationship to a parental object and a severed oedipal couple—was present in the session, in the patient's material and the countertransference. This is not always the case, but if it is and is sufficiently understood it can be taken up and brought together by the therapist in the session.

In this case the work of integration was done first of all in the nurse–therapist supervision. The integration in the minds of the staff helped nurse and therapist to repair their own relationship and experience the patient in a different way. Their understanding of the patient and different approach to her helped her to integrate some of these aspects for the time being. Later, when the impending discharge stirred up powerful feelings, some of these issues came up again, as illustrated in the first vignette.

Conclusion

In-patient psychotherapy is not just psychotherapy in an in-patient setting. It takes place within a complex structure and a network of relationships and requires an effective integrating function. As analysts, we are particularly interested in the phantasies and mental functioning behind the external structure. We have described the setting of the Cassel Hospital as well as some of our ideas about the dynamics of mental functioning in patients and staff.

The patient projects his internal objects and object-relationships into various parts of the hospital and, by way of re-introjection, creates a hospital in his mind which reflects parts or the whole of his internal world. His phantasies are not just about the various objects within the hospital but also about the relationships between them. These phantasies shape his perceptions of the hospital and, via projective identification, can have a powerful impact on the relationships between members of staff. These spread-out and split-off aspects need to be integrated first of all in the minds of staff to enable the patient to introject a more integrated view of himself, and this requires a lot of work and working-through in the countertransference. Sometimes the integration can take place within the therapist's mind from the material brought to a session, but often it needs additional and painful work by the whole team in different arenas to bring together the fragmented aspects.

CHAPTER FIVE

A psychoanalytic hospital unit for people with severe personality disorders

R. Vermote & M. J. Vansina-Cobbaert

Patients with severe personality disorders do not lend themselves very well to classic psychoanalytic psychotherapy, in which the focus is on interpreting transference and relieving repression. In addition, the disruptive character of their symptoms or a lack of motivation often hamper such therapies. The purpose of this chapter is to describe an in-patient setting that endeavours to bring about a psychoanalytic process in such patients and to achieve a permanent change in the way that they deal with their inner world and relationships. In in-patient settings, much emphasis is often put on the object-relations that patients play out, as in a theatre. Perhaps the distinctive feature of our work is that we are also concerned with the disruption of symbolization, and we stress working with the process of "mentalization". We also believe that work in an in-patient setting is not very different from what would be done in an out-patient setting. Many people assume that psychoanalytic group therapy in an institutional setting has to be different from such work in an out-patient setting, while we have tried to build a setting in which this is not the case. Attending to the therapeutic frame of psychotherapy within an institution is as important as in out-patients, and it comprises fifty percent of the work with severe borderline patients. Our institution is organized in a way that is in line with our theoretical ideas, which are derived largely from Bion. Had we adhered to Kohutian ideas, for instance, this would have led to a different organization and set of attitudes towards the diagnostic categories of patients.

In the first part of the chapter, R. Vermote gives a sketch of the theoretical background and the structure of the setting; in the second part, M. J. Vansina-Cobbaert illustrates how psychoanalytic group therapy is an essential part of this institutional psychotherapy.

The treatment setting and concepts

The unit is part of the psychoanalytic department of the Saint-Joseph University Psychiatric Centre in Belgium, a hospital with 400 beds, and was created more than twenty-five years ago by Professor S. Verhaest, the head of the department. The setting provides room for thirty-four patients.

The *target group of patients* consists of persons with severe personality disorders and corresponds most accurately with what Kernberg (1996a) describes as "borderline personality disorders". These are patients with diffusion of identity, primitive mechanisms of defence, and often superego problems. In DSM IV-terms, this group can be described as borderline, narcissistic (borderline with a grandiose self), antisocial personality (malign narcissism with superego problems), schizoid and schizotypal personality disorders (where the inner borderline world is hidden), histrionic (showing more symptoms in a sexual realm), and hypomanic and paranoid personality disorders.

Counterindications for the setting are severe toxicomania and acute suicidal tendencies, the setting's openness being the main reason. The setting does offer opportunities to patients with superego deterioration, but they have frequently to be refused in order to protect the other patients.

During the intake interview, an assessment is made of the extent to which the patient is capable of being in contact with his psychic suffering. This is a useful indication for predicting whether a psychoanalytic process is possible or not. The capacity for change is more important than insight.

This patient group has specific *clinical characteristics* that gives the here-and-now a prominent place. The therapeutic relationship is intense but fragile. Frustration tolerance is low, and psychic tension is easily acted out. Splitting brings about strong distortions in the externalized psychic reality and the experiencing of others. Feelings are aroused in others in order to communicate or get rid of them, because verbalization is at first impossible. The analytic relationship is more important than interpretations, and there is a great deal of sensitivity towards the therapeutic frame, to which the patient really clings but at the same time often attacks (Godfrind, 1993). As a consequence, a lot of work is done with the patients concerning the therapeutic frame of the setting. During the intake sessions, the rules are discussed at great length and agreements are made concerning love relationships at the ward and all kinds of "acting", especially alcohol, drugs, and self-mutilation. These patients manifest a need–fear dilemma towards the strict therapeutic frame. There is a dynamic tension between offering a firm holding within the setting and enough freedom. This is worked out continuously at the large group meetings and the weekly patient–staff meeting. Safeguarding the therapeutic space and frame of the setting is the main topic of these meetings. Ways of attacking this therapeutic space and blocking growth are discussed at length and illustrated with what happens on the ward. The nurses and the psychiatrist of the ward often reformulate individual problems from this point of view in individual contacts with the patients.

From a *theoretical point of view*, the clinical picture of these borderline patients as it manifests itself in the therapeutic setting may be caught under two different concepts, which are closely related to one another: on the one hand, object-relations, which are reflected in transference–countertransference, and, on the other hand, disorders in symbolization (Vermote, 1997). In most of the literature on institutional psychotherapy, it is mainly the object-relational point of view that is stressed. In our way of working, fostering the mentalization is very important. There is a link between the regression from an object-relational point of view and the development of mentalization.

As far as object-relations and transference are concerned, it is the severe splitting that is most typical. In splitting up the internal objects, the good things that were experienced by the patients in their early childhood are usually kept separate in order to protect them. At the same time, they became idealized. Bad experiences were split off from the good ones in order to evacuate them. Ideal internal objects are created, but at the same time they give rise to annihilating, persecuting, destructive internal objects. These internal objects of all kinds may be organized in what Steiner (1993) calls "psychic retreats"—pseudo-organizations that are often found in people with personality disorders. Malign narcissism and antisocial personalities are telling examples of organizations in which the internal bad objects are idealized and used to hide the fragile self. The lack of good experiences often creates an immense void, a fundamental deficiency. Patients with personality disorders try to evade this feeling by arousing body sensations.

The object-relations described have a certain impact on the process of symbolization, or *mentalization*. Indeed, thoughts are formed by the ability to support some kind of psychic pain. In their turn, these thoughts create a protective layer, a psychic skin, to allow the patient to deal with new tensions more easily (Anzieu, 1974; Bion, 1962; Vermote, 1995). When tensions are vented by transferring the disagreeable sides of the self into somebody else and controlling them there by projective identification (Klein, 1946) or by acting them out largely through physical surface experiences—that is, self-mutilation, alcohol, anorexia (Tustin, 1986)—then this mentalization process does not take place.

The objective of the treatment is to facilitate a psychoanalytic process in the patients. This psychoanalytic process is not only the classic one with the focus on resistance, interpretation, and working-through. The psychoanalytic process that we discuss also takes place at a much more basic level. It aims at a better integration of the internal objects and at bringing about basic trust that permits the mentalization of psychic pain. In order to be successful, therapeutic regression is a prerequisite. Five different therapeutic entrances are used to facilitate this process (Vermote, 1996).

1. In *psychoanalytic group therapy*, we run four different groups corresponding with the "slow-open" type, and each attends a 90-

minute session three times a week. The internal objects and their dynamics are distinctly brought to the forefront in the group scene. The topics that are discussed in the sessions are often related to experiences from other therapeutic contexts, which has a mobilizing effect. Patients with fewer psychic abilities often open up after recognizing the topics from other group members. Group cohesion, mutual respect, and trust in the basic goodness of the group allows an emotional regression to take place in which pathological defensive psychic organizations can be released. Participation in psychoanalytic group therapy is preceded, however, by attending group psychotherapy, in which the sessions are less frequent and no transference interpretations are given in order to keep the level of anxiety low. This introductory group was inserted in the treatment to make patients with pronounced disorders of mentalization aware of their inner world first and teach them to stand still instead of acting out their emotions. For instance, in patients with acting out, attention is focused on what happens in the patient at the moment he decides to do something, and we try to create a space between impulse and acting, concentrating on what a patient feels and how he deals with it, instead of concentrating on meaning. Many patients use this introductory psychotherapy group to come to terms with great anxiety and are often present for weeks without talking. They start with the group analysis only at the moment that they feel ready for it. It is the patients themselves who, in consultation with the staff, decide how long they will be attending group psychotherapy before moving to the psychoanalytic group therapy. Working this way has significantly reduced the drop-out rate.

2.   The patients' inner world is also reflected in the *daily life at the ward*. Three times a week, the medical staff calls small group meetings, during which the specific handling of all kinds of practical matters such as rules and planning are discussed. On these occasions, the team treats the patients with a great deal of respect, without viewing them as helpless, and keeps putting their faith in the analytic process. When faced with painful and strong emotions, the team actively stays with the patient. In this way, an atmosphere is created that patients often experience for the first time; here they feel safe to abandon the defence mechanisms and ways to act out

emotions. This containment and holding attitude largely boils down to preserving the therapeutic frame, which then can be internalized. At this level, no interpretations are given. What is carried out at this relational level is of a major changing value. Frequently, it is at this stage that an analytic process is catalysed. It is the level that, according to Balint (1968), can be described as "basic" transference. It requires a permanent commitment of the team members to maintain such an attitude. Their attitude is unremittingly attacked by splitting, idealizations, and envy.

3.   The framework used in the *expressive therapy* is also one of three 90-minute sessions per week. Patients are free to use any material they wish. The way they choose material, and deal with it, reflects how they get in contact with their inner world. To many patients, this is tangible and often their first introduction to this psychic reality. For instance, a patient may cling anxiously to the same tools, with which he only copies paintings from an artbook. He sees how other patients work and succeeds in working with larger sheets of paper and starts to paint instead of working only with pencils. He arrives at a point where he can let himself go, and he is then amazed to see what appears on the paper and realizes that the painting occurs not by coincidence but is related to what he feels inside. Topics such as control, provocation, despair, emptiness, creativity, aggression, and sexuality often first come to the fore in this expressive therapy, before they are verbalized and shared in the psychoanalytic group therapy. The expressive therapist refrains from psychoanalytic interpretations; he only uses his own medium. But his attitude fosters the opening of an intrapsychic space, which is essential for most of the so-called lower borderlines.

4.   *Psychomotor therapy* follows the same pattern. It is about discovering or rediscovering the experience of one's own body, especially stressing the relationship between the emotional and physical aspect and all kinds of group interactions flowing from the activities.

5.   During *music therapy*, which takes place twice a week, virtually direct contact is made possible with the patients' emotions. This therapy gives access to experiences that are hard to verbalize.

Moreover, a non-verbal kind of communication emerges within the group, allowing group processes to be shaped in specific ways.

* * *

All these therapies focus on facilitating the analytic process. It is striking how the various therapists end up describing the same inner processes in patients, using totally different forms depending on the medium that is used. It is paramount that each therapist works in an authentic way, taking his own medium as a starting point and thereby refraining from pseudo-analytic interpretations (Vermote, 1996).

The most important difficulty of this intensive approach to severe personality disorders is the possibility of the occurrence of *pathological regression*, which involves the therapeutic regression brought about during the sessions being pursued outside the context of these sessions. This, however, may be counterbalanced by calling upon the healthy parts of the patient's personality through offering optional activities outside the therapeutic programme, such as theatrical performances, garden workshops, dance, exercise such as running, and courses of autogenous training. Furthermore, the isolation ward and seclusion of patients is avoided since in this population it highly coincides with the acting out of primitive object-relations as punishing, being held, and exploring limits. In addition, in the weekly patient–staff meeting the elements encouraging pathological regression and opposing therapeutic culture (for instance, the creation of cliques of people, alcohol abuse) are discussed at great length.

* * *

A follow-up study (Callens & Vermote, 1994) of 132 discharged patients shows that, despite severe pathology, 55% of them went through an analytic process, irrespective of the number of prior hospitalizations. Going through an analytic process clearly correlates with later well-being and the absence of rehospitalization. Statistically speaking, the outcome is less favourable for the group that did not go through an analytic process, although even half of those patients are satisfied with the result of the treatment. In order to reach an analytic process, a six- to twelve-month treatment programme is needed. This rather long period does not seem to be an obstacle to later integration into society; besides, many patients had got completely stuck before. For the past two years, hospitalization has been shortened because of the possibility of continuing the psychoanalytic process in an out-patient formula, after a couple of months in the ward itself.

Psychoanalytic group therapy in this setting

For many years I have worked as a psychotherapist, as well as with training groups, and I have often been amazed at the possibilities that groups hold to foster change and development. Therefore, to me, group therapy is not a second-best choice—on the contrary, especially for severe personality disorders, it often provides prospects that exceed by far those contained in individual analyses.

The therapy groups that I work with have at most eight participants, and we meet three times a week for an hour and a half.

The advantage of psychoanalytic group therapy over individual analysis is based upon several factors. To quite a number of people, the group, featuring more active and direct participation combined with dispersed transference reactions, feels much safer than the dual relationship, the silence of the analyst, and the possibly intense and exclusive transference that belong to the psychoanalytic encounter. Often, very disturbed people feel relieved when they have the impression that they share the responsibility for the analyst's interventions with other participants, while they like to observe the different reactions of the analyst to different group members. This provides them with the reassuring feeling that they know the analyst well and have obtained some predictive sense of his interventions.

Therapy with borderline and narcissistic personalities in a hospital setting means that one tries to work in the presence of a restricted level of symbolization and with difficulties in accepting the "as-if" quality of certain experiences. This makes it difficult for the analysand to understand, let alone accept, transference interpretations. Here, the demonstrative potential of the group provides invaluable help. One of the classic and revealing situations occurring in my groups is when some male participants who are convinced that I prefer—and therefore privilege—women over men find out that, based on exactly the same "facts", a few women hold the opposite belief. It is thanks to experiences like these, which make transferential elements directly visible, that thoughts arise about the existence of an inner world, individually differentiated through personal life experiences and through the meaning they obtained. An inner world colours our perceptions and concerns.

Something similar happens when it comes to dreams. Some members of the groups that I work with have never before paid attention to their dreams, and at first they regard me with suspicion when they see that I take dream stories seriously. It is when they observe the work we do, and when they witness the revealing qualities of dreams, that they are amazed initially, then pensive, and finally start telling their own dreams.

Like Bion (1970), I am convinced that it is through thinking about and understanding the emotional experiences of intimate relationships that the mind can grow and develop. I also believe that, in this respect, a therapy group provides unique possibilities. Here, the emotional experiences pertaining to the intimate relationships between the group members become directly visible and explorable in their full complexity. In individual analysis, the analysand will never know if, maybe, the sorrow or the anxiety he experiences in a session belongs to his analyst, who is herself at most dimly aware of those feelings. The analysand can express the supposition, but it will never go beyond that, because in individual analysis projective identification is explored only one way—going from analysand to analyst—and even then the analyst will not express her own experience directly. She will only use it as the basis for her interpretation. In groups, on the other hand, this becomes a two-way exploration that provides participants with a rich and important view of the psychic life of other people, and of the many factors that play a part in it. Let me illustrate this with a clinical vignette taken from the story of "Lucy".

Lucy is a young woman who often talks about her mother. She does this in two different ways. In a more general way, she describes her mother as a real saint: a person who is always concerned about the well-being of others, always busy helping the needy, and never demanding anything for herself. In a much more concrete way, however, and especially on Mondays, she describes the interactions between the two of them in terms of : "I said so and so, and then my mother said this and that and the other", or: "I did this and that, and my mother did this and that and such and so". Even before Lucy finishes her Monday story, the whole group is furious with this mother whom they experience as selfish, insensitive to the feelings and the suffering of her daughter, and exclusively concerned with keeping up a nice front.

When the situation repeats itself, the group members start exploring their anger. Are they angry with Lucy? Because she lets herself be taken in, and doesn't want to see reality? Yes, certainly, . . . but most of all they feel angry towards this mother! I draw their attention to the fact that their anger towards Lucy's mother is the consequence of the stories that Lucy tells us. And Lucy is all amazed: "How is it possible that people get so angry at such a good mother!?"

And, of course, history has to repeat itself many times. But meanwhile Lucy has told us that during one of the graphic-expression sessions she painted my picture, a fact that she presents as a sign of her positive feelings towards me. One of the group members remarks that, even so, she used a lot of black in it; and I comment that maybe, once in a while, she would like to "blacken" me a bit. At first Lucy reacts with shock—how could I possibly think this about her, she who likes me so much! Yet when somebody helps her to remember that she really is sometimes angry with me, Lucy admits her angry feeling and attributes them to the fact that I never give her any good advice, while she needs it so badly. To this, one of the other young women cries out in amazement: "You wouldn't want Marie-Jeanne to act like your mother, would you!? By now your mother's endless good advice must pour out of your ears!" I add that maybe Lucy would like me to tell her what to do, because then she would not have to think for herself and make up her own mind about what is going on here in the group whenever she tells the stories about her mother, nor would she have to think about what's happening in her life with mother outside the group. By now the circle is closed: Lucy recognizes her angry feelings towards me, I become connected to her mother, and there is a clue about the background for Lucy's anger.

The next time that Lucy brings up one of her interactions with her mother, the group seems about ready to lynch the mother. I repeat that the anger expressed by the group members is provoked by what Lucy tells us. When Lucy looks around once more in utter disbelief, I add, talking very slowly, that maybe she can retain her exclusively positive feelings towards her mother, and even idealize her, because, thanks to the way in which she is telling her stories, she manages to put her criticism and anger towards her mother into the other group members, who express them for her.

For Lucy, my intervention meant the beginning of a long and painful period during which she re-integrated those feelings of anger that scared her so much. She became more aware of the complex ambivalent feelings and the intense anxiety that she experienced in the relationship with her mother. She finally gained some insight into the origin of those feelings.

For the other group members, interventions like this create an immediate feeling of relief, because it frees them from a burden that, for a while, they carried for someone else. Moreover, as such interventions provide the whole group with a view of the way in which the human psyche functions, they may get an exploration going of the way that they, too, deposit parts of themselves into others. One of the findings pertaining to their relationship with Lucy was that, at times, some of them had tried very hard to make Lucy say to her mother some brutally confronting things which they would have liked to tell their own mother.

Although, after this evolution, Lucy became much more conscious about her experiences and her feelings connected to them, I would not describe the evolution that took place as a process whereby the unconscious becomes conscious, because I believe that something quite different has been taking place. That "something" is what I like to call "mentalization". Originally, Lucy's psychic space was filled up with memories of actions about which she could talk (mother said or did this and that; I said and did this and that), but which were disconnected from their emotional quality and unavailable for thinking. Her emotional experiences pertaining to this part of her relationship with her mother were thrown out and put into the group members, who had to contain them but put them into words and eventually think about them. To me it seems that, over time, this space that the group provided for containing, expressing, and thinking about the complex emotional experiences of Lucy's intimate relationships, belonging to the there-and-then and being linked-up with the here-and-now, became part of Lucy's mental world. It is a process analogous to a child taking in its mother's alpha function. From then on, Lucy will be able to keep together, within herself, the bits and pieces of her sensory experiences, link them up with their emotional counterparts, stand the pain and anxiety that accompanies them, and use the whole to think and maybe talk about, rather than to throw the different elements around in the external world. The "inner space" created in this way has some of the characteristics of a transitional space. It provides room for "play" with images, words, and thoughts, whereby new and more complex links can be created and explored; it therefore also provides the transition from being compelled to act, to the possibility of choosing an action.

Related to the previous point is a another important attribute of group therapy: it creates the possibility for the participants to look into each other's inner world. For people with serious personality disorders, this is apparently something that they have never dared or been allowed to do. At first, it seems like a very scary business, and they go about it in a rather awkward way, alternately spilling or trying hard to contain their anger and aggression, their excitement, and feelings of triumph. As they learn—partly through seeing how I go about it with diffidence and care—they gain confidence and start to take pleasure in their own capacities to be considerate and caring. Finally, they enjoy the use of their newly found reparative capabilities. Often, it is only at this point that they can start talking about all the mixed feelings of the initial phase, while it becomes clear how these mixed and disturbing feelings are related to the way in which they were themselves carelessly intruded upon and were victims of psychical or physical abuse.

My intervention technique is based upon, but not restricted to, Bion's views on group dynamics and interventions in small groups. I address both the individual and the group: the individual, only if the group functions according to the work-group mode; I focus on the group whenever it functions according to one of the basic-assumption mentalities (Bion, 1961, 1970). But I also turn to the group whenever its way of working reveals an underlying phantasy about the meaning of the group for its members, or about the relationship between the members—including me—that is independent of the basic-assumption mentality.

Let me illustrate this last point (the others were already visible in the "Lucy" vignette and will also become clear with the help of a vignette in the next section).

> Imagine a group during the final session before I leave for my summer vacation. In a pleasant mood, the participants try hard to round off the ongoing work. They take up unfinished matters and link together certain issues of different people; they associate, elaborate, venture some interpretations, and I almost don't need to intervene. After a while, I notice that I look with satisfaction at what happens and find myself wishing that this would occur more often. The only thing missing is an elaboration of the approaching end. It is mentioned, but only casually. When we have about fifteen minutes to go, while it seems to me that the on-going work has come to an end, I say that it is as if the hard work they have been doing, and to which I had only little to add, was not only a way to attend to some unfinished business, but perhaps also served the purpose of showing themselves and me that they need not be afraid of the coming interruption. They have demonstrated that they can manage quite well even without my help, and maybe at the same time they were giving me a sort of a vacation present, so that I will remember them with pleasure and will be glad to come back.

> One could not possibly say that this group was working according to basic-assumption flight. On the contrary, they were showing a piece of good, hard work, and it was a pleasure to

watch them do it. Yet, the good work also had the function of avoiding confrontation with their anxiety about my leaving. This avoidance, however, was realized through a very constructive move, which had nothing to do with manic defences and, rather than hinder, enhanced personal and group development. For indeed, if they are capable of working like this, they need not be afraid of the approaching vacation period.

The hospital setting is often viewed exclusively as a hindrance for psychoanalytic group therapy. I do not think that this is correct. On condition that living together is well organized, I believe that the advantages of the situation outweigh the disadvantages.

It is certainly true that people who have to live together often hesitate to speak their mind for fear of creating tensions that may make daily life rather difficult. Yet, in as far as the nursing staff manages to provide a structure and to maintain a climate of openness, in which everything can be said as long as it is voiced in a non-aggressive language and is put up for exploration, then the hesitations are easily overcome. The work that goes on in the context of various ward activities provides excellent preparation for adequate functioning in the analytic group. It is exactly this supportive and preparative work that allows me to function in the in-patient psychoanalytic group in the same way that I would in an out-patient setting.

It is also right to say that people who live together and do other forms of therapy together have a tendency—when in a psychoanalytic group—to talk quite a bit about what they did and about the behaviour they observed around them. But I have never found it difficult to help them move to the level of hidden concerns and emotional experiences that accompany the doing. However, if the group contains some more experienced members, they often make that move all by themselves. Moreover, these shared experiences play a significant role in some important confrontations. It is sometimes almost unbelievable how the description that people give of themselves, or the way in which they behave in the analytic group, differs from the way in which they appear in other situations. If their fellow patients bring in their own observations, the therapeutic work moves faster and becomes richer, because in this way we are able to reach some areas of the personality that otherwise would probably be omitted. Think, for example, about what happened to Lucy, thanks to the input from one of the group members about the black colour that Lucy used in her painting of me.

As far as transference reactions are concerned, there is no doubt that they are different in these groups from others. They may be less striking, more subtle. They often pertain to part objects. But they are certainly abundant and permit all the work that one can wish for. A somewhat longer clinical vignette may help to illustrate some of the preceding remarks.

> When "Howard" joins the group, he is a very anxious and disturbed young man. But he integrates rather easily into the ongoing group, and, over time, he becomes one of its active and influential members.

> Within a few months his suicidal tendencies disappear, and during the next year and a half the origins of his homosexual preferences are identified and worked through. He becomes an attractive young person, with a keen interest in women his own age. He prospers and blooms, and it is a pleasure to see him develop.

> Then, everything comes to a standstill. Howard starts to miss sessions, and, when he does come, he looks like a senile old man. He wears his slippers, drags his feet, and is badly groomed and dressed. He claims that all this leads to nothing, that nothing ever really changes.

> In several ways the others tell him to stop this comedy, and they describe to me his habitual behaviour on the ward or on outings, where apparently he acts like a charming and alert young man. I suggest that maybe it is this attractive guy that he wants to hide from me. But he disagrees: he assures me that, as always, I am missing the obvious—namely, he just can't change!

> This situation drags on for a couple of months. At times, the material indicates that envy plays a part in what is going on, but this never becomes clear enough to permit an interpretation that hits home.

When we discuss Howard's evolution during our team meeting, all of us agree that this man no longer needs hospitalization, and that—if he so wishes—psychoanalytic therapy can continue on an out-patient basis. The ward psychiatrist discusses our findings with Howard, and together they decide that he will leave the hospital and resume work within a delay of at most three months.

Shortly after this decision took place, the group is gathered for their Monday session. A woman talks about the anxiety that she experiences whenever she thinks about her plan to leave the hospital, because she is not really sure that she is ready for it. Voicing her feelings, she frequently uses the expression "be ready/getting ready", which in Dutch also means having an orgasm (the equivalent of the English "to come"). I intervene in this context, because an important part of the work that this woman did concerned her frigidity.

Meanwhile, Howard moves restlessly about in his seat, and the woman expresses her amazement at the fact that he does not join in the exchange, as he, too, feels uneasy at the prospect of leaving the hospital. But Howard shakes his head: "No, no, he does not want to talk." A group member adds : "Yes, especially when it comes to 'getting ready' he sure feels uneasy", and he tries to convince Howard of the necessity to talk about what happened last night. After a rather long detour, Howard starts speaking.

Yesterday he went to see a prostitute. Not because he wanted a sexual relationship, but because he needed to talk. One of the men exclaims with astonishment: "It can't be possible: who would want to spend his money on talks, when we can talk here all through the week?!" Apparently the prostitute, too, thought that talking wasn't part of her job, for she proposed to masturbate him. Howard accepted, but he saw to it that he had no orgasm. He assures us that this does not mean that he did not enjoy it, only that she was not aware of it.

Now the whole group talks at once: "How is it possible? This is really him!" Then someone asks explicitly: "But why?" When he responds, Howard's face radiates with pleasure: "Well, now she can doubt for the rest of her life whether she's a good prostitute."

I am so amazed and taken by surprise because of what becomes clear just there and then that in my intervention I use a swearword, and say something like: "Jeepers! Isn't that what has been going on here too, for the past few months? That you saw to it that the group and I got the feeling that we couldn't help you to get ready, while all the time you hid the pleasure you take in the work that we do together; maybe because you want me, too, to doubt for the rest of my life about my qualities as an analyst?"

It is as though a wave passes through the group. Everybody moves, chatters, and acts as if the last couple of minutes hadn't existed. The man starts talking again about the stupidity of wanting to pay a prostitute in order to talk, and the others join in. I leave them for a while to give them a chance to come back on their own to what I said. But when they don't, I intervene and suggest that maybe they could not stay with what I just said because of my unusual choice of words, but also because I compared what happened between Howard and a prostitute to what happened here between Howard and me, and that all this was rather scary.

This enables them to come back to the many things my first intervention had provoked, and, from there on, Howard manages to do an amount of work that I would have thought impossible during the time-span that we had left. The material he produced in the context of the group relationships made clear that his envy of me, in connection with his doubts about his own professional qualities, had only a minor influence on what had happened. The most important factor for the stalemate proved to be his phantasy that if he were to show or recognize the positive results of our work, I would take all the credit for it and would not recognize the important part that he had played in it. His dominant anxiety had been that I would steal his success, in exactly the same way that his mother had always done, sometimes even before success was accomplished.

This vignette demonstrates how important the knowledge that participants have about each other through living together can be for the progress of therapeutic work. If one of the participants had not known and talked about "what happened yesterday", we may never have solved the impasse. It also demonstrates how I became a transference object, exactly in the way that "Lucy's story" shows how the other group members can serve the same purpose. Finally, it illustrates the way in which I move from talking to an individual, to taking to the group, and back, depending upon the level at which the group operates. When my unusual way of expressing myself, together with the disturbing comparison I introduce, makes the group retreat to basic-assumption flight, I tell them about my view of the reasons behind their flight movement, thereby opening the possibility for working through the complex emotional experiences that my intervention provoked. Even while this work is in progress, and certainly after it is done, I can go back to the experiences of individual members.

* * *

The source of change in psychoanalytic group therapy is, in the first instance, not different from the change agents active in individual analysis. On the one hand, it is a benevolent exploration of anxieties, defences, needs and desires, their interrelationships, and the meaning that they seem to get in the context of what is going on between the participants. On the other hand, it has to do with the experience and introjection of a person, the analyst, who is capable—at least most of the time—of containing her own emotional experiences, mulling them over, and using them through her interventions to the benefit of the analysand, instead of allowing them to spill over in emotional outbursts or actions.

Apart from that, I believe that groups provide some extras. They certainly permit the practice of new behaviour in a more tolerant and safe environment than the one provided by "everyday life". But, as I have elaborated elsewhere (Vansina-Cobbaert, 1996), there is something much more important. Especially in the instance of serious personality disorders, the change in the individual is, perhaps, more a consequence of the introjection of the qualities of the group in which he participated, than of the interventions and interpretations made by the analyst. In this respect, important group qualities are, first of all, the existence of reciprocal intimate relationships, intended to be thought about and talked about in an exploring way, while nobody is forced to accept the others' truths. Then there is the participation in a system that permits mutual reparation, which stresses the existence and the strength of the good parts, the constructive forces that are present in the participants themselves.

Finally, and possibly the most important, are the capacities for containment present in the group: containment of the content of the sometimes horrible personal stories, containment also of the intensity of personal affects as, for example, love, hate, jealousy, and envy. I believe that it is the introjection of such group qualities that provides the basis for the development of authenticity, affection, generosity, patience, and an adequate form of self-control in the individual. Unfortunately, such complex developmental processes defeat illustration through clinical vignettes.

CHAPTER SIX

"How hard can you kick a baby before it dies?": psychotherapy in an institution for disturbed children

Valerie Sinason

This chapter looks at the work of a child psychotherapist in an institution for disturbed children who were unable to be managed in other special provision. It follows several days in the life of the unit—through the individual and group sessions, a mothers' group, staff meetings—and thereby focuses on the way that the nightmare lives of three boys percolate through the structures and boundaries of the unit.

"Steven" was 8 years old, mute, mildly brain-damaged, and severely delayed in his learning. He was covered in bruises and dirt and dressed in clothes that were too small for him. He had enormous eyes, which he powerfully fixed on all staff members, and a beautifully shaped head, which was too large for his body. His baby-like qualities and appearance evoked powerful maternal responses in the predominantly female staff. Compassion for his muteness, his abusive home, and an awareness that his mother wanted to keep him as a baby coexisted with tension and shock caused by his suicidal gestures.

At the unit, he would suddenly launch himself from the top of a staircase, a low wall, a chair. He behaved as though he knew he was dispensable. We were concerned that he was being physically and sexually abused. We noted all his bruises and painstakingly tried to differentiate between those caused by his own "accidents" and those that were inflicted by others. He came with black eyes, limbs in plaster, and infected cuts, and he continued to damage himself in the unit. It took time to realize that the largely female staff (teachers, psychiatric team, and myself) were joined to him by an umbilical cord of pain. Outwardly gentle, without any of the shouting and extreme external violence generated by the other disturbed children, he was weakening the life of the institution.

Staff meetings were full of safety concerns. We wanted to put netting over the side of the stairs so that if he jumped and we did not catch him in time he would still be alive. We wanted to put locks on windows in the toilets to prevent him jumping out. We wanted to lop the lower branches of trees and remove all stones and rocks from the grounds. The fear of him succeeding in killing himself took precedence over any other clinical discussion.

We realized, then, of course, that we could not make the unit death-proof and that our task was to provide more staff containment. Steven's fearlessness and destructiveness had attracted the death-wish in the older boys, and a gang process began in which the female staff struggled to round up the disaffected violent boys. "Linton", especially, began to pull bricks off the body of the building and then hurl them across the playground. Whereas Steven was short, white, and silent, Linton was large, strong, black, and noisy. His punches and kicks were very damaging. He was hyperactive, unable to learn, and highly eroticized; his sexual and physical violence towards the female staff members was chilling. His father had died of AIDS. Whilst Steven's hurt and fury tore the unit apart through his silence, Linton's noise was the counterpart.

Linton, aged 10, was referred to us after violent sexual attacks on female staff members at his last unit. And then there was "Johnny", aged 8, tiny, thin, and on the child-protection register for failure to thrive. He would sit for hours in trance-like states, moving his hands or feet in strange patterns. He would come out of these states either desperately offering himself for sexual attention, presenting his buttocks to the older boys or thrusting his pelvis, or else suddenly throwing himself into violent action with no apparent warning.

Changes in the external organization, due to Health Service restructuring, affected internal morale. The previous male consultant had taken early retirement and was missed for his "fathering" abilities as well as for his analytic skills. Steven would remember the way that the consultant had mended a broken bike and fixed a leaking roof. Without him, and with only one part-time male staff member, the unit felt—at times, for the staff—like a battered single mother, and it took us time to realize that for the boys the experience was of a battering one. It was after the staff concern when the very fabric of the building itself was under attack, with bricks thrown and pictures torn—particularly by Linton and Johnny—that I decided to take both Steven and Linton into individual twice-weekly therapy and Johnny into group therapy.

In Steven's first session, with difficulty he stared at me, opened his mouth, moved his lips soundlessly, and then, with great force, with his fists clenched, said the single word "Kill". As William Golding wrote (1980), "Not only did he clench his fists with the effort of speaking, he squinted. It seemed that a word was an object, a material object, round and smooth sometimes, a golfball of a thing that he could just about manage to get through his mouth, though it deformed his face in the passage."

The terrible word that hurt his face coming out—the terrible birth that damaged the fantasized body of his mother—turned out, in fact, to be the embodiment of his mother's death wish towards him. It was not the baby Steven who destroyed his mother by being born. However, the unwanted child, as the child of an unwanted child, became the receptacle for disowned hatred. Steven, in his silence and in his single word, carried one of the two secret unbearable keys to the day unit—infanticide. Rascovsky and Rascovsky (1968) comment that our professional neglect over cruel parenting is due to universal resistance to acknowledge "the mother's filicide drives, undoubtedly the most dreaded and uncanny truth for us to face."

Linton carried the second key. In therapy, he started making a double bed out of the cushions and blankets. He flung himself down on the right side of the bed and punched ferociously at the empty space on the left, screaming "Mother-fucker, mother-fucker". Then he burst into tears (something I had never seen from him) and started kicking a locked cupboard so hard that it splintered. I said to him that he had made a double bed and it sounded as if it was for him and a mother, and that this made him feel angry and excited. He stopped kicking the door and stood still with his back to me—frozen with tension. I said he was not allowed to kick my cupboard and suggested that he sat down on the chair. With his eyes covered, he shuffled to the chair and sat down, making a loud humming noise.

I waited a moment until he stopped. I said that he was pleased that I did not want my cupboard broken into—and perhaps that allowed him to hope that I did not want to break into his space. He burst into loud sobs, kicked the pillows on the "mother" side of the bed violently, and shouted, "She makes me sleep in her bed at night."

Stewart (1961) considers that the feminine equivalent to the Oedipus complex is not the love of the daughter for her father, but the incestuous wishes of the mother for her son, whom she regards as part of herself. I consider the term "mother-fucker" a diagnostic feature in boys who have been tantalized at best or seduced at worst by their mothers. But the taboo and the hurt are so great that the male child has to take responsibility for the act. Hence, the most dangerous insult in many institutions is never "son-fucker" but "mother-fucker".

As Mannoni comments (1967): "Where we are dealing with a child caught in the death-wishes of his parents, it is their words first of all which must be unravelled." In a piece of research on bad language used by children and adolescents in another institution for disturbed children I found that the swear-words provided an iconography of the first hurt (Sinason, 1989).

With Johnny, came the third layer of secrets. Every week he came for group therapy, calling, "Give me blood" in an ogre-like voice. I wondered to myself what horror film he might have been watching. However, during this particular week, I became suddenly aware that I was not properly thinking about Johnny's words. They worried me so much that I had turned them into video nasties in order to distance myself from them. Therefore, on this particular day, when Johnny walked in calling, "Give me blood", I made the comment, "Somebody seems to need a lot of blood today". Johnny went white, shook, and hid under the table. "How did you know?", he asked. I said that there was something I had not known for a long time, but today I seemed to know some things better. Whilst my co-therapist concentrated on the other boys (who were drowning the baby dolls), I focused on Johnny.

"I am going back now. I am a ghost", he said.

"How did you get to be a ghost?", I asked.

"Well, it's better being a ghost, because if you are dead they can't hurt you any more."

I felt enormously sad.

"Poor ghost", I said, "then it is a good job you can find a way of surviving."

"Yes", he said, suddenly restored, "and now I am going back to hell."

"Right", I said, "that must be a difficult place to get to. How do you get there?"

"By the trapdoor next to the cooker in my kitchen", he replied.

A chill entered the room and into myself and my co-therapist. We had opened yet another door of the children's terrible private lives. However, outside the clinical situation there was insufficient forensic evidence of possible abuse for further action to be taken (Sinason, 1994).

Two days in the life of the unit

It was 8 a.m. on a sunny Tuesday morning as the teacher-in-charge hurried to the entrance of the unit. In the shadow of the porch, she took the doorkeys out of her bag and walked nervously in. It was all right! The illuminated fishtank in the entrance hall hummed quietly. The three goldfish had not only survived the first night without the children, but, more importantly, had survived the children's attentions for one day and the children had allowed them to survive. The fish were a sign of hope that the unit itself would survive, as well as being a magnet for the fears, experiences, and destructive fantasies of the children.

On Monday, the day that the fish had arrived, Johnny (who had been sexually abused by both his parents) had promised his teacher: "I am going to kill them." Seven-year-old "David", who feared he had contracted AIDS from his abusing father, agreed: "I am going to put poison in the water to kill them." In her therapy session with me, 6-year-old "Mary", neglected and abused, dropped a baby doll in the sink. "Oh dear!", she said with fake concern, "I've killed the fish and I have killed the baby. Never mind! It is easy to get more, and the police don't believe mummies do anything bad."

After I had taken Mary back to the classroom, the new female doctor was walking down the stairs with her head downcast after returning 8-year-old "Chris" from therapy. The Consultant noticed her slow walk and then joked, "You're not bleeding are you?" She lifted her wrists, and they were pouring with blood from wounds caused by Chris, who had stabbed at her with his sharp lead pencil. A psychiatric team meeting that afternoon decided that Chris needed two workers—two parents to contain his violence.

Fish, babies, blood, AIDS, and death surfaced in words, play, symbolic activities, and as symbolic equations in the classrooms and therapy room of this National Health Institution for disturbed children. They wove their way into the community meeting, too—a 30-minute, once-weekly meeting for all the children and adults. An attack on the baby—the result of intercourse, of two people coming together—is a central issue in all therapeutic work. However, in looking at a Bionic attack on linking (Bion, 1959) when working with abused children, we need to look very carefully at how the adult concrete actions have set the terrible sequence in motion. The attack on linking can be a double one, the mental process being a continuation of what was begun concretely on the body and mind of the child.

Mary rocked up and down on the chair, poking her finger in her mouth in an explicit way and opening her legs. "It's fishy", she giggled. "It's the Mummy fish." Linton covered his face with his jumper, and his teacher said he had been worrying about some of the things his Mummy said and did. David, whose father had died of AIDS, cried that the fish might catch something and die. Johnny jabbed me with his elbow, and when I held it to stop being poked he proudly showed the wart he had at the end of his elbow and said that I had been touching it. I said to the group: "Johnny is saying hello to me with his elbows. He doesn't like being alone with a wart. He wants me to have one too. Lots of people today are showing us how they have had painful things happen to them, and they think it will be catchy, or they want it to be catchy. Perhaps they think it will be the same for the fish." Chris and David agreed. The others were silent. "Ahmed", aged 8, spoke of illness in his family in India. "Gemma", aged 11, who needs two escorts to bring her to the unit, leapt up from her chair and pushed Ahmed onto the floor. Two staff were needed to restrain her.

A nursery nurse commented that Gemma's father was dying of cancer and she could not bear thinking about anyone being ill. Isabel, whose twin had died, spat at Gemma, who erotically lifted her dress high over her head, wriggling her buttocks. "Pooey—you are pooey", shouted the formerly silent Steven. "Pooey" echoed the other children, all except for "Ken", aged 10, who sat in a dissociated trance state, making strange hand movements. Gemma threw off the two female staff who were holding her and ran out of the room, slamming the door. We adults debated whether to send someone after her.

A teacher suggested that the group should find names for the fish. David said that the fish wouldn't need names as they were going to die. Ken came out of his trance state to say in a hypnotic voice: "Everyone is going to die. I know." Steven jumped up and did a stamping dance. Gemma, who had been hiding outside the door, ran back in on hearing the noise. She joined in with the stamping. For a while, despite staff attempts, the noise continued. However, something in Steven's concentrated dance eventually silenced the other children. There was a moment when the whole group looked at him. "How hard can you kick a baby before it dies?", he asked. "Fucking hard", screamed Mary. "It's the wolf! It's the wolf!", shouted Gemma, speaking in a Disney cartoon voice.

There was a painful silence. The baby-killer, baby-fucker, and baby devourer had entered the community meeting, the heart of the unit, and now we could consider it together.

After the community meeting, Mary brought two fish puppets she had made to therapy. One had a hard head and sharp teeth, and one was soft. She said that the hard-headed one was a cruel bad Mummy fish who was sometimes kind, and the soft one was kind, and they were both friends. She asked me to be the bad fish puppet. I asked her how bad the fish was—how bad was I to be? "Well, she can't stop biting people and tickling their tummy and cunts, but then she can be nice." So each time her puppet came near me, at a certain point I went "grr" and made my puppet bite hers on the neck and then apologize.

> *Mary* (*as fish*): But why do you do such bad things?
>
> *Me*: I don't know. Why do you think?
>
> *Mary*: Because you can't stop it.
>
> *Me*: I suppose that's right.
>
> *Mary*: It's not good for you—it makes everything worse. I'll get you some medicine. (*She does*) How's that?
>
> *Me*: Well, it makes me sleepier but—grr—I still want to bite.
>
> (*She laughs uproariously*)
>
> *Mary*: Give me a ride on your back.
>
> *Me*: Well, you can, but it might not be safe.
>
> *Mary*: Well, promise it will be.
>
> *Me*: How can I promise that? I don't know what will happen.
>
> (*Her puppet had a ride, and I kept throwing it off and then apologizing. She giggled and then changed the pattern: she made her puppet start falling off by itself before mine even began to attack.*)
>
> *Me*: Oh dear, now you have learned to be in danger all by yourself—without me having the pleasure of hurting you. But it's quite nice for me, because now you take the blame.
>
> *Mary*: Why did you start doing that to me, Mummy?
>
> *Me*: My parents bit me and tickled me.
>
> *Mary*: I'll tell you what I'll do. I'm going to tell them not to.
>
> (*She moved away, knocked on a door and told the parent dolls not to bite their daughter fish any more because she was biting her children. They promised to stop.*)

Mary: They've promised, so you mustn't do it anymore.

Me: Do you think I can stop?

Mary: Well, you might carry on a bit all by yourself.

Me: I suppose I might.

Mary: Let me have a ride.

(*She had a ride, with her puppet knocking itself over so violently that I decided to make my puppet feel worried.*)

Me: Oh dear, now you are hurting yourself before I can hurt you, and that makes me worry.

My voice tone was transitional—I was no longer sounding like the mother-fish as I felt that Mary was ready to explore this real bad object more carefully. I commented to her that maybe the daughter-fish had found a way of surviving terrible parents by hurting herself first, so that what her parents did could not hurt so much. She left the therapy room saying that she hoped the fish would stay alive.

Shortly afterwards, Steven came for his session. He picked up the square musical toy that I had in the room. This toy provided the opportunity for making different sounds—bells, whistles, drums. He bashed it. Then he tried to blow its whistle. I said that he wanted to see if it still had a voice after it was hurt. He put the toy in the sink and poured water over it. He said that the water was ice-cold. Then he tried to whistle desperately through it again. I said that perhaps it was a voice-box like his and that he was seeing how much he could do before the voice died. He nodded and said, "It goes to heaven. Then it flies—it is a ghost—a dead voice." He looked at me very seriously: "The fish is still alive." I said that yes, it was, and it seemed very frightening for him—worrying how the fish would manage and how everyone would manage. I commented on his worry at the community meeting about how hard you could kick a baby before it died. "I don't really think you want to kill me", he said, leaping onto the window ledge. I caught him up and carried him down, saying that he was offering to hurt himself first to stop me hurting him—I seemed such a dangerous, bad mother. He agreed.

It was then time to meet with the educational psychologist for our children's group. Only three of the children were present, but we decided to hold the group for the whole time. Ken, David, and Johnny came eagerly from the classroom with the class teacher, sensitively saying that they would wait to have the special story until after the group.

Inside the therapy room, the children rushed for the sink and filled it with water. Ken began to drown the baby dolls. David dressed up in women's clothes and said that he was the baby's mother. "Shall I feel your willy and then feel your arsehole?", he asked in an eminently reasonable voice, while coming to join Ken at the sink in holding the baby doll's head under water. Johnny dropped plasticine on my co-therapist's head. "Shit to shit, piss to piss", he intoned, as if saying a prayer. I said that it sounded like terrible things were happening, and yet everyone seemed perfectly nice about it all.

One hour later was the mothers' group. All the boys who were referred for violent behaviour lacked a father who either lived with them or provided any consistent attachment (Rosen, 1979), and they all, like Linton, made pointed use of one poignant and key phrase—"mother-fucker". Everything else about the boys—their academic levels, class, race, and religion was different. But all of them, often after a destructive act in the classroom or the therapy room, blurt out that they share a bed with their mothers at night. They take care to say "share a bed" instead of "sleep with", as the sexual connotation is so powerful in the latter. Some do have their own bedroom, but their mothers insist that they share the double bed. Others do not even have their own bedroom and give up on all friendships from shame at what other children would think if they found out that they had no bedroom of their own.

At the mothers' group that I ran with the social worker, we heard a story told by different mothers from different cultures, each of whom slept with her son. There is this one son, aged around 8 to 11 years, that they all have (Sinason, 1996). He is terrified at night, they say. They stress that initially they do not like it: they want a proper night's sleep; they hate being woken up by his nightmares. "I am so tired", they all say. "I just let him go to sleep with me, and then I get a better rest." "It's the culture", they say. "I haven't got enough rooms", they say. But something stays wrong.

We leave the realms of culture and kindness and find a very specific abuse—the emotional abuse of the sons by the mothers, and the earlier abuse of the mothers when they were children:

- "I am the mother. He came out of me, so he is mine. Nothing else is mine. He is not a man. He is just a child."

- "He's got a better willy than his dad."

- "A little prick. You should see him try to hide his erection in the morning, as if it mattered."

- "In my country anyone could sleep with you if they were lonely. I was lent out to my grandma, my granddad, and my uncles—so why shouldn't I have that comfort too?"

- "If he turned that thing on me in the night I'd cut it off—he's a little boy—he's my baby.

In all these cases, the child is a no-thing—not a person. Estela Welldon (1988) comments: "Mothers who display perverse tendencies towards their offspring do so within the first two years of their children's life." The baby becomes the sexual toy, the missing penis. For a man, the perverse act is against another; for the woman, it is her own part-object, herself or her child.

After the mothers' meeting, I suggested to Linton's mother that we should meet, as Linton had asked me for help in stopping her from sleeping with him. I first checked whether he was telling the truth, and his mother agreed happily. When I carefully suggested that now he was getting older it might be difficult and sexually disturbing for him, her eyes lit up in a sexualized way. "Why, the sexy little beast!", she giggled. The abusive parent projects onto the child their own disowned animality, bestiality, sadism—and, of course, unsurprisingly, she too needed work to deal with her prior abuse.

In the beginning, under the Goddess religions, infanticide was widespread, random, and acceptable. Slowly it was processed into ritual child sacrifice. With a male God, early Judaism sought to curb this process. Abraham tried to kill Isaac but was stopped at the last moment by God. This attempt to move from infanticide did not work completely, and the painful point of contact between Judaism and Christianity is the murder of a child—Jesus—whose special sign was the fish. Once a male God was dominant, the frightening aspects of the Goddess were split off. Woman was idealized as mother the life-giver. The counterpart, Kali, the mother as destroyer, was too painful to think about in the Judao-Christian cultures. We have to go back to the Greek tragedies for that understanding. Euripides has Pentheus (in the Bacchae) pleading to his priestess mother Agave: "Mother, it is I, thy child, thy Pentheus. . . . Have mercy mother! Let it not befall through sin of mine that thou shouldest slay thy son" (I, 1115–1120). But Agave dismembers him, seeing him only as a wild animal, a sexual beast.

Discussion

Brett Kahr (1993) has written of the infanticidal introject, exemplified here by the way that Steven took his mother's death-wish into his heart. Through the day unit, the children, and their death-wishes, we meet the wolf-mothers in whose hearts their own childhood suicidal introjects bruise.

In the childhood fable about the wolf and the three little pigs, the piglets were sent off into the world, usually by a single mother, to build their own homes. Where the walls were not made of strong enough substance, the wolf could break in and kill and eat them. The threat of the wolf is to huff and puff and blow the house down. This is destruction of the container. As Obholzer and Roberts (1994) comment, our need to have containing institutions is to protect us from layers of anxiety.

Where the children were imbued with death-wishes, their physical and emotional attack on the body of the unit was a lethal one. Without a good-enough father, internally or externally, to protect young boys from women—and women from boys—the unit was under threat. Initially, the female staff were unable to deal with these mental and physical projections and saw danger everywhere. We were in identification with the children, unable to contain their deadly anxieties. With no containment and with a largely female staff, the most primitive fear was the primary cannibalistic fear of being devoured.

It is the third little pig who has both the mental equipment to build a house of bricks with firm foundations, and the ability, as Bettelheim (1976) points out, to delay gratification for the sake of the reality principle. However, even with a strong house the wolf is able to climb through an orifice—the chimney. The little pig—to survive—needs to find an internal defence and attack system that will keep the wolf from his door.

In many fairy tales, the wolf either stands for the disowned, devouring, cannibalistic part of us, or else he represents hatred of the mothering function. He enviously kills or kidnaps children—sometimes simulating a pregnancy by incorporating a female child, or simulating a female identity (the grandmother in Red Riding Hood). The wolf can therefore be a split-off: the murderous, infanticidal mother or grandmother assuming, for disguise, a male identity. This split is the counterpart of the negligent mother who abandons her young or who finds a male to carry out her own murderous impulses.

Whilst the staff identified with one half of the maternal imago that these children carried—the battered single mother—it was hard to recognize that for the children they represented the other half—the infanticidal mother. In the absence of a father, the close relationship with women evoked worrying incestuous fantasies and a corresponding fear of a devastating punishment by a missing father. The attacks on the building were also a desperate communication, a message in a bottle, asking for fathering, for a strong father to appear. However, because of the painful experiences of the children, the strong father all too quickly was transformed into a violent one. As many of the children had witnessed violent attacks on their mothers and had been the victims of violent attacks by their mothers, they also feared a combined object of ferocity.

Some of the attacks on linking (Bion, 1959) could come from a realistic awareness that if both parents realistically were dangerous singly, then the combination was lethal. I refer to Melanie Klein's concept of the combined parent figure: an extremely cruel and dreaded fantasy (Klein, 1929). Indeed, it is a tragedy, for children and adults alike, when their experience of reality coincides with their fantasies.

The female staff have had to learn to "run with wolves" without becoming them. In the absence of adequate male support, they have needed to provide mental containment and physical strength. The child psychotherapist in such an institution has a powerful chance to see—through the individual, group, family, and community work—the hurt-lines, the wear-and-tear lines, the breakdowns and breakthrough of the physical and mental structure. The fish died a normal death of old age, and, despite the daily fears, the boys are all alive too. Staff get bad backs, injuries, colds. The building is attacked and repaired. New children find holes in the structure just when we think we have made the unit safe, and we realize that our task is to be prepared to face sudden attack. Such traumatized children can never be easily contained. However, if we make room for their nightmares, they get a chance to sleep and wake and repair, and so do we. The baby, although kicked, does not die.

CHAPTER SEVEN

Treatment and management of the sexually deviant and criminal: an out-patient facility

Robert Hale

The Portman Clinic is a large Victorian house in Swiss Cottage, North London; it is indistinguishable externally from the neighbouring residential properties, most of which have been divided into flats for the prosperous middle class. The only identifier is a small sign by the front door. It has a large, well-kept garden with shrubs and fruit trees. An admiring comment on the garden is often a patient's opening remark. The hallway has the original tiles; leading off it and within sight of the receptionist are the patients' toilets, men and women. A small sign marks the reception and the waiting-room. A glass partition separates the receptionist from the patients in the waiting-room. Patients are called for their appointments as "Dr Jones' patient" or "Mrs Smith's group". Anonymity can thus be preserved. Stairs lead to the consulting-rooms, each bearing the marks of its occupant—a few pictures, pot plants, and professional books—but less intimate than the average private analytic consulting-room. A couch, a desk, and a few easy chairs positioned so the patient can *escape*. Some of the rooms are large enough for groups.

This clinic treats people who "have carried out criminal acts or consider themselves to be suffering from sexual deviation". The words are carefully chosen. It offers out-patient psychotherapy, individual and group, often long-term. It is part of the National Health Service, and the patients' treatment is paid for by a series of contracts with local health authorities as part of the internal market which was introduced a few years ago. With the Tavistock Clinic it makes up one Trust, which is the trading unit within the internal market; the Portman is much smaller than the Tavistock, accounting for approximately 10% of the total budget.

All the staff are psychoanalysts or analytic psychotherapists, and because of the nature of the work there is only one trainee. We have an active training programme for other professionals and offer consultation to other institutions. In Britain, the Portman Clinic is the centre for the gradually emerging profession of forensic psychotherapy—a development that is being paralleled in other European countries.

The history of the clinic is interesting and relevant. It was founded in 1933 as the Institute for the Study and Treatment of Delinquency (ISTD). The prime mover was Dr Grace Pailthorpe, a farsighted woman of enormous energy, who had run a field ambulance unit in the Balkans in the First World War. She then became interested in the application of psychological and psychoanalytic theories to criminals and criminal acts. In 1932 she published a report, *Studies in the Psychology of Delinquency*, the result of a study she had carried out on the inmates of a prison in Birmingham. The work was funded by the British Medical Association: already we can see the links with law, health, and psychoanalysis which characterize the Portman Clinic today.

In forming the ISTD, she gathered around her a group of psychoanalysts, the most influential of whom was Edward Glover—his writings in subsequent years were the seminal works in the subject. These pioneers recognized the need for political and social influence. The early patrons included not only Adler, Jones, Freud, and Jung, but luminaries from the scientific and literary world—Havelock Ellis, Cyril Burt (the most eminent contemporary psychologist, whose works were subsequently discredited), the writer H. G. Wells, the Poet Laureate John Masefield, and the eminent Shakespearean actor Miles Malleson. Apart from the obvious protection and support that such patronage gave, this connectedness represented a realization that the organization had a social and political function to fulfil.

The clinical service started as the Psychopathic Clinic but subsequently changed its name to the Portman Clinic due to its location in central London close to Portman Square. In 1948, the organization split: the clinic joined the newly formed National Health Service, and the ISTD remained an independent charitable body—an interest group in the field of criminology, organizing conferences and publishing the *Journal of Criminology*. This division into a clinical and a scientific branch was no doubt necessary and prudent at the time, but it did have consequences. The clinical services were now clearly funded from the health budget—a paradox, since the benefits of our services accrue more to the Home Office than the Department of Health. Put another way, we keep people out of prison rather than out of hospital. The problem that this now poses to our funders will be obvious. The clinic thus sits adjacent to law and health—perhaps in a no-man's land, where our patients need it to be—but administratively it is part of health.

The patients who come to the clinic are referred by psychiatrists, forensic psychiatrists, general practitioners, probation officers, lawyers, and law courts. Some come reluctantly, some freely; we see a small number of self-referrals. The two largest groups of patients are those who have committed a sexual offence—usually paedophilia or incest—and those who have been violent, including murderers. Our patients would be characterized as having major personality disorders rather than being psychotic, the latter being the province of forensic psychiatrists within the Medium and High Security Units. Many of our patients have spent considerable amounts of time in prison. We often see people for assessment for a court report prior to trial, but we are keen to allow the judicial process to run its course before we embark on therapy, for only then can we and our patients begin to know their true motivations—which are always complex and often contradictory.

What, then, is this institution—the inside of this Victorian house—like? How was it designed, and how does it function?

Whilst we fondly believe that we, as professionals, design our institutions, the truth is otherwise. It is my contention that our institutions arise out of the interaction between the unconscious anxieties of our patients and the largely unconscious defensive structures, both individual and collective, of the staff.

The anxiety brought by the patient will vary according to the disorder. In the general hospital, the fundamental and specifically medical anxiety is that of disease and dying, with the attendant physical pain. In the psychiatric hospital, it is the fear of insanity—of falling apart psychologically—that dominates, coupled with the fear of sadness. In the forensic setting—the prison, probation, or, I would propose, the drug addiction service—it is the anxiety associated with corrupt and corrupting forces, the anxiety of being coerced, seduced, or taken for a ride.

It is, then, the function of the professional and the institution to recognize, contain, and counteract those unconscious anxieties. The patients of the Portman Clinic inhabit the no man's land bounded on three sides by fears of:

1.   badness—moral disintegration;
2.   sadness—depression and loss;
3.   madness—psychic disintegration.

Their capacity to move from one perimeter to another—to change the clinical presentation and the countertransference response evoked—is characteristic of these patients. Some would say that the chameleon quality is one of their hallmarks.

Clinical example

I saw Mr J in 1983. He was 57. In the first interview, which lasted an hour and three quarters, he seemed concerned but not particularly depressed about his predicament. His main motivation seemed to be his wish not to go back to prison. In the past eight years, he had served two sentences for homosexual paedophilia, and he had been released six weeks previously. On both occasions on release from prison, he described how his attraction for children became particularly strong. He said that he was not frightened that he would "break down and do something silly, but I want help to live with this very strong attraction". He told me about the two offences.

The first was while he was a headmaster of a primary school. He had taken a group of children to his caravan for a holiday, the children being aged between 7 and 11 years. On five different occasions he took a child into bed with him and simulated intercourse by placing his penis intra-crurally from behind. One of the children told his parents, and he was charged with buggery. He claimed that this had not taken place and felt aggrieved that he was found guilty and received the first prison sentence. After leaving prison, he was not allowed to continue in the school service and, after being unemployed for a couple of years, obtained his present job.

The second offence for which he was charged was as follows. Mr J was a strong Catholic. A young woman moved into the street with a boy aged 9 years, and Mr J "noticed him". He got to know that the family were Catholic and, on the pretext of informing them of the local church, insinuated himself into the family. It turned out that she was a "wanton woman" and was, to all intents and purposes, a prostitute. However, Mr J "fell in love with her", and she used him to look after "Keith", her son. She even went away to the Continent for five days, leaving him in his care. Just prior to this occasion, Keith had said to him, "don't go into the kitchen". However Mr J did and found a man who had obviously just emerged from the bedroom. Mr J was "a bit upset", as it confirmed what he feared—namely, that Keith's mother was indeed a prostitute. Shortly afterwards, Keith was left in his care. "Unfortunately, I only had one bed— I was a surrogate father to him—I've always wanted a son." Again the same interaction took place—intra-crural intercourse and masturbation. Subsequent to this, Mr J looked after Keith for eighteen months without any overt sexual encounters. Eventually, a person moved into the area who knew his previous activities and remarked that Keith was spending a lot of time with him. One day, Mr J was asleep in the afternoon (he did a night job), and Keith came and rang on his doorbell for half an hour. When he answered it, Keith said, "I thought you didn't love me", and then ran away. Shortly afterwards, the police came and arrested Mr J: Keith had told his mother he had been buggered. Mr J described his time with the police, whom he saw as unsympathetic, and how he wanted to save Keith from going to court. He therefore admitted the buggery. His counsel tried to persuade him not to do so; in retrospect, he thinks Keith was probably buggered by other men whilst on holiday, and there was a long history about how that had taken place.

Later in the interview I asked him about other sexual encounters, and he agreed that there had been episodes of mutual masturbation, with boys, throughout his teaching career. On one occasion, he had taken a young girl, who was very much a waif, home with him, and in the course of erotic horseplay he had ejaculated and thought that she, too, was aroused. (That the child was aroused is important, because we often avoid the fact that there may be sexual arousal in the child; this is what makes it so different from other forms of child abuse and thus so damaging.)

At this point, most of us would have sent this man to prison and had little sympathy for him. We would feel revulsion and moral outrage and would be of the opinion that castration might be letting him off too lightly. Mr J is eliciting the superego control that he apparently lacks. To be more accurate, he disowns his own superego, which is sadistic, inconsistent, and corrupt, and projects it into the institution. Let us look, though, at this man's childhood.

He says the first six years were idyllic; he was the third of four children, spaced a year apart. He can never remember his father being with his mother, as they were divorced when he was 5 years old. "He turned up in the home, he was a stranger who gave me a penny." There was no affection from his father. His mother, on the other hand, was enormously affectionate and demanded a great deal in return. He described how the children would run home from church in order to be the first to make her a cup of tea. One day, shortly after his parents divorced, his mother put him and his younger brother into the bath. Apparently this was an unusual event. His mother said: "You're going away tomorrow." It turned out that it was to an orphanage, a convent. His mother was getting rid of the children because she was due to marry again. As the story unfolded, it emerged that his mother was "really quite a flighty piece". She subsequently remarried three times.

When he went to live at the convent, his sisters went to live with their paternal grandmother. His impression of his parents' marriage was that his mother always wanted the good times. She commented that her husband only touched her four times, and each time she had had a baby. He seemed to be unable to maintain her in the lifestyle to which she would have liked to have become accustomed.

Mr J described the orphanage in some detail. It was for both boys and girls, but there was very strict segregation: if you talked to a girl you were thrashed. There was no affection from the nuns, and consequently all of the children turned to one another for comfort. It was "a hive of sexual activity", and he was adopted by a 14-year-old boy. "There was masturbation and cock-sucking—I'm sure the nuns were aware of it." He described an episode when his pet fly which he kept in a matchbox, and whose wings he had taken off in order to stop it from leaving him, died. He went into the lavatories to find a replacement, saw a bluebottle on one of the doors, and climbed up to catch it. But he realized that one of the nuns was watching him. He was taken back into the refectory where all the children were assembled, stripped naked, and left for half an hour before being thrashed. He said that it was not the thrashing that he minded, but the humiliation of being left alone, naked. He described how many of the children were incontinent or doubly incontinent. They were given no underclothes, and on Saturdays the nuns would inspect their shirt-tails for evidence of shit. On Friday night, the children used to suck their shirt-tails.

His father came to visit him occasionally, as did his mother. "The thing that cut me right inside was when my mother came at Christmas and loaded me with toys. I started to cry as she was going, and she turned to me and said: 'What's the matter— do you want some more toys?'"

The children from the convent went to the local school. They were known as convent children and segregated. They were punished more than the other children, because the teachers knew there would be no come-back. They were dressed shabbily and always smelled. The story then turned to his adolescence and how he himself became an abuser; how he chose a child, who more and more approximated to the age that he was when his own abuse started.

I provide those two parts of the history deliberately, because both pictures presented are true: the neglected and appallingly abused child, and this abhorrent creature who repeated that very self-same history. The clinical history now reveals sadness bordering on madness. The victim within the perpetrator is now obvious. The institution must recognize both but not fall into the trap of being naively therapeutic or cynically retributional. It must remain adjacent to the psychiatric services, connected to them yet not part of them; equally, it must remain adjacent and connected but not part of the judicial process. It cannot be the agent of either. (In this respect, perhaps the title "clinic" is a misnomer—it connotes attachment only to the health service and the sickness part of the individual.)

A feature that Mr J displays, which also defines all those who come to the Portman Clinic, is the propensity to act out. Perhaps a brief recapitulation of the concept is appropriate here.

Freud originally used the term "acting out" to describe the phenomenon of a patient, whilst in psychoanalytic treatment, carrying out an action that in symbolic form represents an unconscious wish or fantasy that cannot be experienced or expressed in any other way within the treatment. Over the years, the term has been broadened to describe a general character trait in which a person is given to relieving any intrapsychic tension by a physical action.

Acting out is the substitute for remembering a traumatic childhood experience, and unconsciously aims to reverse that early trauma. The patient is spared the painful memory of the trauma and, via his action, masters in the present the early experience that he originally suffered passively. The actors in the current situation are seen for what they are now, rather than what they represent from the past. Furthermore, the internal drama passes directly from unconscious impulse to action, short-cutting both conscious thought and feeling. The crucial element is that the conflict is resolved (albeit temporarily) by the use of the patient's body, often in a destructive or eroticized way.

The person will implicate and involve others in this enactment. The others may be innocent bystanders or have their own unconscious reasons for entering and playing a continuing role in the patient's scenario. The patient thus creates the characters and conflicts of his past in the people of his present, forcing them (by the use of projection and projective identification) to experience feelings that his consciousness cannot contain. He gains temporary relief, but as the players in the patient's play disentangle themselves from their appointed roles, they return to the patient his projected affects. Because he knows no other solution by which he can escape his inner conflicts, the patient is forced to create anew the same scenario in a different setting. This is the essence of what Freud referred to as "repetition compulsion" (Freud, 1914g).

The process of reducing this propensity is long and difficult. The treatment must be guided by two factors. Firstly, the culture in which the patient is managed must minimize the propensity for the staff to join in acting out, which the patient will inevitably invite them to do by cancelling sessions, breaking confidentiality, writing punitive reports, accepting presents, even becoming drowsy in sessions—the possibilities are many. Indeed, at the Portman Clinic we divide the roles of therapist and manager between two clinicians. The therapist sticks to therapy, whilst the manager negotiates all the interactions with other agencies in the outside world—writing reports, speaking to relatives and other professionals, arranging admission if necessary, and so forth.

Only when this culture is operating can the second factor take effect—the process whereby the patient internalizes the therapist's capacity to *think* about material presented—having first identified the concomitant affect—a capacity sadly lacking in the caregivers of the patient's childhood.

An important concept that guides our treatment is the core complex described by Glasser (1979). It is a state of mind in which the patient lives a life bounded by two sets of anxieties. The first is that of proximity. For these patients, intimacy is seen as merging engulfment and loss of identity. Separation, on the other hand, is seen as being abandoned to starve. The person thus lives in a narrow corridor of safety, controlling his partner by acts of coercion or cruelty, never allowing the partner to make his or her own choices. Very often, the partner in the relationship will share or mirror this pathology, and thus the two become locked in mutual distrust. From this description, it will be clear that if this relationship is repeated with the therapeutic institution, no psychic change will take place; indeed, it is likely that the patient will reject any offer of treatment.

An organization that in its physical appearance is too much like an impersonal institution will be seen as repressive and uncaring (and potentially corrupt), whereas one that is too informal and friendly will be seen as ensnaring, intrusive, seductive, overwhelming, and equally corrupt. In each case, the institution will be seen as having its own agenda and ignoring the needs of the patient/client.

It is the lot of the psychopath that he will bring out the worst in an institution and in the professionals working within it. The psychopath will need to project, to seduce, to split, to corrupt, and ultimately to be rejected by that institution, thereby repeating his own history and proving that nothing changes. It must therefore be the function of the institution to contain and counteract these destructive forces and to replace action with thinking (and feeling), and splitting with integration.

I hope that it will be evident from this account how important both the functioning and the physical structure of the Portman Clinic are to our clients. Two examples of this: one patient carried a photograph of the Portman Clinic around in his wallet—he would look at it when he felt tempted to re-offend; another would drive past the clinic at weekends to check that it was still there. To our patients, the physical reality is desperately important.

CHAPTER EIGHT

Children in torture-surviving families: child psychotherapy within a family-orientated context

Liselotte Grünbaum

Psychoanalytic psychotherapy with psychosocially disadvantaged children and adolescents demands special awareness of the familial, institutional, and societal contexts of treatment. This is especially the case when the child comes from an exiled, torture-surviving family. Governmental persecution and torture violently transgress personal, familial, and societal boundaries and affect the tortured member of a family and his or her spouse and children. Thus, the entire family may have lived through pervasively chaotic and terrifying events. Such lived experiences of extreme human evil may, in the inner world of the individual, produce unthinkable, uncanny feelings, which tend to get an interminable life of their own in intrapsychic and intrafamilial chaotic processes (Gampel, 1996; Gustafsson, Lindkvist, & Bøhm, 1987). Thus, increased vulnerability and risk of disintegration of both personal and familial cohesiveness and integrity follow in the wake of torture. For the members of the exiled family, the traces of past trauma and strain may be multiplied further by current strains connected with exile.

When such a child is referred for psychotherapy, not only the referred child but also siblings and parents are often in urgent need of treatment. The family as a whole may be in a highly unstable and fragmented state, and parental care of the children may more or less have broken down. Thus, the state of the family may seem to prevent child psychotherapy.

Children cannot be considered fully independent, either from a psychobiological or a legal point of view. In most European countries, the rights and obligations of parents, as well as the limitations imposed on them, are consequently regulated by detailed legislation concerning, for example, legal custody, child protection, education, and health. From the beginning of child psychoanalysis, pioneers were aware that parents could be decisive with regard to the outcome and therefore must be included in discussions concerning the treatment of the child (A. Freud, 1926–45; Klein, 1932). Child psychotherapists accordingly are careful to facilitate cooperation with the parents in order to minimize the risk of conflicts of loyalty and to prevent premature termination of therapy. Thus, it is commonly acknowledged that some work with the parents has to be included in the overall treatment plan, as a minimum regarding, for example, discussions of time-scheduling, important events in the everyday life of the family, the effect and termination of treatment, and so on. However, the child psychotherapist's regular contact with the parents creates a dilemma in so far as the transference relationship to the child may become complicated and diluted. For this reason, many child psychotherapists working in institutional settings prefer that someone else works with the parents whenever this is possible (Harris, 1968; Sandler, Kennedy, & Tyson, 1980).

All this is taken for granted and is most often part of the unnoticed, silent background of psychotherapy, part of a context that need not be given special thought. However, for the child psychotherapist working with children from psychosocially strained families that are heavily dependent on public support and child protection, this background is not at all silent. On the contrary, for periods the child's family life intrudes into the therapy as the troubled centre of attention and intervention.

This makes the work done with the parents especially important. The assignment of a special therapist to do this work introduces the idea of a therapeutic team working together at the institutional level. Whether we want it or not, some families evoke quite an intensive teamwork process because of their intrafamilial interaction, parenting, and relations to important community-based institutions. Sometimes the therapeutic team must also include, as supplementary participants, child-protection authorities, social welfare offices, schools, and daycare institutions in an extended effort to provide some continuity and predictability in the life of the child.

* * *

In the following I want to express some thoughts about child psychotherapy in this context. I illustrate my thinking by a clinical example, taking as my starting point some theoretical considerations about the child in the torture-surviving family.

On torture-surviving parents and children

In the following, the term "torture" means governmental torture—that is, any act by which severe pain or suffering, whether physical or mental, is intentionally inflicted on a person for such purposes as obtaining from him or a third person information or a confession, punishing him for an act he or a third person has committed or is suspected of having committed, or intimidating or coercing him or a third person, or for any other reason based on discrimination of any kind, when such pain or suffering is inflicted by or at the instigation of or with the consent or acquiescence of a public official or other person acting in an official capacity.

In 1997, 102 countries had ratified a United Nations convention prohibiting the use of torture (United Nations, 1984, p. 2; 1997). However, it is common knowledge, and also established by the daily press, that torture is still a reality in many countries, even in some that have ratified the convention.

The effects of torture are a problem for many refugees. Among different groups of adult refugees seeking asylum in Denmark, 18–28% had, according to their own statements, been tortured in their country of origin or during escape through other countries.

Prevalence varies between different groups and may be higher in some populations (Baker, 1992; Kjersem, 1996; Montgomery, 1996). In a recent survey including 311 children of parents from the Middle East seeking asylum in Denmark, it was found that 51% of the children lived in families in which at least one member had been tortured in the past (Montgomery, 1996).

On the effects of torture on parental functioning

The psychological effects of torture are often long-term and extensive and include severe posttraumatic symptoms such as chronic irritability, sensitivity to noise, increased suspicion, fits of rage with loss of control, sleep disturbances with nightmares, and loss of vitality and of hopes for the future. Traumatic re-living of specific episodes of imprisonment, torture, and loss is common and may include flashbacks with temporary loss of reality-testing. The torture victim may experience his personality as changed and may have difficulties coping with close emotional and physical contact (Baker, 1992; Somnier, Vesti, Kastrup, & Genefke, 1992).

The consequences of the above on the relationship between parent and child have been extensively discussed with regards to the Holocaust (e.g. Barocas & Barocas, 1980; Bergman & Jucovy, 1982; Grubich-Simitis, 1981; Yehuda et al., 1995). Clinical experience and research indicate similar difficulties for torture-surviving parents and their children and imply that the children may have an increased risk of emotional, psychosomatic, and behavioural disturbances (Allodi, 1989; Cohn et al., 1985; Lukman & Bach-Mortensen, 1995; Montgomery, Krogh, Jacobsen, & Lukman, 1992). The torture experienced by the parents appears, other things being equal, to involve an increased risk of anxiety symptoms in the child. This is even true for children whose mothers were tortured long before pregnancy and birth-giving (Montgomery, 1996). The above-mentioned studies did not include learning difficulties, but it should be mentioned that the children often have problems in this respect too, as is commonly seen in clinical practice.

The effects of torture on the parent may cause changes in the emotional atmosphere in the family; for example, they may lead to a conflict-ridden, anxious, and secretive climate. Often the tortured person and other members of the family tend, more or less unconsciously, to avoid thinking about past evil and suffering. The wish of most parents to spare their children the pain of uncontainable knowledge may enhance the tendency for such avoidance. The massive denial of mental pain may result in a deadly standstill of mutual emotional communication within the family. This tendency has been understood as a partly unconscious "conspiracy of silence" about the past between members of the family, resulting in the avoidance and tabooing of certain topics, emotions, and forms of interaction (Danieli, 1981, 1984; Krystal, 1971, p. 225; Krystal & Niederland, 1968, p. 189). The hidden and denied aspects of former suffering and loss may come to life again as unacknowledged, uncontained, and destructive aspects of dynamic interaction between parents and children, introjected by the children as frighteningly empty, silent areas of their inner world (Laub & Auerhahn, 1993).

In some families, the torture-surviving parent's difficulties of containment may take the form of an endless soliloquy, pouring out fragmented aspects of former suffering without any awareness of spouse and children being present and listening. This may affect secondary traumatization of the children through the repeated exposure to inconceivable atrocities without any possibility for an inner creation of a meaningful narrative through a dialogue with the parent.

These and similar consequences of torture for parental care may have a cumulative traumatic effect on the child (e.g. cause a permanent state of watchful anticipation and related survival strategies: Grünbaum, 1997). This may interfere with separation–individuation in the growing child, and thus separation anxiety is often part of the reason for referral of the child. The anxiety may be enhanced by the behaviour of the torture-surviving parent towards the child, as he or she may experience difficulties in coping with the growing child's age-related expressions of aggression and autonomy.

The traumatized child in the torture-surviving family

From the perspective of the child, chaotic processes in both external and internal reality are recurrently set in motion by war, organized violence, governmental persecution, and torture (Gustaffson et al., 1987). The above-mentioned study concerning children from the Middle East (Montgomery, 1996) showed that slightly less than 90% had experienced war in their country of origin, 78% had taken shelter against air raids, 60% were separated from one or both parents for more than a month because of persecution and escape, and 20% had suffered the loss of one of the parents due to death or disappearance.

Such simplified figures concerning environmental circumstances may conceal overwhelming traumatic experiences connected with events such as brutal separation from parents; witnessing humiliation, torture, and death of parents and family members; detainment as a hostage of family members; imprisonment with or without parents; physical and mental abuse or torture from figures of social authority; exposure to personal danger and physical injury because of bombings, sniping, land mines; and witnessing and maybe participating in atrocities in the streets.

* * *

Exceptionally threatening events like these are clearly outside the range of experiences normally expected in childhood and are likely to cause pervasive traumatic distress. However, whether and how a specific event produced a traumatic reaction in the child is not easy to ascertain (A. Freud, 1967; Kris, 1956; Sandler, 1967). Although all torture-surviving parents and their children have to come to terms with experiences of evil as part of human existence, not all children in torture-surviving families are traumatized. For this aspect to be explained, a clinical assessment of the individual child must be performed (Gaensburger, 1995; Scheeringa, Zeanah, Drell, & Larrieu, 1995; Terr, 1991). In such a preparatory exploration it is important to keep in mind that for prolonged periods most of these children have also experienced less manifestly dramatic events, but which were, nevertheless, possibly equally traumatic or in other respects quite as harmful. These may include:

- a family context of repeated loss, in which family members disappear and return from prison and torture in a changed state, without any explanations being offered to the child;

- chronic and pervasive fear for life;

- isolation and expulsion from peer-groups;

- unjust and humiliating treatment from teachers and other figures of authority, who also may have thrown suspicion on the parents and questioned the child about private family affairs;

- periodical deprivation of basic needs (e.g. food, opportunities to play with children of the same age, education, medical care);

- failing parental capacities and family conflict due to the effects of torture;

- periods of escape, hiding, and the related life-threatening events, when without preparation the child has to leave behind toys and other objects invested with feelings of security and predictability;

- last but not least, the often prolonged period as asylum-seekers, waiting in uncertainty for a legal residence permit without a functioning language, together with exhausted and anxious parents.

* * *

To sum up the above, in the lives of these children a complex mixture of accumulative strain and repeated exposure to sudden shock trauma tends to affect whole developmental periods. We have to recognize the interaction of cumulative strain and trauma within the family with recurring traumatic exposure to extrafamilial violence within a broader social environment of chronic danger and estrangement (Pynoos, Steinberg, & Wraith, 1995).

Child psychotherapy and family breakdown

One starting point for child psychotherapy is the supposition that a distinction between the unconscious phantasy world of object-relations and the child's current external interactions within and outside the family can be made. On the basis of this, we substitute everyday interactions by a secluded relation to a child psychotherapist in a recurrent pattern of sessions. Implicit in this arrangement is the assumption that the child can introject and integrate the therapeutic relationship in such a way as to increase his capacity for reclaiming adequate parental care and making meaningful use of whatever possibilities for development the present environment has to offer.

However, for some children in torture-surviving families this may be a momentous and nearly impossible task, as torture of the parents may be followed by fragmentation of the family as an emotionally cohesive and caring unit. The process of disintegration may for a time have been detained by the efforts of escape and survival. However, while waiting for legal asylum in the new country, the mental and physical condition of the tortured parent is likely to deteriorate considerably (Kjersem, 1996). Thus, what was still a psychically caring family context at the time of arrival may be in a state of breakdown by the time of the referral of the child for treatment. Sometimes it is part of a sad reality that past violent, societal oppression may be unconsciously repeated through repressive and violent relations within the family—for example, as humiliating and aggressive parental actions towards each other and the children.

As is commonly acknowledged, every child has fundamental needs of a containing framework for everyday life in which reasonably predictable personal love and understanding are offered, as well as adequate possibilities for play, education, and health care (United Nations, 1959). For most children, this is taken care of by their parents with support from those social institutions to which some of these functions have been delegated: for example, schools, daycare institutions, and institutionalized recreational activities. When the bounded, protective space of the family breaks down, the child is left psychically uncontained and "may or may not be homeless, but he is psychically unplaced" (Britton, 1983, p. 105). Such family breakdown does not necessarily imply legal and conspicuous disintegration of the kind that immediately evokes concern and community intervention. Nevertheless, the consequences are the creation of serious problems in the further development of the child.

In a disintegrated family context, the child may display a host of serious indicators of trauma, personality disturbance, and psychopathology. This is especially so when talking about massively traumatized children. The current environmental breakdown thus tends to re-evoke the inner chaotic conditions of past trauma, creating a flux in which it is hardly possible to differentiate between traces of past trauma and present traumatic reactions to environmental deficiencies. In this situation, we must take care lest our countertransference reaction to the inconceivably evil events of the past overrules our ability to think. Thinking about the present, acute needs of the child for the restitution of a predictable and caring family context is therefore sometimes much more fundamental than rushing to initiate psychotherapy prematurely. The child suffering because of family breakdown does not primarily need the uncovering and working through of past trauma, but first and foremost the re-creation of an adequately bounded and caring framework for everyday life.

* * *

The therapeutic intervention in the context of parental care may be the precondition for the development of a psychotherapeutic relationship in which forgotten trauma of early childhood can be dealt with. As pointed out by Britton (1983), the absence of important parts of psychic and emotional parenting thus creates a diffuse transference situation, which renders therapeutic work difficult. As a consequence, both the child and the therapist may experience confusion relating to the difference between wanting a parent–child relationship with each other and having such a relationship. In general, the working-through in the transference of this differentiation contributes decisively to the child´s increased ability to differentiate between inner phantasies and external reality.

This is of special importance in relation to traumatized children from torture-surviving families. Thus, traumatic exposure to extreme human evil may affect a breakdown of differentiation between the external, horrifying reality and the most primitive and aggressive parts of unconscious inner phantasy, leaving behind an increased vulnerability in reality-testing. Consequently, it is of special importance that the therapist maintains a position vis-à-vis the child that elucidates her task as not connected with literal parental care, but with the working through of psychic suffering and internal trauma.

The countertransference reactions of the child psychotherapist and other professionals involved with the family may enhance confusion. The empathic strain involved in the mental processing of unwanted knowledge of ultimate human evil and suffering thus easily evoke attitudes of over-identification or avoidance in the professional (Wilson & Lindy, 1994). A guilt-ridden desire to compensate the child for past and present abuse, loss, and deprivation may, for example, manifest itself as enmeshment and loss of boundaries. This may provoke evil circles between the family and the involved professionals giving too much care; that is, not therapeutic care, but literal care. The predicament of the child may evoke massive concern, which at times understandably may find outlet in the form of pressure on the child psychotherapist and the clinic to take over casework responsibility and do something "real", meaning something else and more than psychotherapy. The uncontained countertransference feelings may also have the seemingly opposite effect and evoke numb withdrawal of empathy. This may, for example, find expression as a rigid insistence on bureaucratic rules and procedures, or as resigned and indifferent attitudes, as expressed by an overburdened teacher from an inner-city school: "What do you expect? Eighty per cent of our pupils are immigrants, and in any case they are so understimulated and deprived that nothing can be done." The tendency to refrain from a conscious awareness of the individual child's severe traumatization may be further enhanced by the conspiracy of silence going on in the family. Thus, mutually reinforcing processes of denial may affect therapeutic and professional work on all levels around these children.

In order to render psychotherapy of the individual child feasible, continuing teamwork with community agencies in charge of child protection, social welfare, and education may be necessary. The aim of this is to support the parents in their parenting, which at times entails a proper warning that ongoing chaos and violence may have consequences for the custody of the child.

Clinical example

The referred child, "Nabil", was 8 years old, the youngest child of three in a family from the Middle East; his two sisters were considerably older. He was referred by the parents, who were both torture-survivors and had recently started treatment at the clinic. Nabil suffered from severe separation-anxiety and a host of anxiety symptoms, including frightening nightmares. He allegedly refused to sleep alone, and frequently his mother slept with him. He panicked when away from his mother, asked incessantly for her whereabouts, and could not be soothed by other family members. After school, he often found the apartment empty and would then not dare to enter, but would remain crying before the front door. Panic was inevitably induced by a certain hammering sound emitted frequently by the radiator in the apartment. In general, Nabil was described as a vulnerable child who often cried for no apparent reason. He had quite a hard time at school, feeling mocked by both teachers and children.

The family had arrived in Denmark as refugees two years previously; both the parents and the extended family had for many years been victims of governmental persecution due to their political resistance against the rulers of the country. Both parents were highly educated, but as dissidents they were denied work within their professions. According to the mother, Nabil's early development was unremarkable. However, she recalled very little apart from the fact that he grew up in an atmosphere of war, prevailing fear for life, and recurrent periods of mourning due to persecution and death of close relatives. His father was absent during most of his childhood being in hiding, in prison, or at war. Nabil was present during several violent house searches by government soldiers looking for the father. During one of these, the soldiers smashed up the home and brutally raped the mother in front of the child.

After their arrival in Denmark, the family had to wait in an asylum centre for over a year before a legal residence permit was granted.

The institutional setting

The Rehabilitation and Research Centre for Torture Victims (RCT) in Copenhagen is a humanitarian, non-political, and non-government institution founded in 1982 with the dual aims of rehabilitation of torture victims and contribution to the prevention of torture. The clinic offers out-patient medical and psychosocial treatment to torture-survivors and their families. In addition to the clinic, the institution undertakes an array of national and international activities, including documentation, research, and propagation of knowledge and skills concerning the occurrence and consequences of torture, as well as clinical assessment and treatment methods. The rehabilitation programme is based on a multidisciplinary, holistic treatment approach emphasizing psychotherapy. The programme also includes medical assessment, physiotherapy, nursing, social counselling, and cognitively orientated supportive social group-work. Most of our patients do not speak Danish very well, so a selected group of interpreters assist in the work.

Originally RCT aimed at the treatment of adult torture-survivors. However, the tortured parents gradually opened the eyes of the staff to the fact that the family as a whole, not least the children, also suffered from the consequences of torture. In 1993 this recognition formed the basis of the establishment of a specific child and family department to receive the referrals of families with children (aged 0–17 years); among these are also those children and adolescents who themselves have been tortured. Most children received at the clinic are referred by parents already in treatment at RCT, but some are referred by outside agencies: for example, social welfare offices, schools, paediatricians, and institutions working with the integration of refugees into Danish society.

Thus, the psychotherapeutic treatment of the child takes place in the multidisciplinary context of different treatment approaches simultaneously aimed at several members of the family. This context in itself leads to extensive teamwork in which widely different perceptions, perspectives, and methods are brought together and hopefully made to function as a containing space for rehabilitation. The treatment planned around an individual family is, in principle, designed uniquely for every new referral, and the intensity and scope of the treatment vary both with regard to the referred families in general, and also with regard to individual members of the family. A minimum requirement of teamwork around child psychotherapy is the ongoing cooperation with a social worker and most often one or two therapists who work with the parents. An effort to establish links with important community-based institutions involved with the child is also included in the teamwork: for example, caseworkers from social welfare offices and teachers from school and/or daycare institutions.

The context of the family

Before I first met Nabil, the whole family had been seen at a session in which every single member of the family—except Nabil—put forward pressing needs for treatment. No mention was made of acute strains connected with current relations and parental care, but the older sisters asked to be seen individually. After some reflection, I agreed to see each child in the family for one or more individual consultations before deciding on psychotherapy.

Nabil initially gave a description of his worries, which very well illustrated the traumatized and vulnerable child´s confusion between inner phantasy and external, frightening events. The following is an extract from case notes of the first session with Nabil:

Nabil is a handsome, polite, and slightly overweight boy. His command of the Danish language is good enough to do without an interpreter, but not quite without effort; sometimes he is at a loss for words. He seems to handle this mostly by asking me to provide him with the missing concepts. He appears to be in a state of acute misery and anxiousness (e.g. wringing his hands incessantly). He immediately starts pouring out his anxieties, only once in a while pausing to catch his breath. He starts by saying that he is afraid all the time that his father will attack them, especially that he will hit the mother. One night, not long ago, he was awoken in the middle of the night by loud noises because the parents were arguing. He then saw the father attack the mother with a big knife, but then the mother took Nabil to his room and stayed there with him. Nabil had taken the knife away from his father even though he is a child and much smaller than the father. His father beats up the mother even if she doesn't do anything wrong. He himself protects his mother and sleeps together with her, because then the father can't beat her. He implores me not to tell his father that he had said this, because then he is sure to be beaten up himself. When the mother is cooking dinner, the father beats her and throws the food, pot and all, onto the floor. At this point, Nabil cries silently while wringing his hands. He cries while saying that he is teased at school. The children—the Danish children, that is—call him fat, and so does the teacher, so he is mean too. His teacher says that Nabil eats too much, and sometimes the children shout "Fuck your mother and father" at him. Nabil pauses, seems unable to say anything more, and blows his nose. He mentions that he has one good friend in the class. During the whole session, he completely ignores the box of toys. At this point he takes a piece of paper and draws the crying face of a woman, a coffin, and a cross and says that this woman is grown up, she is a mother, but her grandmother is dead, and she can't stop crying.

While Nabil is talking, I experience a feeling of overwhelming hopelessness as well as a mounting anxiety that something catastrophic may happen in the family.

Several parts of this session relate to unconscious infantile phantasies concerning, for example, greed, envy, persecution anxiety, and frightening images of a combined parental couple. In the transferential attitude, Nabil seemed to oscillate. At times, he tried to gain my collusion in a split relationship as a good, maternally providing object, with all evil located in the parental object; at other times, he pondered suspiciously whether I was a mean, teasing Dane allied with the mean teacher and children (Klein, 1952b). This may seem to be a natural starting point for a psychotherapeutic process in helping Nabil to sort out inner and outer events. However, the details of his complaints of the behaviour of the parents seemed to warrant concern for the present family situation.

The sessions with Nabil's sisters confirmed this. The sisters concurrently talked about violent arguments and fights between the parents, who seemed to have stopped speaking to each other except for sudden outbursts of violence. The children often got involved as they tried to protect the mother against being beaten. The sisters described the father as incessantly roaming around the apartment, mumbling and shouting as though he were speaking to somebody, sometimes shouting loudly about past humiliations, loss, and torture, sometimes in sudden outbreaks of fury shouting wild accusations of robbery, conspiracy, and sexual promiscuity against spouse and children. He allegedly monitored their every movement with suspicion and in a manner more reminiscent of formerly experienced governmental persecution and house searches than of the traditional close protection of female family members in many Arab families; for example, several times a day he minutely searched their rooms for proof of his suspicions. They also complained that they often did not get enough to eat. The sessions thus pointed to a precarious family, in which marital relations and parental care had more or less broken down.

The ongoing, mad events in the family were bound to evoke unconscious, infantile anxiety in Nabil, and as a consequence inner phantasy life traumatically became real and was perceived as external reality. Thus, the primary need of Nabil at this stage did not seem to be child psychotherapy, but more urgently that somebody took on the responsibility of intervention. The therapeutic team (including the two therapists working with the parents, the social worker, and myself) had to consider if and how to intervene in this highly unstable and threatening context of care. Before reaching any firm conclusion, Nabil's worried teacher telephoned and informed us that he had cried at length at school, telling about violent incidents and beating at home. The following events forced an emergency intervention.

One morning, the mother presented herself unannounced at the clinic, bringing one of the sisters, who had a black eye and a bruised arm. The two of them together were seen by the mother's therapist and myself. They told us that during another furious fight the night before the father lost control and tried to strangle the mother. The injuries of the sister occurred as the children tried to free their mother from his hold. The mother and children had locked themselves up in a room and had spent the night there listening to the noises of the father trying to force open the door, while threatening to kill them all. At this, we felt we had no option other than to suggest temporary placement of the mother and the children at a crisis centre, although we were well aware that such a decision would be very difficult for the mother and was sure to provoke the furious resentment of the father. As expected, the mother refused our proposal. She was convinced, probably for good reasons, that this would destroy any future possibility of reconciliation. She stated that she wanted us to talk to the father about his behaviour, and then she would return to the family home and once more lock herself and the children up.

After this, we considered handing over further case responsibility to the child-protection caseworker at the social welfare office. We asked for the mother and children to stay at the clinic while this was discussed in the therapeutic team. Finally, a decision was made to consent to the mother´s wish that we should talk to the father, but on the following conditions:

1. If the mother insisted on going home the same day, she would not take the children but would allow temporary placement while matters were sorted out with the parents.

2. We would immediately arrange one or more couple sessions to discuss the consequences of further violence at home.

3. The clinic would inform the child-protection caseworker at the social welfare office, in order (a) to make sure that an emergency placement of mother and children together or the children alone was available in case this became necessary, and (b) to discuss what further intervention might be considered.

The mother agreed and proposed herself that she and the children could stay temporarily with some relatives, and this was then arranged.

In the discussions with both parents, the consequences of continued violence were raised, including a warning that it might lead to a child-protection care order regarding the youngest child. While stressing that the treatment of the parents´ torture-related sequelae could proceed, it was pointed out that requested treatment of Nabil demanded some peace and stability at home. The outcome of these discussions was that the father agreed to see a psychiatrist to discuss medication; the mother clearly stated to the father that unless the beatings stopped, she would move out with the children; and both parents stated that they still wanted treatment of Nabil and agreed to the involvement of child-protection authorities for the planning of support and temporary intervention in case of emergency.

The subsequent teamwork included several meetings between the parents, the child-protection caseworker, and the teacher of the youngest child, together with the social worker and child psychotherapist from the clinic. As a small improvement, Nabil joined an afternoon recreation centre so that he would not have to come home to an empty apartment. Some months later, matters at home were apparently brought more under control by the parents, although one further episode for a short while again caused the mother and children to stay with relatives. The following year, the parents made good use of their own treatment, and family life slowly improved.

Some general perspectives

In a disintegrated, chaotic family context, the out-patient clinic working with children at risk has to consider whether the following aspects can be safely contained in the treatment plan:

1. Does psychotherapeutic intervention prevent further violence and significant harm in the family to a large enough extent?

2. Can legal role responsibilities related to child protection be integrated in the teamwork in such a way as to preserve possibilities for psychotherapy of the child?

The described treatment took place in a complex institutional setting in which several members of a family were referred for treatment simultaneously. In some respects, this renders therapeutic teamwork complicated, especially so when the legal boundaries of child protection have also to be considered. The combination of adult- and child-orientated perspectives may, however, offer specific opportunities for the creation of a containing context in which psychotherapy with children from disintegrated families is possible. This often demands a prolonged family-orientated explorative assessment of individual needs for treatment.

As pointed out by Copley (1987), one obvious indication for family exploration is the presence of severe relational problems within the current family, especially when considerable fusion and splitting in the relationship between the children and the parental couple are encountered.

In the above clinical example, the same child psychotherapist performed consultations with all the children of a family. As depicted, this posed a complication for later transference development. However, the advantages of this approach were probably highly decisive for the outcome of the treatment. Thus, the child psychotherapist for a time became the link between each individual child's experience of present family life, which was a precondition for obtaining a sufficient overview of the deficient and unstable state of parental care at that time.

One may ask why we proceeded with individual assessment and not meet either with the whole family or with the three siblings together as a group. Family sessions were considered but were not possible, because of the mother's absolute refusal. The considerations of the team concerning sibling sessions dealt with aspects related to: (1) the age range between the youngest and oldest child in the family; (2) the tradition in many Arab families for segregation of the sexes; and, most importantly (3) the expressed wish of the older sisters to be seen individually, which might suggest that something important could not be talked about in front of the rest of the family. It should be mentioned that clinical experience shows that quite a few children of torture-surviving parents have kept personal experiences of extrafamilial violence of the past as their own private secret, not to be disclosed to parents and siblings.

One may also question why the siblings should be seen by the same psychotherapist, rather than by three different ones. On second thoughts about the countertransference involved in this decision, one answer is connected with the necessity to adapt treatment plans to the external reality of a limited availability of child psychotherapists. However, our unconsciously perceived risk that current family life would erupt in violent acting out and disintegration was probably more critical in the decision. The involvement of five different psychotherapists in one single family is a massive intervention, prone to overrule the family´s own resources for coping, and difficult to keep together in a constructive teamwork.

* * *

Copley (1987) stressed that explorative work with families most often leads to a transference relationship to the therapist not primarily as a specific person, but rather as a representative of the clinic. In accordance with this, the connected feelings and phantasies are primarily related to the institution, rather than to the therapist as a private person. It is interesting to note that during the explorative stage of the treatment, Nabil and his family formed a transference relationship to the clinic and the therapists that in many respects resembled the traditional delegation of authority in the extended Arab family. The therapists thus, for a period of time, were attributed certain functions that are usually attended to by the older members of the extended family. In the country of origin, this family had lived in a close relationship with grandparents and the siblings of both parents. In case of marital conflict and problems of parental care, the starting point for seeking help would not be the involvement of professional psychotherapists, but rather to seek out the help of those members of the extended family to whom the authority had been transferred—for example, a grandparent or an elder brother. In exile, the extended family had disintegrated and was scattered between several countries. Thus, for a time the clinic was entrusted with similar "grandparental" authority, implying that the therapists were given an emotionally legitimate right to intervene in family affairs concerning marriage and upbringing. This authority was temporarily accepted and contained by the clinic. At a later stage the parents had regained enough strength to cope with conflict themselves, which included an effort to recreate the functions of the extended family in times of difficult decisions and conflicts by seeking out the help of an older relative living in exile not too far away.

This transferral of authority to the psychotherapists is quite common among our torture-surviving families, especially those from the Middle East. Among other things this tendency reflects that governmental persecution, torture, and exile not only imply loss of family members, language, and identity, but that the culturally rooted strategies for coping with family conflict may also be lost. In a broader perspective, this should remind us that when working in a cross-cultural context, it may be very important for the child psychotherapist to be sensitively tuned in to specific manifestations of transference occurring in a culturally bounded space.

Concluding remarks

At a more theoretical level, I want to finish with a few comments on the concept of the therapeutic setting in child psychotherapy.

The primary focus for psychoanalytic child psychotherapy is the understanding of the inner world of the child as this is expressed in the immediacy of the transference relationship at any particular point in time. However, the development of transference depends heavily on the creation of a mentally and physically bounded space, inside which these processes can occur. The boundaries of the therapeutic space in general are constituted by what we call the therapeutic "setting". In child psychotherapy, the setting is often understood as including aspects such as (1) the analytic thinking and attitude; (2) certain physical aspects of the immediate environment such as the therapy-room, the play materials, and so forth; (3) an appointed structuring of time; (4) certain basic methodological rules such as free association in play, containment, and interpretation of the transference (Meltzer, 1967).

* * *

I have advocated here the view that child psychotherapy implies an initial consideration of environmental aspects both of the child´s current life and of the institutional frames for psychotherapy with regard to familial, organizational, cultural, societal, and legal aspects. Furthermore, these aspects must sometimes be contained during treatment through a continuous, comprehensive therapeutic teamwork. From this perspective it seems that we need to reconsider our understanding of what constitutes a workable therapeutic setting, making space for teamwork with the parents, sometimes also with the family as a whole, as well as with community-based institutions. This may be of especially vital importance for the outcome of child psychotherapy with psychosocially disadvantaged and/or massively traumatized children such as, for example, children in torture-surviving families.

The inclusion of the idea of teamwork in the concept of the therapeutic setting should remind us that the protective framework of a reasonably predictable, caring human environment is a precondition both for the psychological development of the child and for the development of a psychotherapeutic process that is able to contain traumatic traces. I should like to add that finding ways to integrate psychoanalytic thinking and methods with social-psychological understanding of teamwork at an institutional level may also be a precondition for the fruitful integration of child psychotherapists into public service institutions.

CHAPTER NINE

The adolescent psychotic and the context of residential treatment

Michael Günter & Reinmar du Bois

The emotional situation of adolescent psychotic patients has its peculiarities. The normal demands of pubertal development leave their mark on the course of the illness. Consequently, the psychotherapy of psychotic adolescents has to adjust to the special situation and the needs of this age. This applies especially to the residential treatment of severe schizophrenic psychoses, where the patients should not only receive an adequate treatment in the narrow sense, but be in a therapeutic milieu that facilitates emotional growth and is adapted to the needs of the adolescents, which should be an inseparable part of every help (du Bois, 1996).

Some special features of this treatment should be mentioned: many psychotic youths exhibit considerable maturational deficits. Such retardations of maturity are frequently encountered, especially in early pubertal onset of a psychotic illness and in conditions that are later classified as hebephrenias. They are characterized by infantile modes of experience and patterns of coping; by difficulties in social relationships and emotional attachments, especially towards their peers; and by a lack of development of social skills, extending to simple everyday tasks like taking a bus, shopping, and age-appropriate leisure activities. These deficits are often evident long before the onset of the illness (du Bois, Günter, & Kleefeld, 1987).

Moreover, juvenile psychoses can be conceived as expressions of a severe crisis of development (Laufer & Laufer, 1984). According to this concept the normal pubertal weakening of the ego, the adolescent separation conflict, and the precarious balance between regressive and progressive tendencies are not only aggravated but, as a consequence of the severe illness, undergo decisive changes. However, we share the common opinion that the predominant part of all overt psychopathology does not reveal the "primary" disease process, but is indicative of defensive and coping attempts. Thus, we comprehend the manifold and rapidly changing symptoms essentially as attempts to seek protection from psychotic anxiety and from the experience of "catastrophic change" (Bion, 1963, 1970; Eigen, 1985). This is achieved by externalization (for instance, delusions and hallucinations), by control of external reality (for instance, by means of compulsions and antisocial acting-out), and possibly by lowering the level of emotional vitality (for instance, by means of negative symptoms) or raising the threshold of stimulus control, as in catatonia.

The adolescent psychotic symptomatology expresses a strong hunger for relationships and a desire for containment: to hold and order to counter the patient's chaotic experience. These needs are directed at the person immediately face to face. In adolescence, such spontaneous relationship patterns are sought with much greater intensity than later in adult life. This is a challenge for the therapist but at the same time a therapeutic chance. One has to consider that it is the first time for the adolescents to come into contact with such completely incomprehensible and highly frightening experiences. This occurs at a phase in life when ego functions are at their most vulnerable and no established social roles are yet available as a hold and point of reference. All adolescents lay special emphasis on their immediate experiences, yet run a high risk to surrender to them. This is why adolescents are to be viewed as especially vulnerable towards psychotic breakdowns.

Every treatment of psychotic adolescents has to consider the normal age-specific behaviour, with its balance of regressive and progressive tendencies (A. Freud, 1965), rapid changes between the depressive and the paranoid-schizoid position, and a tendency to counter all anxiety and inner tensions by means of a high cathexis of everyday activities and acting-out. The thrill of immediate action is meant to expel the ghosts of unbearable internal forces.

In the following, we would like to deal with some core problems and tasks of residential psychotherapeutic treatment, as they present themselves from the everyday perspective of therapeutic contacts with our patients on the ward. We then move on to a discussion of the basic setting and the framework of such treatments.

Separation from infantile patterns of relationship

The majority of juvenile psychotic patients have great difficulties among existing or new relationships to rely on themselves as independent individuals and to build a relationship, maintain it, or gradually withdraw from it. These patients are arrested in a seemingly infantile dependence from their idealized parental figures, while feelings of extreme proximity and deeply rooted feelings of hatred, being persecuted, or being engulfed can prevail in turn. The fixation of these infantile patterns must again be understood as an attempt to deal with psychotic fears of being deserted and annihilated, as well as an attempt to deal with the ensuing destructive impulses. These mechanisms have repeatedly been described by different authors: for instance, by Klein (1952a) with her concept of a "paranoid-schizoid position", or, more recently, by Glasser (1979, 1992) with respect to perversions, using the term "core conflict".

In practice, these badly demarcated states lead to a situation where emotions and even body sensations fluctuate between patients and parents or their substitute on the ward—a key worker, for instance. The exchange of non-verbal signals becomes the para-

mount type of object-relation, to the same effect as projective identification.

During the time of one of my [M.G.] patient's acute psychotic
illness, I had regular therapeutic appointments in our small and
very quiet swimming pool. One day, while I was dressing after
the event, I was suddenly convinced that the patient had taken
my underpants and put them on. I pointed this out to him, but
he assured me that this was not so. As I was unsure how to
regain my reality control at that moment, I eventually walked
back to the ward with only my trousers, shirt, and shoes on
but with no underpants. Months later we discovered that in
the patient's family the following arrangement existed: every
week, when the regular family treatment sessions took place,
the mother brought seven clean pairs of underpants. They were
hidden in a paper bag under some fruit. We expected the patient to use our hospital washing-machine and wash his own
clothes, but he used to throw his dirty underpants out of the
window. The soiled underpants were retrieved from under the
window, taken home, and washed by the mother. Next, they
were passed on to the patient's brother. After the next washing,
they were then once again returned to our patient, using the
fruit and paper-bag method. The father, as we subsequently
learnt, was only excluded from this recycling process because
he weighed some 30kg more than his two sons.

As the family, under the aegis of the mother, dealt with the
underpants, thus it handled feelings and emotional ownership
in general, which in our view explained a considerable part of
the relationship pathology.

We have chosen this vignette primarily because it conveys an
impression of the contagious quality of such badly demarcated
emotional states that the therapist could no longer realize clearly
that the patient did not wear the therapist's underpants. Transference psychoses and psychotic countertransference reactions often
seem to converge if one really commits oneself to a therapeutic
relationship. It is the task of a functioning therapeutic team, with
its firm organizational, informational, and supervisory structures,
to enable a continuous reflection of induced countertransference

reactions, as had occurred in our case. Thus the therapeutic process could be advanced.

Such a tight clamping of emotions and such hardly noticeable exchange of emotional signals in psychotic relationships are partly reminiscent of early infantile interactions (e.g. see Dornes, 1993; Stern, 1986). The subtle tuning-in between infant and mother can also be interpreted as an attempt to control psychotic anxiety by the forming of a relationship on the most basic level (Winnicott, 1952, 1963). Primitive patterns of relating become apparent during everyday contacts on the ward: the patients try to entangle the staff in unpleasantly obtrusive, yet seemingly inextricable situations; or they become inaccessible by withdrawing into delusional and phantasmatic worlds, thus enabling themselves to defend the illusion of a fusion with an idealized mother. The countertransference of the team is infused with feelings of hopelessness, paralysis, inability to act, and a sense of being caught in endless repetitions.

The pathological involvement of the parents leads to strong feelings of guilt and fierce attacks on the treatment, which can lead to a break-off. The treatment can only continue if the parents, together with the child, manage to a certain extent to liberate themselves from their highly ambivalent and highly loaded relationship, despite their fears of loss (Becker, 1987).

Regressions

Regression signifies a patient's retreat to a more primitive psychic organization. Early infantile wishes to be nursed and cared for are revived. At puberty, especially in emotional crises at this developmental stage, stronger regressive tendencies are becoming noticeable. They often go together with a weakening of ego structures. Severe forms of psychotic regression occur in half of our adolescent schizophrenias (du Bois et al., 1987). In these cases, the regressions lead to a state of utmost helplessness. The patients become passive, dependent, and unable to make decisions concerning even the simplest routine jobs. The temporal dimension is missing from their experience. The patients forgo language as a means of communication, and instead sounds are uttered as a more primitive signalling function. Oral and anal libidinous needs reappear; thus, regressed patients can reject the uptake of solid food and may have to be fed pap or even through a gastric tube. The patients may also neglect their body care, and bed wetting and even faecal soiling can re-emerge.

In the severe cases, the permanent presence of a care person may be necessary, and in extreme cases we have had to maintain such a regime of intensive care over several months. In these treatments, the provision of proper and comprehensive nursing care is the core element. Only such care is seen as being able to satisfy the physical needs and at the same time convey the experience of being held according to Winnicott's (1960) holding function. This will only succeed if the entire treatment team accepts and supports the fact of overt regression in a patient and views the nursing of such a patient as a rewarding task with respect to his future development. The team must, however, be put in a position to tolerate the primitive relationship patterns and remain free from anxiety. The expressed fears that a patient may plunge into a malignant regressive condition are completely understandable, as the staff have to commit themselves extensively to the psychotic world with its fears of death and loss. Regular supervision is therefore required not only in order to ensure the capacity to work but also to be able to renew constantly one's understanding of the patients' subtle and penetrating messages.

We would like to state three reasons why we are not seeking to prevent such regressions in favour of a speedier restoration of ego-functions, if at all possible:

1. In our experience, a considerable proportion of the patients exhibit strong regressive tendencies because of the milieu on a psychiatric and therapeutic ward, which inevitably promotes regression. Even if it was our intention, we could not always take effective measures against regressive trends.

2. In the past twenty years, we have never seen a patient slip from our control irretrievably. On the contrary, we were able to convince ourselves that profound regressions were self-limiting conditions.

3. The patients, as they go through their regressions, achieve a

stability and soundness in their therapeutic relationships that is unparalleled in other courses of treatment of schizophrenia. Also, such stability persists far beyond the end of the profound regressions (Günter, 1987). According to our clinical impression, these treatments on the whole run a more favourable course than others.

Psychosexual developmental delay

A considerable number of our patients have been delayed in their psychosexual development long before their psychotic breakdown. Signs of developmental delay are most marked in patients with the Asperger type of early infantile autism, who become psychotic. We observe characteristic perseverances in selected areas of infantile functioning, including difficulties of contact, little peer-group integration, poor social skills, lack of age-appropriate sets of behaviour, and delays in sexual maturation. Modes of experience that are specific for childhood still prevail; for instance, the use of the sense of smell to explore new objects, magic ideas, and imaginative companions. These must be distinguished from genuine hallucinations.

Treatment of these patients can only be successful if generous educational work according to the principles of developmental training is given high priority. Some thought must be given to how appropriate sex education of these adolescents can be achieved and how certain kinds of social behaviour can be rehearsed. During their stay in hospital, they learn how to apply adequate body care, how to go shopping by themselves, how to find their way, how to keep arrangements, and how to take responsibility suitably for plants, animals, and finally other human beings. They also learn how to approach a vocation, and so on. The practising of these abilities and the achievement of social competence is a lengthy process. In view of the often dogged resistance, the team—especially the key workers—must be careful not to give up prematurely. In our view, this can only be achieved if the defensive character of the refusal has been understood and if the actual behavioural manifestations have been recognized as a transference phenomenon.

One of our present patients was transferred to us from an external hospital with the remark that the treatment, despite high-dosage depot neuroleptics, had reached stalemate. We were further informed that the patient was still psychotic, wanted to go home, and refused treatment. During his stay with us, we managed to reduce the medication to a minimal amount without the productive symptoms reappearing. Still, we were confronted with a conduct-disordered, underperforming, academically dull boy, who often refused activities in bizarre ways by pretending he was asleep in his bed for many hours. Reactions of anger and resignation by the team followed, until they began to understand better his reactions as a biographically based mixture of infantile identifications: on the one hand, he identified with his severely depressed mother, as if to say: "I am your small disabled child". On the other hand, he identified with and yet was disappointed about his father, who wanted him to become a football star. This understanding opened new ranges of thinking and acting, which allowed the team to view this painfully slow work as meaningful and worth continuing.

A further difficult problem in the treatment of such adolescents can only be mentioned in passing: it is often nearly impossible to find suitable post-residential placements. Therefore, we have established our own rehabilitation unit.

Rapidly changing ego-states and fluctuations of affect

It is generally known that juvenile psychoses are characterized by rapid changes and shifts of symptomatology and by an equally rapid switching of ego-states and alternating movements between extreme closeness within relationships and abrupt rejections. All of this can be demonstrated if one looks at the extreme fluctuations of drive, the sudden emergence of panics or bouts of impulsive behaviour, the extended compulsions by which reality is to be reconstructed, and the general changeability of productive symptoms. Manic episodes and depressive or dysphoric states can, in certain cases, switch several times within one day. We often observe that the patients erect a narcissistic façade while denying their persisting problems (Günter, du Bois, & Kleefeld, 1989).

The apparent self-reliance of such patients, who might be classified as partly remitted, is, however, situated on shaky ground. The social conduct, however adapted it may seem, follows rigid patterns. The mood can be hypomanic, irritable, and provocative. Inside the hospital, for long periods they can keep themselves free from disturbances, whereas in unaccustomed or critical situations—as, for example, when being caught having trespassed or having committed an offence, or when under the influence of alcohol—they can suddenly be strikingly insecure, fearful, or even openly psychotic.

The key workers are frequently put under pressure to react and make decisions. The patients would noisily demand that the rules be relaxed or drugs be discontinued. Owing to the pressure exerted by the patients, it is sometimes difficult for the team to remain at all conscious of the artificiality of the demands. The team members are in danger of ignoring the underlying fragility of the patients' ego structures and forgetting the serious nature of the underlying conflicts. In the everyday context of dealing with patients like this, one is well advised to create as precise and constant an image as possible of a patient embracing his entire range of abilities and risks.

The management of critical situations depends decisively on keeping a middle distance, which strikes the balance between the extremes of being too close, with a high emotional pitch and the risk of explosions, and being too detached and cold-blooded. It is a relief for both the key worker and the patient if, in such critical situations, a neutral third party can be called upon, and this will often relax the scene. Of course, a severely agitated psychotic state may still require intravenous application of a sedative.

Drug treatment of psychotic adolescents generally follows the principles that have been established in adult psychiatry. In our view, it is, however, indispensable that the cathexis of a drug and its significance in the transference–countertransference relationship is observed and reflected. Only by recognizing the stabilizing effect of drugs on the ego and their effects on the structure of relationships can the neuroleptic treatment come to its full effect and be fully utilized within the therapeutic process (Danckwardt, 1978; Günter & Becker, 1990). In this way, negative transference reactions on drugs, especially a marked paranoid cathexis, can be avoided.

Framework and organization
of residential treatment

Despite some limitations, the term "everyday" is the central catchword for our therapeutic concept. Of course, the everyday life in a hospital is a special construction standing out and contrasted against the life that the patient had previously lead in his family—and so it should be. On the other hand, it is in many ways a reflection of the previous life. It should by no means be a special situation obeying completely different laws and thus alienating the patient, as can easily be the case in an adult psychiatric hospital stay.

Fortunately, we can rely upon our adolescents to bring with them the dynamics of everyday life—even if they are severely mentally ill—thus making it easier for us to re-create the features of normality of such a life. One could almost formulate that the youths enforce everyday life and a certain measure of normality—against all the odds, despite all obstacles, and regardless of the fact that at the time of admission they often find themselves in complete chaos. Everyday life is introduced from the outside world into the internal space of the hospital.

The patients use everyday life as their stage. This is where they settle their quarrels. Such behavioural models apply to adolescence in general, but in our case the situation is more complex. Even the psychosis is transported into the structures of everyday life, while at the same time the patients try to defend elements of normality. Everyday life under such circumstances is obviously a most endangered life, which can easily be confused and destroyed soon after having been resumed.

We like to formulate that everyday life under such clinical circumstances is, on the one hand, a facet of the real life; on the other, it is a screen for manifold projections and even becomes an outwardly turned representation of inner problems. Thus, the team members are real objects as well as transference objects. Hence, it follows, for example, that we cannot just observe or share a patient's everyday life benevolently or leave it to itself. Also, we must not act for or against this life at our own discretion, but we have to make great efforts to reflect and defend it constantly against the encroachment of chaos and help to shape it and re-erect it when it is destroyed.

A simple example will help to demonstrate the complexity of everyday life issues. An adolescent on his admission to residential treatment asks if he can bring his stereo and his guinea-pig on the ward. The bureaucratic and institutional answer to this could be, for example, that electronic equipment and pets are not allowed in a hospital. A somewhat rigid and rarely adopted counterpoint would be the dynamic contention that certain rules and frameworks of the treatment—and thus the rules of an institution—must not be attacked and the basic setting of a treatment process must be preserved. Admittedly, such a view has a lot in its favour if violent outbreaks are threatening and the vital safety of the therapist is at stake. In other cases, the negative label of "acting out" is, however, granted too lightly, and an inability on the part of the patient to "internalize" his problems is rather too often feared as a serious impediment to successful treatment. One has to accept that adolescents do apply acting-out behaviour as a common, age-specific defence mechanism, which is, moreover, supported by powerful elements of youth culture.

Thus, in all therapeutic work with adolescents a third pathway must be pursued, leaving aside stern institutional objections as well as orthodox therapeutic reservations. We would start at the assumption that the so-called acting out—as a behaviour that is dominated by conflicts based in reality and aiming at rules and other obstacles—is the only way in which our patients can present themselves, move forward, and achieve emotional growth. In our therapeutic team, comprising both nursing and educational staff and academic therapists aided by external supervision, we would always consider the actual and symbolic significance of a battle such as that concerning the pet and the hi-fi. We would ask ourselves which message we would convey if we agreed, and, alternatively, what the message would be if we refused. In any case, we would commit ourselves to serious negotiations with the patient about these matters. At the instant of a psychiatric hospital admission for a young patient, such negotiations can be the all-important issue, and we should adjust our clinical priorities accordingly.

Of course, a professional team can at the same time and behind the banality of some everyday events recognize the urgency of the need for help in a catastrophic situation. This is at first a task that is limited—for instance, by the number of days spent in residential treatment. At the same time, our team has a sense of the limitlessness and infinity of the task of helping some of our most severely ill patients. We start our work in a situation of utmost threat and confusion. Responsibility is taken on for a long period and with an open end. The hospital has to provide and to represent virtually everything a patient needs to survive emotionally and physically. Above all, the everyday life in a psychiatric hospital is conceived as a novel and first-time alternative to the previous everyday life, which the patient has spent in his family and which has failed.

* * *

After long struggles in the late 1970s, fundamental institutional changes have evolved in our units in Tübingen and Stuttgart which now enable all members of the hospital to join forces in several integrated teams and to view the creation of a therapeutic milieu as their primary common task. To achieve this task, typical hospital hierarchies had to be weakened, and the classic professional roles of doctors and psychologists, educational and nursing staff had to be levelled. The wards were transformed into living quarters for the patients. Offices and special treatment rooms were removed from all living areas. Educational and nursing staff were united to form a new professional identity as key workers. New informal hierarchies and qualifications developed across the professions according to individual experience and competence, which proved itself during the team sessions and everyday work with the patients. Aspects of transference and countertransference were observed and reflected throughout all ranks and professions. A sense of responsibility for the entire treatment process grew among each member of the team. At the same time, we were still aware of the importance of maintaining the remaining hierarchies of a hospital in order to preserve the capacity of the staff to work; to safeguard the necessary distance and boundaries; to defend the reality principle; and to distinguish between self and non-self, internal world and external world. The separation of different roles in a hospital setting facilitates the growth of different patterns of transference, which can be utilized for treatment. In any case, the therapeutic function of a person who works in the hospital is not automatically tied up with a professional role, but varies widely from case to case, depending on the treatment course and transference reactions. A typical example for the deconstruction of hierarchies is the participation of academic staff on the wards if a patient is severely regressed and in need of basic care. A typical example for the *preservation* of such structures is the utilization of the neutral and respected position of a consultant in a case of acute crisis management.

Psychiatric residential units for adolescents have very vivid group dynamics. Therefore, groups of about eight patients should be the maximum, if intensive treatment is to remain possible. Adolescents relate to each other intensely, and strong dynamics of mutual projection and identification take place. As a further peculiarity, adolescent groups join up in confrontation against the adult world. This applies even if the members of the group are extremely weak and emotionally at risk. These dynamics cannot simply be ignored, relying on the motto that the child should pay attention to his own problems. It would be wrong to assume that these group dynamics simply reflect problems of the individual. We are looking at an age-specific process of emancipation and liberalization seeking its rightful developmental place. This process can indeed set off maturational powers. They are, however, as one is painfully aware, fatally contaminated by the profound helplessness resulting from the psychotic illness.

Frequently, we have to separate patients from the group—during meal times, for instance. Repeatedly, patients have to be nursed or entertained separately in their bedrooms. Passionate quarrels inside a group have to be interrupted, sometimes to the extent that reserved areas on the floor are marked with adhesive tape.

Therapeutic events and individual treatments

The patients receive a high degree of individual care. Two key workers are allocated to each patient and spend firmly agreed times with them, apart from being responsible for the overall care and the structuring of everyday activities for the whole group. The arranged meetings are not meant for verbal reflections. Instead, various matters are "taken care of" or "taken up" together. Typical activities include sports, games, drawing, building and repairs, shopping, and cooking. These activities should be approached as routinely as possible, the only difference being that the patients have exclusive access to their key worker.

There are also arranged therapeutic sessions with the academic psychologist or psychiatrist who is in charge of the case. These sessions are deliberately set at a somewhat greater distance from the ward. More often in these meetings, verbal techniques are applied; techniques applying body experience also have a major place in our concept. But, again, this depends on the needs of the patient and the stage of the treatment process. Especially in adolescence, the disruption of ego structures is accompanied by abnormal body sensations. Self-manipulative behaviour is a typical attempt to prevent even further disintegration. Hypochondriacal anxiety is most prominent. The treatment attempts cautiously to support the reconstruction of the ego by enhancing or modifying proprioceptive body experience using a wide range of physiotherapeutic techniques within an analytic framework (Pankow, 1976; Schilder, 1935).

All therapeutic activities are controlled by a tightly knit system of conferences and supervisions. Apart from the usual daily ward conferences for all the team, there are weekly or fortnightly meetings of all the people who are engaged therapeutically with one particular patient. Thus, if a ward has eight patients, there would be eight separate weekly meetings of 30 minutes each comprising the two key workers and the academic therapist, sometimes supplemented by the teacher or someone else who is engaged in extramural activities with the same patient. The circle is deliberately kept very small. From a transference point of view these meetings comprise the "good parents", who need constantly to exchange their views and adjust their work. Here, all therapeutic planning and most interpretative work takes place and is then passed on to the large ward meetings. The meetings are regularly supervised by an external supervisor. We are traditionally reluctant to introduce further persons from outside the ward to offer special therapies. All therapeutic action should be centred around the group of key workers who are closest to the everyday life of the patient.

Rules as part of the therapeutic framework

Everyday life on a therapeutic adolescent ward requires only a few universal rules referring to the social life of the group and its interplay with the institution. Individual rules that have been arranged with individual patients prevail. The patients negotiate about rules concerning meals, going-out times, spending money, contact with parent, other social contacts, shopping, body care, smoking, and so forth. These rules offer the patients a concrete way of experiencing everyday life.

At the same time, the rules are representations of internal difficulties, as they indicate a kind of interpretative adaptation to the patients' internal conflicts. These are made tangible and visible, as they become translated into patterns of everyday life experience. Such rules could be signified as a canonization of mutual knowledge about the patient's difficulties being held by and secured within the relationship between key worker and patient. Both may fight vigorously about the content of these rules. The rules assure the patient that his most threatening conflicts have come under control, and that as he tries to master them he can count on the help of others.

A practical example for such rules are agreements concerning the cigarette consumption of restless and agitated young patients. Without rules, such patients would smoke incessantly and become even more disorganized. If restrictions are arranged, the patients subject themselves to them most readily. The rules pertain to issues such as the time, quantity, and place of cigarette smoking. The rules should also demand that the patient be accompanied by another supportive person whenever he smokes. The patients make constant efforts to test and negotiate such rules. They want their key worker to be available constantly, and they can hardly accept any other company. Thus, they have to weigh their mere craving for the next cigarette against their urgent need for a strong supportive relationship. They impart and exchange vital information about their inner situation, stability, and object-relations. A wide range of dynamic issues can be addressed without even touching on the more critical psychotic areas of experience.

Each psychiatric unit needs additional rules and structures for the management of dangerous and critical situations. Our wards are only locked when needed. Transfers of a difficult patient from one ward to another do not occur. No ward is specially designed or equipped to deal with particular behavioural problems. Conversely, for each ward there is provision to increase the number of staff in each shift, call up staff from a special on-call staff pool, and temporarily rearrange daily routines, so that a door can be locked and other patients are as little affected as possible. The locked/open status of a ward can change weekly.

Much more could be said about crisis management on an adolescent ward (cf. Günter, Karle, Kleefeld, Werning, & Klosinski, 1997). Suffice it to mention that conflicts should, whenever possible and as far as possible, be personified and personalized and should not prematurely be quelled or distorted by structural violence such as through the appearance of on-call emergency doctors or the excessive application of sedatives or mechanical restraints.

Therapeutic work with the parents

We have already drawn attention to the frequent occurrence of symbiotic relationships and separation anxieties between parents and a psychotic child (Mahler, 1968). Thus, our work with the parents not only enjoys high priority, but also requires considerable skills. Sessions with the parents take place at least every fortnight or more frequently. They are conducted by the academic therapist and one of the key workers. Often the children join the sessions for some of the time. Teachers and other relevant members of the treatment team are invited as required. Some sessions are reserved for the parents themselves. Families of psychotic patients take a long time and many steps forwards and backwards before they have grasped and accepted the fact and scope of the illness of their child. We welcome the formation of parental support groups, which can assist the adaptation process. Not infrequently, our co-operation with parents leads to separate psychotherapy being offered to one of them. Such treatments are conducted by a member of staff who is not engaged in the treatment of the child, but the therapist is regularly invited into case conferences concerning the child.

Extramural spaces of treatment

When we described the patterns of everyday life in a treatment unit, our main concern was to stress that this life reflected a piece of real life, not just one of fantasy or play, and that such reality could be handled therapeutically. However, if a severely disturbed patient is arrested in a confined space for a prolonged period of time, no matter how successfully some pieces of reality can at first be reconstructed, the ward will soon no longer be able to reinforce all aspects of reality to a sufficient degree. In other words, the spaces on the ward are virtually becoming narrower and narrower as time passes. This is why a therapeutic unit for adolescents, in order to defend the everyday life principle credibly, does need yet another periphery of real life surrounding it. It should be located at a middle distance. From there entry or re-entry to the wider and more general reality should be possible. But we have little therapeutic influence upon that last step, when reality at large is to be approached.

All such enlarged areas of reality must be accessible from within the ward; on the other hand, they must be fenced off against the ward in order to preserve their special character. The school is the most important anchor of external reality and should be defended at all costs. Even though the cooperation with the teachers is very close in all our team work, the external position of the school is strictly observed.

For similar reasons, our staff perform numerous outside activities. From the perspective of adult psychiatry, our staff may appear all too pleasure-seeking. But these activities have a firm place in our treatment concept in order to support reality-testing and orientation, which, in contrast to older patients, is in much greater danger of withering. Young psychotics have not had any significant social life of their own before their illness. They have had little social competence and insufficient life experience. In these respects, they are much more vulnerable to suffer hospitalization effects.

An important technique, by which we try to open pathways leading from the wards to the outside world, even if the patients' abilities are still minimal, consists of encouraging them to visit sheltered localities where they can go at certain times. Thus, a new range of movement is achieved, as they take leave from the ward and arrive at the other end, gradually learning to commute between an external school and the ward or between a sheltered workshop or training unit and the ward. At first, they would be accompanied; ultimately, they would manage on their own.

Conclusion

After twenty years of our treatment project and an informal follow-up study (du Bois, Günter, Koller, & Zimmermann, 1990), in which we had the opportunity to meet many of our previous patients for extensive narrative interviews after an interval of five to ten years, we are facing a sobering balance. As is confirmed by other studies, the prognosis of early onset schizophrenias, especially with pre-existing maturational deficits, is anything but favourable. Many of our patients have chronic debilities and live in sheltered accommodation. They cannot fully care for themselves. From our interviews with them and their next of kin, we have, however, gathered that our patients may have achieved a special quality of understanding of their situation and their dependency. We also discovered a quality of self-reliance, which in such patients can easily be buried. Some of these patients had again been hospitalized for some time, but most of them could build a safe existence in a residential home with a fair amount of freedom and easy access to their families. Curiously, most patients had at first returned to their families before taking the next step to move out, for which they had been well prepared through their previous treatment.

Thus what was achieved was that the patients did not remain stuck in their situation of origin. Their experience of psychiatric hospitalization turned out to be more than just a temporary escape from their life at home but, rather, a widening of their experience. They did not develop negative attitudes towards psychiatric treatment and were spared painful antagonisms between hospital and family. At least in the favourable cases, the families had adopted a new, secure attitude towards the illness of their child. They were not put in the dreadful position where separation seems as impossible as togetherness, and only death seems to be able to part a child from his parents.

Our model project was conducted during a period of high public prosperity in Germany, when both public and private health insurances were not troubled by the unusually long hospital stays and, in fact, did not even take any notice. Of course, the overall numbers of patients involved were rather small.

Still, our concept of generously allowing regressions and integrating rehabilitative elements into the features of an acute ward remains disputed. It is in sharp contrast to principles of modern social psychiatry that has firmly set its goals at avoiding lengthy inpatient treatments and advocates speedy discharge from acute hospitals and referrals to special rehabilitation units or even immediate re-integration into society. Even in our own speciality, our model is not unanimously supported, and a sharper division between an initial medical part of the treatment and a subsequent educational and social rehabilitative part is often preferred. Also, questions of costs are becoming more critical.

We ourselves are convinced and concede that our treatment concept is not equally suitable for all courses of juvenile schizophrenia. We must reiterate that our patients were at a developmental stage, where, without our intensive interventions, further growth of limited autonomy outside their families and an orderly retreat from their families would have been impossible. At such an early developmental stage, conventional rehabilitative activities make no sense. Where social and vocational life has never existed, there is no base to build on and nothing to restore. Nobody could prevent these patients from slipping back into either a kind of "hospitalism" inside their families or social degeneration outside.

CHAPTER TEN

Psychoanalytically orientated in-patient treatment

Ulrich Streeck

As early as 1927, Ernst Simmel thought of attempting to apply psychoanalytic knowledge in the treatment of patients suffering from "advanced compulsive neuroses and phobias" and from "hysterical illnesses in which functional organic disturbances impair—often considerably—their ability to live"; patients with addictions or with defective character development, especially where these lead to "social dangers"; as well as patients with "complicated and long-term organic illnesses in which a psychic component clearly hinders and threatens to suspend the process of healing" (Simmel, 1928). Finally, and not least, he was also concerned about patients whose illness "was becoming so extensive that the sufferer was entering a distinctly asocial state" (p. 352).

Today, seventy years after Simmel's first efforts on behalf of psychoanalytically orientated treatment in clinics in Berlin, the diagnostic and therapeutic possibilities of psychoanalysis contribute in many ways to in-patient treatment. From today's standpoint, many of the patients described by Simmel would be recognized mostly as patients with severe developmental disorders (A. Freud,

1965) or structural disturbances, who have now become treatable through the possibilities of psychoanalytically orientated therapy applied to in-patients within the hospital framework.

For all their heterogeneity, the concepts and models developed for this purpose have certain fundamental aspects in common. Thus, there is general agreement that in-patient treatment involves different, specific therapeutic procedures and methods of treatment, applied and combined under a psychoanalytically orientated viewpoint into a concept for a complex, multi-dimensional organization of treatment.

A second aspect of in-patient treatment viewed as fundamental is that the social world of the hospital, with its diverse social relationships and groups, is used for therapeutic purposes during the hospital treatment to replace the social environment in which the patient would normally live. By necessity, the concepts and models of psychoanalytically orientated in-patient treatment must be supplemented by other theories and concepts. In addition to the psychoanalytic theory of mental illness and therapeutic processes, theories and models that contribute to our understanding of social behavior and the interaction of small and large groups and organizations (e.g. Rice, 1965), the therapeutic community (Main, 1946), and the therapeutic milieu (Cumming & Cumming, 1962) are especially necessary.

Finally, there is general agreement that institutional and ecological environment and framework conditions play a vital role and strongly influence the possibilities and limitations of in-patient treatment (cf. Main, 1992; Werbart, 1995). Not least, the size of the institution has an influence on the psychotherapeutic work carried out there. For example, where small psychotherapeutic units are part of a high-tech, large-scale hospital, there can only be a limited realization of the psychotherapeutic milieu, because the sheer dominance of technical medicine and the purely functional hospital architecture "define" (Thomas, 1966) illness and treatment in a way that is not conducive to supporting self-reflexive processes.

Concepts for psychoanalytically orientated
in-patient treatment

Psychoanalytic knowledge of the early stages of mental development, of severe regressive conditions, of narcissistic transference, and of primitive forms of defence have opened up a whole series of possibilities for also understanding those patients whose clinical picture had hitherto been regarded as unanalysable, and for treating such patients with the aid of psychoanalysis and analytically orientated psychotherapy. Moreover, psychoanalysis has contributed significantly to our understanding of small- and large-group processes, families, institutions, and organizations. With the aid of more extensive clinical experience and knowledge of group and organization analysis, the potential of therapy through psychoanalytically orientated in-patient treatment has grown to such an extent that today even such patients as these can be treated effectively—patients who, in view of the severity of their illnesses were usually only kept in custody and treated with drugs (cf. Becker & Senf, 1988; Janssen, 1987).

This is, not least, facilitated by the fact that it is possible under hospital conditions—unlike those where we meet patients only as out-patients—to observe and influence patients' experiences and behaviour both in a *vertical, intrapsychic* dimension and in a *horizontal, interpsychic*—that is, interactive—dimension.

The plurality of therapeutic methods

In addition to psychoanalytically orientated individual therapy (which in in-patient therapy might well be combined especially with group therapy), other therapeutic methods are commonly used: for example, family therapy and those therapeutic methods that provide patients who are not accustomed to introspection and the verbal-symbolical expression of their experiences and feelings with primary and non-verbal means of expression—for example, art and music therapy, but also kinetic therapy methods. Such therapeutic methods—which work mainly through non-verbal, expressive means—can, under the conditions of psychoanalytically orientated in-patient treatment, open up therapeutic access routes in even very severely disturbed patients. Also, socio-therapeutic measures such as work and work-stress trials can play a role in hospital treatment, especially with patients who have been repeatedly hindered by their illness in their social and professional lives. Finally, a central part of hospital treatment is the work conducted along psychoanalytic lines with large groups and ward meetings, as well as therapeutic management of the ward or the hospital environment.

The prerequisite for this, however, is that the different treatment approaches are integrated with each other according to psychodynamic viewpoints and not just added on one after another. The fact that individual therapy for in-patients is of a less private nature can make it necessary to separate clearly the role of the individual therapist from the nursing and community treatment (Bell, 1997).

The focus of treatment

The integration of these different therapeutic methods and access routes is an indispensable factor of psychoanalytically orientated in-patient treatment. In this connection, integration means that the focal points and goals of the treatment determine the therapeutic procedures and their order of application for each patient and his particular disturbance. All of this is individually designed, coordinated, and consolidated to form a complex treatment arrangement. Thus, the therapeutic process here is revealed to be a dynamic process involving a complex treatment organization.

In order to facilitate this, the treatment organization should have, as far as possible, a common focus (Streeck, 1991). The focus thus acquires the function of integrating and controlling the various therapeutic activities. The focus in psychoanalytically orientated hospital treatment encompasses a central aspect of the patient's disorder on which the team members involved in the treatment of the patient orientate their therapeutic strategy. Because most in-patients suffer from development-related disorders, the focus here—unlike in psychoanalytic focal therapy—should chiefly concentrate on characteristic disorders of the self and the internalized pathological object-relations, as well as other aspects of personality organization, but not unconscious conflicts. Since the therapeutic aim of the treatment of these patients does not necessarily lie in exposing such unconscious conflicts, the focus must not be formulated in the form of an interpretation, as Balint recommends for psychoanalytic focal therapy (Balint, Ornstein, & Balint, 1972). The choice of the focus may possibly take the form of a progressively orientated solution or compensation of the basic developmental fault. It is based on a careful diagnosis of the dynamic development of the disorder. A diagnostic assessment of the personality organization, as well as of the strength and abilities of the egos in these patients, is the platform of therapeutic cooperation and should be accorded an importance similar to that which Bellak and Small (1972) highlight with regard to brief psychotherapy:

> Hence an assessment of the strength of individual ego functions gives us information on which functions have broken down or been weakened through the course of the illness and which are relatively well intact. With this the therapist has gained reference points for both the course and goals of the treatment, because now he knows both the personality elements in need of therapy as well as the still healthy ego functions, . . . on which he can rely during treatment. [p. 56]

The frame and its functions

The social environment of the hospital is used in psychoanalytically orientated in-patient treatment as a therapeutic sphere for "playful" interaction, which is defined and limited by a set framework. This framework provides orientation for the patient as well as for the therapeutic personnel. It constitutes the line between the therapeutic space and ordinary social reality, marks out a reliable borderline for patients and therapeutic personnel, offers protection, and provides a transitional space.

It is therefore important that there should be clear treatment agreements and reliable rules for cooperation and behaviour, so that the patients—as well as members of the therapeutic team—can feel sufficiently well orientated and safe from arbitrariness. The framework thus guarantees the possibility of limited therapeutic regression, constitutes a transitional space, and is a binding "law" for the therapists and hence proof of their reliability (Trimborn, 1994).

Whether or not the framework conditions do indeed fulfil these functions is not least a question of how the therapeutic colleagues advocate and employ them. If the members of the therapeutic team adhere inflexibly to the framework agreement, for no therapeutic reason that they can give, as is often the case in "total institutions" (Goffman, 1972), they can easily become abstract instruments of a rigid regulatory power. If, on the other hand, members of the team regard the framework conditions as non-binding rules that can be bent or overstepped with few or no consequences, then the inter-personal sphere in the clinic—the therapeutic space—is threatened by arbitrariness and the patients do not feel sufficiently safe and protected.

Transferences and splitting of transferences

During hospital treatment, the patient actualizes and re-enacts his unconscious conflicts and his internalized pathological object-rela-tionships within a complex social context. Transferences are not concentrated on one person alone, as on the analyst in a psycho-analytic setting, but rather are spread out onto several people or subgroups. In patients with neurotic disorders, this splitting of transferences can easily lead to the danger of conflictual elements of the transference being kept out of the treatment and thereby not being recognized as split-off transference elements. The problems and impairments of patients with so-called pre-oedipal disorders or development-relevant disorders is usually not the consequence of symptoms that have come about as compromise-seeking solu-tions to unconscious conflicts, as is the case with neurotics (i.e. conflict-related disorders), but rather they are the result of a lim-ited ability to control and steer impulses and affects, to regulate the sense of self-esteem, and to adapt with sufficient flexibly to the social environment. Accordingly, such disorders are usually based on an unstable defence organization, the centre of which is a split between contrary self- and object-representations, as well as di-vided supportive defence mechanisms such as idealization and devaluation, denial, projection, and projective identification. In many patients, this becomes a handicap in all areas of daily life.

Some patients tend to a behaviour that is severely self-destructive or destructive to others, are unable to enter long-term relationships with other people, or are entangled in destructive interaction circles from which they are unable alone to free themselves; they tend to psychosomatic crises, move on the borderline to psychotic decompensation, or run the danger of becoming isolated from their social surroundings and dropping out of the workforce by reason of their psychic condition.

For the treatment of these patients, the complex arrangement of the clinic may possibly offer decisive advantages. Patients are adequately protected under clinic conditions, and here in the social field of the clinic they can explore new solutions, while at the same time examining and dealing with their disturbances in the transference arena of the clinic via a division of the non-compatible aspects of their inner object world onto several members or subgroups of the therapeutic team.

A splitting of transference is not a complicating factor in these cases; however, the possibilities for splitting offered by the clinic setting are often an important condition for the treatment of these patients. In order to be able to recognize the mutually incompatible partial-self or partial-object aspects as partial aspects that belong together, the therapeutic team must assume integrative functions.

Spheres of experience and playful interaction

Sometimes patients compare psychotherapy with a game and the therapeutic space in the clinic with a playground. "Serious" psychotherapists do not like to hear this. They warn that therapy is not a game, and they can only imagine a playground as a place for infantile desires and childish regressive experiences. They do not understand that it is often decisive, especially in the treatment of patients with severe developmental disturbances, for patients to be able indeed to use the therapeutic space to move about in a milieu of playful interaction—that is, as a place where the socially serious consequences of interactions are and must be to some extent suspended. The therapeutic space of playful interaction, like the range of play and experience described by Winnicott (1987; cf. also Friedman, 1989), is not subject to the grave and irrevocable consequences of social reality, but nonetheless does not lack seriousness.

The behaviour of patients must also abide by social rules similar to those that are valid in daily social intercourse, but only limited and to some extent non-binding. The patient's behaviour, however, still has genuine consequences.

If this were not so, the therapeutic space would be invalidated by "arbitrariness" and could no longer function as a sphere for playful interaction—just as a game is destroyed by an arbitrary breaking of the rules. If, on the other hand, the same rules applied as in daily social reality, this experience-space and the playful interaction that should take place there would be destroyed.

The insights and experience that the patient gains through the different therapies applied in his treatment can be put into practice relatively safely by him within this play and transition sphere— that is, the social environment of the clinic. He can then, in a next step, work through the experiences that he has made in the inter-personal sphere of the clinic—above all, in individual or group therapy. In this way, the range of experience can be extended step-by-step beyond the limits of the clinic environment and gradually brought closer to everyday social conditions, until the patient is able to meet and deal with the challenges of his daily world by himself.

Furthermore, specific concepts for in-patient treatment were developed for individual disorders: for example, for the treatment of depressions (Neimeyer, Baker, Haykal, & Akiskal, 1995); for borderline and other severe personality disorders (e.g. Armelius, 1991; Bateman, 1995; Hartocollis, 1980; Kernberg, 1982; Rosenbluth & Silver, 1992; Tucker, Bauer, Wagner, Harlam, & Sher, 1992); for patients with multiple personality (e.g. Kelly, 1993); or for severe eating disorders (e.g. Engel, Hentze, & Wittern, 1992; Vander-eycken, 1992).

The integrative task of the therapeutic team

In-patient treatment thus offers especially favourable conditions for patients with severe developmental disturbances facilitating and supporting the integration of different primitive partial-object representations. To be successful, it is important that the members of the therapeutic team participating in the treatment of a patient can cooperate closely with one another in a confidence-building atmosphere that enables them to exchange experiences and feelings with one another frankly. This is the more important as these often difficult patients frequently arouse strong and intensive transference feelings. For this reason, the danger of transference acting out is especially great when it is not recognized that the feelings and impulses often awakened with such strong intensity in the therapeutic work with these patients—and which often try a therapeutic team to the edge of endurance—are a response to the archaic part-object transference of the patients. Under some circumstances, massive conflicts and tensions within the therapeutic team may then develop—for example, when the patient idealizes one subgroup of the team and denigrates the other part, and the team does not recognize that this splitting of their own group is a reflection of the patient's own primitive split.

In view of this often considerable psychic and interpersonal stress, the nursing staff needs a qualified psychoanalytically orientated training (Hughes & Halek, 1991; Winship, 1995), complemented by interactive competence, and the work of the therapeutic team in hospital treatment should be supported by an external psychoanalyst acting in the function of a team supervisor.

Good cooperation among the team members is also necessary in order to be able to coordinate continuously the therapeutic procedures and methods in the treatment process. The team members must feel that the different therapeutic methods that they represent are recognized and respected as being equal and valued parts of a complex treatment arrangement.

Problems in the treatment of patients with serious developmental disorders

Without doubt, the treatment of patients with severe developmental disorders or structural deficits, especially of patients with pre-psychotic and severe personality disorders, is often accompanied by considerable problems and pressures. For one thing, the specific pathology of these patients is almost impossible to recognize from what the patient communicates, because they do not present their illness verbally and symbolically, but, rather, enact the disturbance within an interaction. The dynamics of the disturbance is thus not displayed through fantasies, associations, or dreams—that is, expressed symbolically—but is produced in interaction with real, present objects. In an expression of primitive transference, these patients attempt to force "the other" to assume a particular role (Sandler, 1976) and indeed to behave according to the aspects of the transferred self or object, thus causing psychic reality to take place as outward reality, outside the self. As a result, it is often difficult for the other person to maintain distance and neutrality. Analysts and therapeutic personnel become easily entangled in what could be called enactment dialogues (Klüwer, 1983), one of the consequences being that the behaviour of the other responds "appropriately" to the transference expectations of the patient, thus confirming, in fact, the patient's version of reality.

The language of patients with severe development disorders is thus to a large extent one of manipulation and acting out. But it is not necessarily large-scale acting out (which in most cases is comparatively easy to identify and to decipher the unconscious significance: Chiesa, 1989) that leads to a corresponding transference-conformance behaviour in the other. On the contrary, the patient often elicits this response through the use of subtle, but effective, verbal and non-verbal methods, which are usually not consciously perceived. Treurniet (1996) called these methods "micro-acting out". Micro-acting out is not a simple and crude dramatization, in which memories are replaced and expressed through re-enactment. It is not a means of expressing something, and it is not meant to convey an underlying meaning, but rather to elicit an effect. Borrowing from Piaget, we could speak of methods of senso-motoric intelligence, with the practical purpose of achieving certain results and effects, rather than the expression of truths (Piaget & Inhelder, 1966). Micro-acting out is a means of interaction used to form and direct relationships, in which unconscious communications are carried out, and the other person is manoeuvred in certain ways to participate in scenes that are "engineered" to create reality—means by which the patient is often successful.

That this is the case appears at least questionable when the structure of patients with severe developmental disorders is generalized and dismissed as deficient. These patients seem to be especially competent in interaction, which enables them to direct and influence the other person, so that the patient's psychic reality of interpersonal relationships is transformed into factual reality.

The problems of many patients with severe developmental disorders is displayed in how they deal with the framework. They run headlong against it and seek to destroy it—usually in the unconscious hope of not succeeding, and that the framework will withstand their attacks. Patients ignore the ban on drinking alcohol, threaten suicide, run away without warning, gain too much weight, threaten violence, are unable to be alone—but are also unable to bear the presence of others. They undermine their treatment, without seriously desiring to end it, provoke other patients and the therapeutic personnel, and burn and cut themselves. In their attacks against the framework, they are expressing their enormous fear of dependence and their self-destructive urge for self-sufficiency—but also attempting to challenge measures that maintain boundaries. If the patient does indeed succeed in destroying the treatment organization and its framework, the therapy fails—among other reasons, because the patient experiences confirmation of his fear that his destructive power is uncontrollable. The treatment also fails if the personnel allow the framework to be weakened; this leads to expressions of arbitrariness and destructive acting out, and escalating crises. Sometimes the therapeutic workers feel called upon simply to endure the destructive behaviour of the patient, without setting limits. The patient resorts to ever more drastic behaviour; the therapeutic personnel strive even further to endure their own ever more unbearable feelings. In response, the patient intensifies his destructive actions, and so on.

It is usually these patients who keep the therapeutic personnel and their fellow patients under tension. In cases of severe regressive decompensation with destructive acting out towards themselves or others, patients may need to be transferred for a time to a closed ward. It can often then be observed that, after just a short time, patients begin to feel safer and can be transferred back, because in the closed ward those boundaries were drawn that the patient had been unable mentally to draw himself because of his disorder.

With these patients, the danger is especially great that the therapeutic personnel will become enmeshed in an acting out of transference affects and impulses and respond to the disorganized behavior of the patient with counter-aggressive measures—for example, the treatment organization is managed as a rigid therapy programme, or the conditions of the framework are carried out with force. The interventions then have a poor pedagogic effect at best, and usually serve to satisfy the patient's transference needs.

In the course of favourable treatment, on the other hand, the patient progresses from angry-destructive rebellion against the framework to a joint struggle for framework conditions. This joint striving towards a framework increasingly establishes secure boundaries between self and object. In the best case, they succeed step-by-step in interactively developing conditions that constitute a framework that the patient can endure without running the danger of giving up his autonomy, but also without the necessity of denying an existence of another reality, existing outside and independent of him.

Indications for psychoanalytically orientated in-patient treatment

A psychoanalytically orientated in-patient treatment can be helpful for many patients, including patients with severe mental and psychosomatic disorders. However, this depends to a large degree on the character of the therapeutic institution, the number of therapists, the therapeutic orientation and qualification of the therapeutic staff, its size and location, and whether it is a small therapeutic unit within a general hospital or an independent psychotherapeutic hospital.[1] Such a treatment is indicated, for example, for patients who are unable to have psychotherapeutic treatment as out-patients because of the nature of their symptoms, for in-patients with psychogenic gait disorders or psychogenic attacks, or for patients who are unable to undertake or to maintain a therapeutic relationship with some stability within an out-patient framework and who therefore constantly fall into difficult crises and a state of psychic decompensation between sessions. The indications for hospital treatment are often present for patients who tend towards severe forms of acting out and who need the kind of stable therapeutic framework that cannot be maintained securely enough in out-patient treatment, as well as for patients with a high risk of acute decompensation, for whom hospital treatment, in the sense of a crisis intervention, may represent the continuation of, or a further step in, an already begun out-patient treatment. In addition, psychoanalytically orientated in-patient treatment is indicated for patients whose disorders require psychotherapeutic treatment but who cannot be motivated under out-patient conditions. For them, trials can be undertaken in the clinic, using the therapeutic milieu and the complex treatment arrangements, to find ways of introducing psychoanalytically and psychosomatically orientated treatment. Such treatment is also indicated for patients whose disorder results in grave social, professional, or economic consequences and who need the framework of hospital treatment potentially to halt or interrupt these repercussions.

Sometimes in-patient treatment can become necessary to remove a patient temporarily from a pathological environment and thus create the conditions necessary for psychoanalytic treatment. Also, in cases of multimorbidity, out-patient treatment is sometimes insufficient to achieve complex therapeutic access routes. Finally, treatment in a clinic is indicated for patients who, through the nature and course of a physical illness, suffer secondary severe psychic changes, and for patients with primary somatic illnesses, in whom a hitherto latent neurotic conflict situation or a relatively stable, compensatory personality disorder threatens to decompensate and lead to psychic or psychosomatic destabilization, particularly where this also reinforces physical symptoms.

NOTE

1. I am referring here to experiences with psychoanalytically orientated in-patient treatment in the Tiefenbrunn hospital, a Lower Saxony state hospital with 176 beds founded in 1949 as a psychotherapeutic hospital with different departments specialized for patients with personality disorders and severe neuroses, psychosomatic disorders, psychoses, and for children and adolescents.

CHAPTER ELEVEN

The legacy of power play in societies for psychoanalytic psychotherapy

Serge Frisch

"**P**ower" is not a psychoanalytic term. It is nowhere to be found in the dictionaries either of Laplanche and Pontalis (1967) or of Hinshelwood (1989), and, with the exception of feminist psychoanalysis, few psychoanalytic articles deal with the subject. While periodicals for the "general public" regularly publish pieces on the "Power of Shrinks", it is surprising to see how discreetly psychoanalytic literature handles the idea, and while every analysand attributes some sort of power to the analyst, it seems agreed that this could only be imaginary. The extent to which the notion of power is charged with negative meaning in professional circles is revealed by the fact the forthcoming volume of *Cahiers de Psychologie Clinique* is being devoted entirely to the issue of power; in the announcement of this (1997, Vol. 8, pp. 281–282) it is stated that "domination, greed, ties, seduction, suggestion, manipulation, and interpretation are some of the ways in which the mind structures the difficult relationship with power". There is no question of power being "good" or even, at its limit, "neutral", but only of its having negative and even perverse connotations.

In choosing her profession, a psychoanalyst would appear to deprive herself of gratifications that people seek in the exercise of power (Green, 1992). The aim of psychoanalysis is ostensibly to take individual internal freedom, freedom of thought, and creativity as far as they can go. As analytic work progresses, it opposes conscious and unconscious resistance. To achieve this opening-up and to help the analysand in his development, the psychoanalyst has, in principle, nothing at her disposal but her capacity for analytic interpretation. Yet psychoanalysts often find, despite themselves, that their patients always risk a sort of indoctrination by their own psychoanalytic theories (Kernberg, 1992). There may therefore be more power over other people's minds than we care to admit. The notion of power is therefore omnipresent in treatment, even if in only a shadowy way.

The need to create institutional structures was felt very early on in the psychoanalytic movement. Already in 1910, Freud was hoping to create an international psychoanalytic association. The training institutes were formalized after the congress at Bad Homburg in 1925.

Psychoanalytic psychotherapists draw their theoretical and technical frames of reference from psychoanalysis and the internal organization of the societies for psychoanalytic psychotherapy, and their training institutes are likewise often modelled directly upon the psychoanalytic societies. How psychoanalytic psychotherapists organize themselves to function as groups needs constant review in order to avoid rigidity and the emergence of powers that it could become dangerous to question. Raising such questions seems less complex for psychoanalytic psychotherapists because the Freudian legacy weighs less heavily on their societies than on the psychoanalytic societies.

In this chapter an attempt is made to address the issue of power inside psychoanalytic institutions. These institutions exert very real political power through their selection of candidates and the orientation they choose for theoretical teaching, and therefore they create a sort of analytic "ideology". Reference is commonly made to the formation of "analytic cliques", equivalent to pressure groups within psychoanalytic societies, or even "colonization of the thinking" (About, 1996) of candidates in training by the people training them.

It would be naïve to imagine that the notion of power—and therefore of power struggles—is any less a feature at different levels in psychoanalytic organizations than it is in every other sort of organization. Power is certainly wielded both inside psychoanalytic societies and their training institutes, and between analytic organizations and the social world or in relation to other therapeutic organizations. However, the kind of power exercised can differ. In this chapter we have chosen not to address the most extreme situations, abuses of power, or the iron grip that some analysts have on patients during treatment. If such abuses seem rather rare, Helena Bessermann Vianna's book (1997) describes very poignantly the tragic effects of the way that the dominating hold of one psychoanalyst, compromised by the system of the Third Reich, was passed on to three generations of psychoanalysts. This example clearly demonstrates how important it is in all therapeutic work to analyse in detail precisely how patient and psychotherapist are trying to exert real power over one another in multiple, often insidious and stealthy, forms.

We will suggest that the uneasiness about "power" goes back to one of Freud's difficulties: that of assuming power openly in the analytic movement he initiated, preferring instead to wield it in hidden ways.

*Freud could be father but not president
of the psychoanalytic movement:
or, why does the notion of power have negative
connotations in psychoanalysis?*

With Freud, the beginnings of psychoanalytic *theory* and the psychoanalytic *movement* are inextricably confounded. He developed his analytic theories while at the same time also wanting to create an international movement.

He gave Sándor Ferenczi the task of proposing the creation of the International Psychoanalytical Association (IPA) at the Nuremberg Congress in 1910 and asked him to put forward C. G. Jung as its first president. This provoked the first institutional crisis in the analytic movement, because of the hostility towards Jung of a great number of Freud's oldest and staunchest supporters, grouped under the banner of Adler and Stekel. Freud, playing on their sensibility and guilt, succeeded in persuading them to accept his proposals (Grosskurth, 1995).

Freud would not agree to take a place officially at the head of the psychoanalytic movement and openly take power in it, preferring his power to be hidden. But when conflict between Jung and Freud became inevitable, Freud once again charged Ferenczi with attacking Jung. Jung broke officially with Freud in 1914 by resigning the presidency of the IPA. Freud then himself responded to Jung and his divergent views on the libido by publishing "On Narcissism: An Introduction" (1914c).

Because of Jung's escape from his authority, the departure of some of his first disciples like Adler, and the quarrel with Stekel, Freud enthusiastically accepted the creation in 1912 of a secret committee of his most faithful disciples (Abraham, Ferenczi, Jones, Rank, Sachs, and, subsequently, Eitingon). The members of this Praetorian Guard owed devotion and total allegiance to Freud, who thereby hoped to have absolute control over them. The purpose of this committee, which was, in accordance with Freud's wishes, to remain informal and secret, was to transmit Freudian theory, to give warning of any deviance within the psychoanalytic movement, and to anticipate any attack from without by "personalities and accidents when I am no more" (E. Jones, 1964, p. 416). It is important to be aware that this committee was set up independently of Jung, then president of the IPA, and of the various presidents of the psychoanalytic societies. The IPA was the official showcase of the movement, whereas the secret committee was felt to wield the real power. "Everything conspired to suggest that the only sort of power he would agree to take part in was games of influence and seduction that ran parallel to and short-circuited the rules envisaged by the organization" (Carels & Gauthier, 1996).

Freud spoke of members of the committee as his "adopted children". Because of his personality, but also no doubt because of the nineteenth-century social ideology that put the individual at the centre of his preoccupations, he thought of institutional ties as family ties: he was the all-powerful father, and his disciples were his children. Under Freud's authority, they could therefore never become his equals. According to Berger (1993) this was a narcissistic descent group, typified by unconditional love for himself that was to be had through the others. Could this distortion in the nature of their relationship still be at work today in the conduct of, or powers within, psychoanalytic societies?

Freud therefore undeniably intended to dominate the psychoanalytic movement while being absolutely unable to take power within it, except in hidden ways and by means of personal influence. He could be its father but not its president.

This raises various questions. Might the lack of analytic thinking about power and the different ways in which power is manifested in psychoanalytic societies not be one aspect of a transgenerational inheritance of Freud's own uneasiness in groups and his difficulty in considering and accepting theoretical differences and in assuming positions of power clearly, openly, and not in a hidden way? Might we not also recognize in the way in which power is wielded in certain analytic groups an identification with Freud's rigid exercise of power? Could this not also underlie the difficulties that psychoanalysts experience in taking account of group phenomena in their societies? Might Freud's refusal or inability to analyse the pathological structure of group functioning not underlie the first defections that heralded future schisms?

This might also help in understanding the mistrust that psychoanalysts have always expressed towards those leaders, whether in analysis or politics, who are described as having narcissistic pathologies (Berger, 1993; Orgel, 1990). Such attacks upon psychoanalytic leaders who do not share Freud's idiosyncrasies prevent them from succeeding in the political domains in which he himself foundered. Is there not a danger here that analysts will artificially distance themselves from the realities of the social world around them by focusing all their attention upon dyadic relationships and exploration of the individual psyche?

Right from the birth of his International Association, Freud was painfully confronted with group conflicts and narcissistic group phenomena. He then wrote his papers on narcissism and *Totem and Taboo* (1912–13), his first attempt at political sociology, whose purpose was to establish the basis of social ties from a psychoanalytic point of view.

As Carels and Gauthier (1996) pertinently observed, Freud did not consider the effect that his own institutional situation might have been having upon his theoretical proposals. He (re)created the myth of the primitive horde to explain the nature and transmission of social bonds and the ambivalence that they arouse. The sons of a hypothetical primitive father are supposed to have organized his murder, with a view to possessing his goods and in particular his wives. After a first totemic feast, the sons identified themselves with their dead father, not simply in order to preserve their own lives but to maintain the unity of the group. A shared sense of guilt would therefore have given rise to taboo as a source of social bonding. This first sketchy version of the superego would then have had "a role in establishing and stabilizing social bonds . . . and the group would then give rise to the very structure of our mental functioning, since the family is the concrete place where this inheritance is cashed in" (Carels & Gauthier, 1996, p. 10). Freud therefore cast into mythical times a drama that he was actually living out in various psychoanalytic circles and especially since his International Association had been up and running. He does not, therefore, seem to have connected what he was currently living through with the development of his theory of social bonds. As Carels and Gauthier point out, by projecting and displacing the drama of a primitive father into archaic times, he tends to blind us to the specific features of the situations that we actually live in, or, in other words, to their particular historical imprint.

In view of all this, it is not surprising that psychoanalysts since Freud have continued to privilege individual mental functioning at the expense of reflection on group psychic functioning and the practices of psychoanalytic institutions. Even today, it is simpler to send anyone who criticizes the institution back for another slice of analysis than to look into the institution's possible malfunctioning. It seems evident to me that psychoanalysis is not an individual but a group exercise, in the sense that each candidate analyst is individually chosen by the analytic group into whose workings she will be admitted, sometimes painfully.

Power and therapeutic societies

For Kernberg (1992), the very structure of psychoanalytic institutions, with their excessively strict if not excessively rigid hierarchies, sets limits to the development of psychoanalytic science.

Here he is issuing a fundamental criticism by suggesting that the institutional structures secreted by psychoanalysts inhibit the development of psychoanalysis and that the involution or current crisis in psychoanalysis could be self-produced.

Starting from some very pertinent remarks in the psychoanalytic literature, reflection could begin upon the internal organization of societies for psychoanalytic psychotherapy, the structure of their training bodies, and the organic links that unite them.

Paraphrasing Bion's formulation, I would be tempted to say that as soon as two people meet there is indeed a relationship, and also a power relationship.

Every structured society of whatever kind needs to define hierarchical positions and positions of power so that those who hold them can make the group function. The same is true in psychoanalytic societies. But this sort of political power, which I regard as normal, can change into pathological power as soon as it becomes a stake to be played for or represents relations of strength between sub-groups.

Psychoanalytic societies are therefore one of the places where psychoanalysts wield the actual power that they deny themselves in their professional situation. In just the same way as in absolutely any other group, society, or even political party, struggles amongst divergent interests—which means power struggles—also go on in psychoanalytic societies. At the very most, one might hope that among analysts such contests ought to be more muffled, more symbolic, or less impassioned.

However, psychoanalytic societies have always been sites of ferocious power battles from the very beginning of the psychoanalytic movement, with the expulsion or departure of such persons as Jung, Adler, Rank, Stekel, and so on. Later, and in other circumstances, these battles ended in schism (Kutter, 1992), as in Germany, Austria, France, Sweden, Switzerland, and Norway, to cite but a few European countries. In England, the sometimes impassioned controversies between Melanie Klein and Anna Freud ended in the coexistence within the British Psychoanalytical Society of more or less autonomous groups, which avoided a de facto schism. But behind the "Controversial Discussions", which bore on theoretical and technical issues, there loomed the equally stark question of the predominance of one or other orientation for control of the European analytic movement.

In recent years, many psychoanalysts have reflected in highly critical terms upon the workings of the psychoanalytic societies in an effort to democratize and improve their internal functioning. One of the most pertinent authors is undoubtedly André Lussier (1992), who stigmatized "the disastrous aspects of our institutes, namely their rigidity and the oppressive dogmatism that prevails in them, our inability to attract candidates with creative minds, and the pathogenic effects within them of unanalysed transferences and counter-transferences, with their trail of idealization, paranoid reactions, etc." (p. 483).

Lussier felt that it was necessary to take a fresh look at the hierarchical structure of the psychoanalytic societies, to "eliminate the oligarchy of a small group and reduce the risks entailed by indoctrination and blind affiliations".

Didier Anzieu (1975) observed that "psychoanalysis as a social institution was erected in defence against Freud's initial, excessively revolutionary, discovery". Psychoanalytic societies have tended to take in conformist candidates at the expense of ones who are creative but perhaps less conformist and amenable. This could be due to leftover bits of unanalysed transference and counter-transference and to phenomena of idealization together with the paranoid reactions that they entail (Lussier, 1992).

We can understand some of these difficulties as inherent in the profession of the psychoanalyst. As Eishold (1994) shows very well, belonging to an analytic "school" forms part of every analyst's identity. "Internalising their training as part of their identities, their mode of thinking is a reflection of their distinctive points of view as members of particular schools" (p. 789). The less secure that identity is, the stronger the need may be to lay claim rigidly to membership of their own group and to want to impose their point of view on others without compromise. Now, as the "Controversial Discussions" (King & Steiner, 1991) have shown, these theoretical divergences are habitually underpinned by political and philosophical oppositions.

Eishold (1994) also argues that the formation of pairs tends to crystallize a very specific concentration of power in psychoanalytic societies: pairs made up of an analyst and his psychoanalytic patient-candidate, or a supervisor and his supervisee-candidate, and so forth:

> The real danger against which the overbounded analytic systems are defending is not external or objective: it is the psychological power of the pair. The systems have to be rigid, confining and authoritarian because the primary allegiances of its members are to the psychoanalytic pairs of which they are part, and to the lineages, the interlocking chains of pairs, of which they are descendants. [p. 793]

Psychoanalytic societies are the only structured groups into which new members are admitted while keeping secret their relationship with the person to whom they owe their admission, namely their psychoanalyst. These societies are therefore made up of "enclaves of secrets". Down the generations, these enclaves of secrets become "family secrets", whose potential for inhibiting the development of individuals in families beset by such secrets is only too well known. Unfortunately, very little has been written about this phenomenon at the very core of the psychoanalytic societies.

If the psychoanalytic societies cannot change very much in this, apart from continuing to think about it or only accepting members analysed in other societies, it seems to me that important implications do emerge for the societies for psychoanalytic psychotherapy, as I hope to demonstrate below.

Power and reproductive function

"Every wish to make or engender runs up against the inverse wish to deform, break, or split others apart" (Enriquez, 1987). This doubtless explains the impressive number of schisms that have split the psychoanalytic societies following disagreements about training issues, and it is proof that it is not only difficult to contain but, even worse, to accept theoretical differences within these societies. Training thus becomes another place where real power is wielded by analysts. This reproductive function is where the centre of power is located.

According to Anzieu (1975), psychoanalytic training seems to degrade slowly into an apprenticeship as it is institutionalized, reflecting, in Kernberg's (1992) words, "an atmosphere of indoctrination rather than free scientific development".

As Lussier (1992) said, a contradiction seems to reside in the fact of wanting to promote candidates' internal freedom by freeing them from paralysing internal constraints through a personal psychoanalysis while at the same time subjecting them in their training to a rigid and controlling framework. "The candidate hears it said that . . . he needs a mind that carries the plague while at the same time he is given to understand that the route into this profession is by way of submitting to strict rules that sometimes smack of rigid ritual" (Lussier, 1992, p. 484). A critical mind would be permitted only if it served to confirm the theory defended by the majority in the society in question (Kernberg, 1996b).

Some analysts, functioning both as analysts and as training members and representatives of the institution, privilege the latter position. The institution's welfare then takes precedence over candidates' personal analysis. This means forgetting that if psychoanalytic theory can be passed on (or taught?), *being psychoanalytic* can only develop in a personal analysis.

The question of the purpose of a training analysis now arises sharply: should it be for the candidate's benefit, or is it in fact a professional licence whose sole purpose is to secure self-reproduction? "Does it tend to insure the dominance and the control of the old guard at the expense of the analytic freedom of the candidate?" (Eishold, 1994).

Even in institutes without the system of reporting analyst, training analysts do hold some institutional power because they participate in the selection and promotion of candidates as analysands in accordance with a particular analytic ideology that is current in their institution and in which they share by the very fact of performing their function.

In a most interesting article, already cited above, "Thirty Methods to Destroy the Creativity of Candidates", and with a grating humour unusual in psychoanalytic literature, Kernberg (1996b), gave a range of "advice" to training committees for destroying candidates' creativity as thoroughly and as quickly as possible, by systematically retarding their institutional progress, favouring repetitive rather than critical teaching of Freudian texts treated as Scripture readings, and making teaching a religious rather than a scientific exercise by only presenting theoretical approaches monolithically and refusing to discuss theoretical approaches not deemed in conformity with the official approach, etc., etc.

When a psychoanalyst is conversant with only a single theoretical orientation or when a psychoanalytic society accepts only a single orientation, we may postulate a risk of abusing power. The scientific level has been abandoned for that of blind faith and sectarian fundamentalism.

André Green (1992) pointed out that power resides in theory teaching, by virtue of a theoretician's personal charisma, seduction by a strength and elegance of thought that may nonetheless be invalid, or reconquest through intellect and reason of powers relativized by psychoanalytic experience, or by a desire to become part of a tribe that is subject to the mechanisms of *Group Psychology and the Analysis of the Ego* (Freud, 1921c).

While analysts may consciously deny any desire for power where treatment is concerned, some do accumulate administrative power (taking a leading role in their institutional agencies) and power from training in the training institutes, sometimes also connected with power as an analytic theorist. In this case, the analyst "works to gather to himself all the imaginary, real, and symbolic effects of power . . . and approaches an omnipotence that is a target for splitting" (Green, 1992).

The social activity of these societies therefore seems to be self-reproduction. Candidates find that the people training them hold hierarchical positions and key posts in the society, which produces a very particular dynamic that induces multiple confusions from which they protect themselves by splitting. The combination of training functions and hierarchical functions in the society produces serious irregularities and incompatibilities, and stems from the false premise that one function automatically qualifies a person for the other. This confusion of roles, associated with fantasies of sadistic intrusion, arouses paranoid and claustrophobic fears based on the widespread difficulties that psychoanalytic societies experience in presenting clinical or theoretical research work.

What consequences can be drawn from this for the organization of societies for psychoanalytic psychotherapy?

Most psychoanalytic psychotherapists have a personal analysis with a psychoanalyst, who is thus not a member of the psychotherapy society to which the future psychotherapist will later belong. This therefore avoids all those enclaves of secrets within the psychotherapy society which I was describing earlier. I would therefore plead very strongly for a requirement for personal work with a psychoanalyst who is a member of a psychoanalytic society distinct and separate from the one to which the future psychotherapist will belong. I am against psychotherapy with a psychoanalytic psychotherapist who is, by definition, a member of the society to which the candidate in training will later belong.

Because of the difficulties already mentioned in apprehending group phenomena, candidates training in psychoanalytic psychotherapy are still too often perceived as individuals in a group. The group of candidates is only very seldom approached as an ensemble with its own group identity, in which group processes influence the candidate as much as the candidate's psychic functioning influences the group in return. The training of psychoanalytic psychotherapists needs to take the group dimension of training into consideration all the more urgently because individual psychoanalytic thinking stems from dependency upon the thinking of the analytic community and because the majority of psychotherapists work in institutions, which means in groups. Could we not conceive of trainings that would include an "observation of an institution" in their curriculum, in the same way as infant observations are already done?

I regard it as important to work towards a high degree of autonomy between training institutes for psychoanalytic psychotherapy and the societies. The point of this would be to clarify, differentiate, and gradually unravel the confusion between these two agencies, with a better separation and wider distribution of power roles. However, such a distinction between the two agencies should not be understood as a general solution in itself, for fear of replicating a mere illusion of independence between training institute and society, such as often actually happens. Training and membership should therefore be located at two radically different logical levels. The hierarchical functions criticized by some authors (see above) might then undergo radical change. The hierarchy of members could be maximally reduced within psychotherapy societies by such a separation because the training and all that it entails would take place in the training institutes. In the same spirit, I would recommend that (all? most?) of the training staff should be psychoanalysts and thus not involved in the conduct of everyday affairs in that particular psychoanalytic psychotherapy society, for all the reasons given in this chapter.

The training institutes, which Kernberg (1992) thinks should become more like art schools or a system of ateliers (Meltzer, 1994), would have the single, unique purpose of training and stimulating the development of students' epistemophilic instinct. Training staff would act as a guide through the body of knowledge that I mentioned above, "a guide who would point places out at the right time and could be seen as representing the good guardian penis who protects the mother's insides. Its protection removes the quality of intrusion from the wish to explore" (Harpman, 1992). In a way, they would not be concerned with what candidates would go on to do once their basic training was over.

Candidates who had finished their training would no longer be automatically accepted as members of a society. Although a basic training is necessary, it does not in fact certify the maturity and autonomous therapeutic capacity of the newly qualified individual. Freud put it as follows: "I leave them to climb an upward path, without leading them to the summit from which they would not be able to get any higher" (Schur, 1975). If training is seen as a process, it is clear that ideally the process would continue after basic training was finished. This would allow societies to have supplementary requirements beyond basic training. In particular, this would allow for assessment of the prospective member's ability to cope with uncertainty, not knowing, and doubt outside any institutional context, would round off her training, and would test her curiosity for exploration beyond the beaten path so as to open herself to new theoretical concepts current in other countries or in theoretical orientations different from those prevalent in the institute where she trained.

The societies would then be places of scientific exchange and places where people who wanted to share the same sort of professional interests could meet.

Power play or complementarity between psychoanalytic societies and societies for psychoanalytic psychotherapy

Freud's desire to control the analytic movement from behind the scenes by means of the secret committee demonstrated a certain mistrust of democratic rules of institutional functioning and, what is more, displayed a certain arrogance towards the external world (Eishold, 1994). This may have been one consequence of Freud's sense of isolation in Vienna and the critical attitude of the scientific world towards his theories. The secret committee ceased to meet after 1925, when rules were established for the recognition of the training institutes. From that time onwards, Freud attended none of the congresses. In this way, he gave the impression that the real value of analysis was to be found in the "splendid isolation" of solitary work, in contrast with social life, from which he no longer expected anything good after all his disappointments.

Psychoanalysis, by definition, faces the internal world, the past, and the world of thoughts and wishes actualized in the transference, not the external world or doing. The external world thus becomes a place into which all sorts of anxiety, disillusionment, indifference, and even mistrust get projected. Thus there arises, as Eishold (1994) describes, a particular analytic culture that sees itself as superior to the world around it. Power battles, political struggles, envious behaviour, and the compromises inevitable in society are regarded with an air of superiority and distance. Could we here be witnessing projection onto the external world of the mistrust that this same world had displayed towards Freud?

These debates are not new, as James Strachey showed in 1943, and I would like to quote him here at length:

> A political problem is not necessarily less important than a scientific one, it requires an entirely different manner of approach. Scientific problems must be faced with ruthless logic and clear-cut consistency: there is no half-way house between truth and falsehood. Administrative problems, with their considerations of expediency, their constant balancing of probabilities, call for flexibility and compromise. Yet there is no contradiction here. Political adaptability is not in the least incompatible with the strictest regard for scientific truth; nor for the matter of that, is rigidity in the application of a belief

any evidence that the belief so applied is a true one. [quoted in King & Steiner, 1991, pp. 602–603]

This withdrawal of the psychoanalytic societies from public affairs could partly explain the rapid growth in the last few decades of societies for psychoanalytic psychotherapy, whose members now greatly outnumber psychoanalysts. This situation has disquieting features for the latter. Directly competed with by numerous forms of "fast-food therapies", they fear a reduction in cases for analysis. They are equally afraid that insufficiently trained and analysed psychoanalytic psychotherapists, who nonetheless make reference to psychoanalysis, are set upon a course that will lead to dilution of the purity of theory and to compromises of the psychoanalytic framework.

At the social or political level, the psychoanalytic societies may also fear that the psychotherapists will cease to defend their own position of political non-engagement, and might be tempted to start discussions with the "powers that be" in order to secure legal status for psychotherapy, therefore implying clearly defined criteria for training. In this case, the psychotherapy societies would be engaged in struggles for real power. Here, in the psychotherapy societies, there may be an omnipotent fantasy of obtaining public powers, experienced as all good, and receiving protection by virtue of an official status. It is true that in countries where such status has existed for a long time, increasingly lively criticism takes place in analytic circles (Gattig, 1996: Lockot, 1988). The powers that be demand in return to have some right to inspect the psychoanalytic training institutes, which immediately lose their independence. Any form of control by the state or health authorities entails, or risks entailing, reduction in freedom of action and, worse still, loss of freedom of thought and thus of psychoanalysts' optimal work. Some psychoanalysts are justified in fearing that the official status of psychotherapist would automatically include psychoanalysts, and that the criteria for training psychotherapists would also be imposed upon themselves. Criteria for training would no longer depend exclusively upon an internal analytic process, but upon social criteria and therefore ones external to the psyche.

We should not delude ourselves: official status will not restore to the psychodynamic approach the lustre of bygone days. The development of a multitude of (psycho?)therapeutic techniques that therapists can assimilate quickly, together with the prospect that in the future psychotherapeutic care will not be given great priority by health authorities, oblige us to consider how to reoccupy the terrain. As Strachey stressed in the quotation above, such political thinking in no way diminishes the rigour of theoretical research.

Such conflicts are, indeed, in danger of masking the fact that amongst psychoanalysts the wider setting of their work is changing greatly, and that during the last twenty years or so the psychoanalytic or psychodynamic model has lost an enormous amount of ground in university and psychiatric hospital circles to biological, cognitive-behavioural, and neuro-scientific approaches. As Kernberg (1992) has shown, the psychoanalytic societies are largely responsible for this situation, although, as he suggests, the prestige that psychoanalysis still enjoys means that they still have a chance of reinvesting psychiatry departments with a strong presence and of re-establishing a constant and steady relationship with institutionalized psychiatry. This "would draw hospital psychiatrists and university psychologists towards the psychoanalytic institutes. . . . Psychiatrists and psychologists in training will go wherever things are happening". Kernberg thus presents the problem with great simplicity and profound common sense. Far from adopting a pious attitude towards "pure" psychoanalysis, I am deeply persuaded of an urgent need to reinvest institutions, especially the psychiatric hospitals, so as to promote and develop psychoanalytic psychotherapy in them.

Work in depth is necessary to adapt analytic theory and technique to the clinical specificities and particularities of the institutions, and especially to confront and collaborate with neuro-biological orientations.

Paradoxically, psychoanalysis could be strengthened by the development of psychoanalytic psychotherapy in the various different institutional spaces. In our own experience, many a future analyst's interest in psychoanalysis was aroused by encountering a psychoanalyst in a caregiving institution. This was not an encounter merely with a certain way of understanding theory in relation to clinical practice but, above all, with a certain way of being that was associated with a particular professional ethic.

Obviously, an increase in the number of psychoanalytic psychotherapists brings a need in the medium term to redefine the respective roles and functions of both of the psychoanalytic orientations, to redistribute responsibilities, and to create avenues for encounter so as to avoid the destructive effects of power play by employing the capacity for dialogue.

REFERENCES

About, E. (1996). Développement et identité. Existe-t-il une colonisation de la pensée? *Journal de Psychanalyse de l'Enfant, 19*: 48–68.

Allodi, F. (1989). The children of victims of political persecution and torture: a psychological study of a Latin American refugee community. *International Journal of Mental Health, 18*: 3–15.

Anzieu, D. (1974). Le moi-peau. *Nouvelle Revue de Psychanalyse, 9*: 195–208.

Anzieu, D. (1975). La fantasmatique de la formation psychanalytique. In: *Fantasme et formation*. Paris: Dunod.

Aparo, A., Casonato, M., & Vigorelli, M. (1989). *Modelli genetivi evolutivi in psycoanalisi*. Bologna: Il Mulino.

Arlow, J. A., & Brenner, C. (1969). The psychopathology of the psychoses: a proposed revision. *International Journal of Psycho-Analysis, 50*: 5–14.

Armelius, B.-A. (1991). University of Umea: the borderline patient project. In: L. E. Beutler & M. Crago (Eds.), *Psychotherapy Research* (pp. 243–250). Washington, DC: American Psychological Association.

Arrigoni Scortecci, M. (1988). The psychopathology of the psychoses: a proposed revision. *International Journal of Psycho-Analysis*, *50*: 5–14.

Baker, R. (1992). Psychosocial consequences for tortured refugees seeking asylum and refugee status in Europe. In: M. Basoglu (Ed.), *Torture and Its Consequences. Current Treatment Approaches* (pp. 83–106). Cambridge: Cambridge University Press.

Balint, M. (1968). *The Basic Fault*. London: Routledge.

Balint, M., Ornstein, P., & Balint, E. (1968). *Psychotherapy: An Example of Applied Psychoanalysis*. London: Tavistock.

Barnes, E. (Ed.) (1968). *Psychosocial Nursing: Studies from the Cassel Hospital*. London: Tavistock.

Barocas, H. A., & Barocas, C. B. (1980). Separation-individuation conflicts in children of holocaust survivors. *Journal of Contemporary Psychotherapy*, *11* (1): 6–14.

Bateman, A. (1995). The treatment of borderline patients in a day hospital setting. *Psychoanalytic Psychotherapy 9* (1): 3–16.

Becker, H., & Senf, W. (1988). *Praxis der stationären Psychotherapie*. Stuttgart: Thieme.

Becker, S. (1987). Loslassen und nicht Fallenlassen: Die psychotherapeutische Arbeit mit Eltern als Funktion der Ablösung von Kindern und Jugendlichen. In: R. Lempp (Ed.), *Reifung und Ablösung: Das Generationenproblem und seine pathologischen Randformen* (pp. 69–77). Bern: Huber.

Bell, D. (1997). In-patient psychotherapy: the art of the impossible. *Psychoanalytic Psychotherapy*, *11*: 3–18.

Bellak, L., & Small, L. (1972). *Kurzpsychotherapie und Notfallpsychotherapie*. Frankfurt am Main: Suhrkamp.

Benedetti, G., Corsi Piacentini, T., D'Alfonso, L., Elia, C., Medri, G., & Saviotti, M. (1979). *Paziente e analista nella terapia delle psicosi*. Milan: Feltrinelli.

Berger, M. (1993). *La folie cachée des hommes politiques*. Paris: Albin Michel.

Bergman, M. S., & Jucovy, M. E. (Eds.) (1982). *Generations of the Holocaust*. New York: Basic Books.

Besserman Vianna, H. (1997). *N'en parlez a personne. Politique de la psychanalyse face à la dictature et à la torture*. Paris: L'Harmattan.

Bettelheim, B. (1976). *The Uses of Enchantment*. New York: Knopf.

Bion, W. R. (1959). Attacks on linking. *International Journal of Psycho-Analysis, 40*: 308–315.

Bion, W. R. (1961). *Experiences in Groups and Other Papers*. London: Tavistock Publications.

Bion, W. R. (1962). A theory of thinking. In: *Second Thoughts*. London: Karnac Books, 1984.

Bion, W. R. (1963). *Elements of Psycho-Analysis*. London: Heinemann. [Reprinted London: Karnac Books, 1984.]

Bion W. R. (1970). *Attention and Interpretation. A Scientific Approach to Insight in Psycho-Analysis and Groups*. London: Tavistock Publications. [Reprinted London: Karnac Books, 1988.]

Bleger, J. (1967). Psychoanalysis of the psychoanalytic frame. *International Journal of Psycho-Analysis, 48*: 511–519.

Bleger, J. (1970). Le groupe comme institution et le groupe dans les institutions. In: R. Kaës, J. Bleger, et al. (Eds.), *L'Institution et les Institutions*. Paris: Bordas, 1988.

Borghi, M. (1991). *Evaluation de l'efficacité de la législation sur la privation de liberté à des fins d'assistance*. Agno: Pro Mente Sana.

Britton, R. S. (1983). Breakdown and reconstitution of the family circle. In: M. Boston & R. Szur (Eds.), *Psychotherapy with Severely Deprived Children* (pp. 105–109). London: Routledge & Kegan Paul. [Reprinted London: Karnac Books, 1987.]

Britton, R. S. (1989). The missing link: parental sexuality in the Oedipus complex. In: J. Steiner (Ed.), *The Oedipus Complex Today*. London: Karnac Books.

Bruni, A. (1985). Il gruppo che non c'è: un riferimento sulla separazione. *Gruppo e funzione analitica, 7* (1): 41–47.

Burnham, D. L., Gibson, R., & Gladstone, A. (1969). *Schizophrenia and the Need-Fear Dilemma*. New York: International Universities Press.

Cahn, T. (1995). Gewalt—Element des psychiatrischen Berufs. *Schweizer Archiv für Neurologie und Psychiatrie, 146*: 109–114.

Callens, K., & Vermote, R. (1994). *Long-term Residential Psychoanalytic Psychotherapy*. Paper presented at the European Congress on Personality Disorders, Nijmegen, 14 June.

Caltagirone, I., & Smargiassi, M. (1997). Therapeutic and non-therapeutic communities. *International Journal for Therapeutic and Supportive Organisations, 18* (3): 167–181.

Carels, N., & Gauthier, J.-M. (1996). Freud, l'individu et le groupe: hier et aujourd'hui. *Revue Belge de Psychanalyse*, 29: 3–32.

Chapman, G. (1984). A therapeutic community, psychosocial nursing and the nursing process. *International Journal of Therapeutic Communities*, 5: 68–76.

Chiesa, M. C. (1989). Different origins and meanings of acute acting-out in an in-patient psychotherapeutic setting. *Psychoanalytic Psychotherapy*, 4 (2): 155–168.

Cohn, J., Danielsen, L., Holzer, K.I.M., Koch, L., Severin, B., Thøgersen, S., & Aalund, O. (1985). A study of Chilean refugee children in Denmark. *Lancet*, 24: 437–438.

Copley, B. (1987). Explorations with families. *Journal of Child Psychotherapy*, 13 (1): 93–108.

Corrao, F. (1982). Psicoanalisi e ricerca di gruppo. *Gruppo e funzione analitica*, 3 (3): 23–27.

Correale, A. (1991). *Il campo istituzionale*. Rome: Borla.

Correale, A. (1995). *Fattori terapeutici nei gruppi e nelle istituzioni*. Roma: Borla.

Correale, A. (1996). *Group Factors in a Therapeutic Community*. Paper presented at the International Congress on "The Therapeutic Community between Myth and Reality", Milan, 7–8 June 1996.

Correale, A. (1997). Le terapie analiticamente orientate delle psicosi: la nozione di campo e la funzione dell'empatia. In: A. Correale & L. Rinaldi (Eds.), *Quale psicoanalisi per le psicosi?* Milan: Raffaello Cortina.

Correale, A., & Rinaldi, L. (Eds.) (1997). *Quale psicoanalisi per le psicosi?* Milano: Raffaello Cortina.

Cumming, J., & Cumming, E. (1962). *Ich und Milieu—Theorie und Praxis der Milieutherapie*. Göttingen: Vandenhoeck & Ruprecht.

Danckwardt, J. F. (1978). Zur Interaktion von Psychotherapie und Psychopharmakotherapie. *Psyche*, 32: 111–154.

Danieli, Y. (1981). Differing adaptational styles in families of survivors of the Nazi holocaust. *Children Today* (September–October): 6–10, 34–35.

Danieli, Y. (1984). Psychotherapists' participation in the conspiracy of silence about the holocaust. *Psychoanalytic Psychology*, 1 (1): 23–42.

De Martis, D., Petrella, F., & Ambrosi, P. (Eds.) (1987). *Fare e pensare in psichiatria*. Milan: Cortina.

Denford, J., & Griffiths, P. (1993). "Transferences to the Institution" and their effect on in-patient treatment at the Cassel Hospital. *Therapeutic Communities, 14*: 237–248.

Dornes, M. (1993). *Der kompetente Säugling. Die präverbale Entwicklung des Menschen.* Frankfurt: Fischer.

du Bois, R. (1996). *Junge Schizophrene zwischen Alltag und Klinik. Alterstypisches Erleben, Betreuungsformen und Weichenstellungen am Krankheitsbeginn.* Göttingen: Verlag für angewandte Psychologie.

du Bois, R., Günter, M., & Kleefeld, H. (1987). Der betreuerische Alltag in der Langzeitpsychotherapie psychotischer Jugendlicher—am Beispiel von Störungen der Reifung und Ablösung—eine Bestandsaufnahme. In: R. Lempp (Ed.), *Reifung und Ablösung. Das Generationenproblem und seine pathologischen Randformen* (pp. 118–142). Bern: Huber.

du Bois, R., Günter, M., Koller, D., & Zimmermann, B. (1990). Die Zeit in der Klinik, die Zeit danach—die biographische Bedeutung der stationären Langzeittherapie anhand von drei- bis zehnjährigen Katamnesen. In: R. Lempp (Ed.), *Die Therapie der Psychosen im Kindes- und Jugendalter* (pp. 196–206). Bern: Huber.

Dupont, J. (1988). Ferenczi's "madness". *Contemporary Psychoanalysis, 24*: 250.

Eigen, M. (1985). Toward Bion's starting point: between catastrophe and faith. *International Journal of Psycho-Analysis, 66*: 321–330.

Eishold, K. (1994). The intolerance of diversity in psychoanalytic institutes. *International Journal of Psycho-Analysis, 75*: 785–800.

Engel, K. M., Hentze, M., & Wittern, M. (1992). Long-term outcome in anorexia nervosa in-patients. In: W. D. Herzog, H.-C. Deter, & W. Vandereycken (Eds.), *The Course of Eating Disorders* (pp. 118–132). Berlin: Springer.

Enriquez, E. (1987). Le travail de la mort dans les institutions. In: *L'institution et les institutions.* Paris: Dunod.

Erdheim, M. (1982). *Die gesellschaftliche Produktion von Unbewusstheit— eine Einführung in den ethnopsychoanalytischen Prozess.* Frankfurt am Main: Suhrkamp.

Federn, E. (1974). Brief eines Entronnenen. *Psyche, 28*: 266–268.

Federn, P. (1952). *Ego Psychology and the Psychoses.* New York: Basic Books. [Reprinted London: Karnac Books, 1977.]

Fenichel, O. (1935). Concerning psychoanalysis, war and peace. *Internationales Ärtzliches Bulletin, 2*: 30–40.

Ferenczi, S. (1928). The problem of the termination of the analysis. In:

Final Contributions to the Problems and Methods of Psycho-Analysis (pp. 77–86). London: Hogarth Press, 1955. [Reprinted London: Karnac Books, 1994.]

Flynn, C. (1993). The patients' pantry: the nature of the nursing task. *Therapeutic Communities, 14:* 227–236.

Fornari, F. (1971). Pour une psychanalyse des institutions. *Connexions, 8:* 90–122.

Foulkes, S. H. (1946). On group psychoanalysis. *International Journal of Psycho-Analysis, 27:* 51.

Foulkes, S. H. (1964). *Therapeutic Group Analysis.* London: Allen & Unwin.

Foulkes, S. H. (1975). *Group-Analytic Psychotherapy.* London: Gordon & Breach. [Reprinted London: Karnac Books, 1988.]

Freud, A. (1926–45). *The Psycho-Analytical Treatment of Children.* New York: International Universities Press, 1955.

Freud, A. (1965). *Normality and Pathology in Childhood. Assessments of Development.* New York: International Universities Press. [Reprinted London: Karnac Books, 1989.]

Freud, A. (1967). Comments on psychic trauma. In: *The Writings of Anna Freud, Vol. V: Research at the Hampstead Clinic and Other Papers, 1956–1965* (pp. 221–241). New York: International Universities Press, 1969.

Freud, S. (1911c [1910]). Psychoanalytic notes on an autobiographical account of a case of paranoia. *S.E., 12.*

Freud, S. (1912b). The dynamics of transference. *S.E., 12.*

Freud, S. (1912–13). *Totem and Taboo. S.E., 13.*

Freud, S. (1914c). On narcissism: an introduction. *S.E., 14.*

Freud, S. (1914g). Remembering, repeating and working through. *S.E., 12.*

Freud, S. (1916–1917). *Introductory Lectures on Psycho-Analysis. S.E., 16.*

Freud, S. (1921c). *Group Psychology and the Analysis of the Ego. S.E., 18.*

Freud, S. (1926d [1925]). *Inhibitions, Symptoms and Anxiety. S.E., 20.*

Freud, S. (1927e). Fetishism. *S.E., 21.*

Freud, S. (1940e [1938]). Splitting of the ego in the process of defence. *S.E., 23.*

Friedman, J. (1989). Therapy, play and the therapeutic household. In: R. Cooper, J. Friedman, S. Gans, J. M. Heaton, C. Oakley, H. Oakley, & P. Zeal (Eds.), *Thresholds between Philosophy and Psy-*

choanalysis: Papers from the Philadelphia Association. London: Free Association Books.

Furlan, P. M. (1997). *Italian Psychiatry Twenty Years after the Reform*. Paper given at the Twelfth International Symposium for the Psychotherapy of Schizophrenia, London, 12–16 October.

Gabbard, G. O. (1990). *Psychodynamic Psychiatry in Hospital Practice*. Washington, DC: American Psychiatric Press.

Gaensburger, T. J. (1995). Trauma in the preverbal period: symptoms, memories and developmental impact. *Psychoanalytic Study of the Child, 50*: 123–149.

Gampel, Y. (1996). The interminable uncanniness. In: L. Rangell & R. Moses-Hrushovski (Eds.), *Psychoanalysis at the Political Border: Essays in Honor of Rafael Moses* (pp. 85–98). Madison, CT: International Universities Press.

Gattig, E. (1996). Rapport de l'Association Allemande de Psychanalyse. *Psychanalyse en Europe, 47*, Bulletin de la Fédération Européenne de Psychanalyse.

Glasser, M. (1979). Some aspects of the role of aggression in the perversions. In: I. Rosen (Ed.), *Sexual Deviation* (pp. 278–305). London: Oxford University Press.

Glasser, M. (1992). Problems in the psychoanalysis of certain narcissistic disorders. *International Journal of Psycho-Analysis, 73*: 493–503.

Godfrind, J. (1993). *Les Deux Courants du Transfert*. Paris: P.U.F.

Goffmann, E. (1961). *Asylums. Essays on the Social Situation of Mental Patients and Other Inmates*. Garden City, NY: Doubleday.

Golding, W. (1980). *Darkness Visible*. London: Faber & Faber.

Green, A. (1992). Préalables à une discussion sur la fonction de la théorie. *Revue Française de Psychanalyse. 56* (2): 507–514.

Greenson, R., & Wexler, M. (1969). The non-transference relationship in the psychoanalytic situation. *International Journal of Psycho-Analysis, 50*: 27–39.

Griffiths, P., & Hinshelwood, R. (1995). *A Culture of Enquiry: Life Within a Hall of Mirrors*. Paper given at the ISPSO Symposium, London, July 1995.

Griffiths, P., & Leach, G. (1997). Psychosocial nursing: a model learnt from experience. In: E. Barnes, P. Griffiths, J. Ord, & D. Wells (Eds.), *Face to Face with Distress. The Professional Use of Self in Psychosocial Care*. London: Butterworth Heinemann.

Grosskurth, P. (1995). *The Secret Ring: Freud's Inner Circle and the Politics of Psychoanalysis*. London: Jonathan Cape.

Grubich-Simitis, I. (1981). From concretism to metaphor: thoughts on some theoretical and technical aspects of the psychoanalytic work with children of holocaust survivors. *Psychoanalytic Study of the Child*, 36: 415–451.

Grünbaum, L. (1997). Psychotherapy with children in refugee families who have survived torture: containment and understanding of repetitive behaviour and play. *Journal of Child Psychotherapy*, 23 (3): 437–452.

Günter, M. (1987). Die therapeutische Regression als Möglichkeit zur Reifung in der Behandlung psychotischer Jugendlicher. In: R. Lempp (Ed.), *Reifung und Ablösung. Das Generationenproblem und seine pathologischen Randformen* (pp. 95–105). Bern: Huber.

Günter, M., & Becker, S. (1990). Psychopharmaka als Hilfsmittel in der stationären Psychotherapie schizophrener Jugendlicher. In: R. Lempp (Ed.), *Die Therapie der Psychosen im Kindes- und Jugendalter* (pp. 153–157). Bern: Huber.

Günter, M., du Bois, R., & Kleefeld, H. (1989). Das Problem rasch wechselnder Ich-Zustände in der stationären Langzeittherapie psychotischer Jugendlicher. *Praxis der Kinderpsychologie und Kinderpsychiatrie*, 38: 250–256.

Günter, M., Karle, M., Kleefeld, H., Werning, A., & Klosinski, G. (1997). Stationäre jugendpsychiatrisch-psychotherapeutische Krisenintervention. Erfahrungen mit dem Management und therapeutischen Techniken. In: G. Klosinski (Ed.), *Stationäre Behandlungen psychischer Störungen im Kindes- und Jugendalter. Brennpunkte und Entwicklungen* (pp. 65–74). Bern: Huber.

Gustafsson, L. H., Lindkvist, A., & Bøhm, B. (1987). *Barn i krig: röster och fakta*. Stockholm: Verbum Gothia, 1988.

Harpman, J. (1992). A propos de la pulsion épistémophilique. *Revue Belge de Psychanalyse*, 20: 39–53.

Harris, M. (1968). The child psychotherapist and the patient's family. In: M. H. Williams (Ed.), *Collected Papers of Martha Harris and Esther Bick* (pp. 18–37). Perthshire: Clunie Press, 1987.

Hartocollis, P. (1980). Long-term hospital treatment for adult patients with borderline and narcissistic disorders. *Bulletin of the Menninger Clinic*, 44: 212–226.

Hartmann, H. (1953). *Contributions to the metapsychology of schizophre-*

nia. Essay on Ego Psychology. New York: International Universities Press.

Haynal, A. (1988). *The Technique at Issue*. London: Karnac Books.

Hinshelwood, R. D. (1989). *A Dictionary of Kleinian Thought*. London: Free Association Books.

Hinshelwood, R. D. (1996). *Cultural Pressure on the Therapeutic Community: Internal and External Factors*. Paper presented at the International Congress on the "Therapeutic Community between Myth and Reality", Milan, 7–8 June.

Hinshelwood, R., & Griffiths, P. (1996). *Actions Speak Louder Than Words*. Paper given at the Day Conference, Maidstone, November.

Hollós, I. (1914). Psychoanalytische beleuchtung eines Falles von Dementia Praecox. *Internationale Zeitschrift für Psychoanalyse, 2*: 376–385.

Hollós, I. (1925). *Búcsúm a Sárga Háztól*. Budapest: Cserépfalvi (revised edition, 1990). [German translation, *Hinter der Gelben Mauer*. Stuttgart: Hippokrates, 1928. French translation, by J. Dupont, *Mes Adieux à la Maison Juane*. Paris: Coq-Heron, 1986.]

Hollós, I. (1946). Letter to Paul Federn. *Psyche, 28* (1974): 266–268.

Hughes, P. M., & Halek, C. (1991). Training nurses in psychotherapeutic skills. *Psychoanalytic Psychotherapy, 5* (2): 115–123.

Irwin, F. (1995). The therapeutic ingredients in baking a cake. *Therapeutic Communities, 16*: 263–268.

Jacobson, E. (1954). On psychotic identification. *International Journal of Psycho-Analysis, 35*: 102.

James, O. (1987). The role of the nurse/therapist relationship in the therapeutic community. In: R. Kennedy, A. Heymans, & L. Tischler (Eds.), *The Family as In-Patient: Families and Adolescents at the Cassel Hospital* (pp. 78–94). London: Free Association Books.

Janssen, P. (1987). *Psychoanalytic Therapy in the Hospital Setting*. London: Routledge, 1994.

Janssen, P. (1993). The evolution of in-patient psychoanalytic therapy in Germany. *Therapeutic Communities, 14*: 265–274.

Jaques, E. (1953). The social system as a defence against persecutory and depressive anxiety. In: M. Klein, P. Heimann, & R. Money-Kyrle (Eds.), *New Directions in Psychoanalysis*. London: Tavistock, 1955.

Jones, E. (1964). *The Life and Work of Sigmund Freud* (abridged edition), ed. by L. Trilling & S. Marcus. Harmondsworth: Pelican Books.

Jones, M. (1968). *Beyond the Therapeutic Community: Social Learning and Social Psychiatry*. New Haven, CT: Yale University Press.

Kahr, B. (1993). Ancient infanticide and modern schizophrenia: the clinical uses of psychohistorical research. *Journal of Psychohistory*, 20: 267–73.

Kelly, K. A. (1993). Multiple personality disorders: treatment coordination in a partial hospital setting. *Bulletin of the Menninger Clinic*, 57: 390–398.

Kennedy, R., Heymans, A., & Tischler, L. (Eds.) (1987). *The Family as In-Patient: Families and Adolescents at the Cassel Hospital*. London: Free Association Books.

Kernberg, O. F. (1976). *Object Relations Theory and Hospital Psychoanalysis*. New York: Jason Aronson.

Kernberg, O. F. (1980). *Internal World and External Reality: Object Relations Theory Applied*. New York: Jason Aronson.

Kernberg, O. F. (1982). Psychoanalytische Objektbeziehungstheorie, Gruppenprozesse und klinische Institution. In: P. Kutter (Ed.), *Psychologie der zwischenmenschlichen Beziehungen. Psychoanalytische Beiträge zu einer Objektbeziehungs-Psychologie* (pp. 313–355). Darmstadt: Wissenschaftliche Buchgesellscaft.

Kernberg, O. F. (1984). *Severe Personality Disorders*. New Haven: Yale University Press.

Kernberg, O. F. (1992). La situation actuelle de la psychanalyse. *Revue Française de Psychanalyse, 56*, 2: 491–504..

Kernberg, O.F. (1996a). A psychoanalytical theory of personality disorders. In: J. F. Clarkin & M. F. Linzenweger (Eds.), *Major Theories of Personality Disorder* (pp. 106–140). New York: Guilford Press.

Kernberg, O. F. (1996b). Thirty methods to destroy the creativity of candidates. *International Journal of Psycho-Analysis, 77*: 1031–1040.

Kibel, H. D. (1987). In-patient group psychotherapy—where treatment philosophies converge. *Yearbook of Psychoanalysis and Psychotherapy, 2*: 94–116.

King, P., & Steiner, R. (1991). *The Freud–Klein Controversies, 1941–1945*. London: Routledge.

Kjersem, H. J. (1996). *Migrationsmedicin i Danmark: vurdering of nogle migrationsmedicinske problemstillinger blandt asylansøgere og flygtninge*. Viborg: Dansk Røde Kors. [Ph.D. dissertation.]

Klein, M. (1929). Infantile anxiety-situations reflected in a work of art and in the creative impulse. In: *Love, Guilt and Reparation and Other*

Works (pp. 210–218). London: Hogarth Press, 1975. [Reprinted London: Karnac Books, 1993.]

Klein, M. (1932). *The Psycho-Analysis of Children*. London: Hogarth Press, 1963. [Reprinted London: Karnac Books, 1998.]

Klein, M. (1946). Notes on some schizoid mechanisms. In: *Envy and Gratitude and Other Works*. London: Virago Press, 1989. [Reprinted London: Karnac Books, 1994.]

Klein, M. (1952a). Some theoretical conclusions regarding the emotional life of the infant. In: J. Riviere (Ed.), *Developments in Psycho-Analysis*. London: Hogarth.

Klein, M. (1952b). The origins of transference. In: *Envy and Gratitude and Other Works* (pp. 48–56). London: Virago, 1989. [Reprinted London: Karnac Books, 1994.]

Klüwer, R. (1983). Agieren und Mitagieren. *Psyche, 37*: 828–840.

Kris, E. (1956). The recovery of childhood memories in psychoanalysis. *Psychoanalytic Study of the Child, 11*: 54–88.

Krystal, H. (1971). Review of the findings and implications of this symposium. In: H. Krystal & W. G. Niederland (Eds.), *Psychic Traumatization* (pp. 217–229). Boston: International Psychiatry Clinics.

Krystal, H., & Niederland, W. G. (1968). Clinical observations on the survivor syndrome. In: H. Krystal (Ed.), *Massive Psychic Trauma* (pp. 327–348). New York: International Universities Press.

Kutter, P. (1992). *Psychoanalysis International. A Guide to Psychoanalysis throughout the World*. Stuttgart: Frommann-Holzboog.

Lanzara, D. (1994). Pluralità delle strutture e differenziazione degli interventi nell'articolazione del trattamento delle psicosi. In: M. Vigorelli (Ed.), *Istituzione tra inerzia e cambiamento*. Turin: Bollati Boringhieri.

Laplanche, J., & Pontalis, J.-B. (1967). *Vocabulaire de psychanalyse*. Paris: PUF.

Laub, D., & Auerhahn, N. C. (1993). Knowing and not knowing. Massive psychic trauma: forms of traumatic memory. *International Journal of Psycho-Analysis, 74*: 287–302.

Laufer, M., & Laufer, M. E. (1984). *Adolescence and Developmental Breakdown*. New Haven, CT: Yale University Press. [Reprinted London: Karnac Books, 1995.]

Leuschner, W. (1985). Psychiatrische Anstalten—ein institutionalisiertes Abwehrsystem, Teil I und Teil II. *Psychiatrische Praxis, 12*: 111–115, 149–153.

Levinson, A. (1996). The struggle to keep a culture of enquiry alive at the Cassel Hospital. *Therapeutic Communities, 17*: 47–57.

Lévy, L. (1957). Obituary of Istvan Hollós. *International Journal of Psychoanalysis, 38*: 280–281.

Lockot, R. (1988). Répétition ou nouveau départ? A propos du rétablissement de la psychanalyse en R.F.A. après la guerre. *Revue Internationale d'Histoire de la Psychanalyse, 1*: 117–131.

London, N. J. (1973): An essay on psychoanalytic theory: two theories of schizophrenia. *International Journal of Psycho-Analysis, 54*: 169–193.

Lukman, B., & Bach-Mortensen, N. (1995). Symptoms of children of torture victims—post-traumatic stress disorders? *World Pediatrics and Child Care, 5*: 42.

Lussier, A. (1992). Notre idéologie de formation. *Revue Française de Psychanalyse, 56* (2): 483–490.

Mahler, M. (1968). *On Human Symbiosis and the Vicissitudes of Individuation, Vol. 1. Infantile Psychosis*. New York: International Universities Press.

Main, T. F. (1946). The hospital as a therapeutic institution. *Bulletin of the Menninger Clinic, 10*: 66–70. [Reprinted in: T. Main (Ed.), *The Ailment and Other Psychoanalytic Essays* (pp. 7–11). London: Free Association Books, 1989.]

Main, T. F. (1967). Knowledge, learning and freedom from thought. *Australia & New Zealand Journal of Psychiatry, 1*: 64–71.

Main, T. F. (1977). The concept of the therapeutic community: variations and vicissitudes. *Group Analysis [Supp.], 10*: 1–16.

Main, T. F. (1983). The concept of the therapeutic community: variations and vicissitudes. In: T. Main (Ed.), *The Ailment and Other Psychoanalytic Essays* (pp. 123–141). London: Free Association Books, 1989.

Main, T. F. (1989). *The Ailment and Other Psychoanalytic Essays*. London: Free Association Books.

Main, T.F. (1992). A few glances at psychiatry. *Psychoanalytic Psychotherapy, 6* (3): 249–260.

Mannoni, M. (1967). *The Child, His Illness and the Other*. London: Penguin. [Reprinted London: Karnac Books, 1988.]

Mannoni, M. (1970). *Le psychiatre, son "fou" et la psychanalyse*. Paris: Seuil.

Matakas, F. (1988). Psychoanalyse in der Anstalt. *Psyche, 42*: 132–158.

McCaffrey, G. (1994). An account of outreach nursing at the Cassel Hospital. *Therapeutic Communities, 15*: 173–181.

Meltzer, D. (1967). *The Psycho-Analytical Process*. Perthshire: Clunie Press, 1979.

Meltzer, D. (1994). Towards an atelier system. In: *Sincerity and Other Works* (pp. 285–289). London: Karnac Books.

Mentzos, S. (1990). *Interpersonale und institutionelle Abwehr*. Frankfurt am Main: Suhrkamp.

Montgomery, E. (1996). *Flygtningebørn fra Mellemøsten*. Copenhagen: Rehabilitation and Research Centre for Torture Victims. [Ph.D. dissertation.]

Montgomery, E., Krogh, Y., Jacobsen, A., & Lukman, B. (1992). Children of torture victims: reactions and coping. *Child Abuse and Neglect, 16*: 797–805.

Neimeyer, R. A., Baker, K. D., Haykal, R. F., & Akiskal, H. S. (1995). Patterns of symptomatic change in depressed patients in a private in-patient mood disorders program. *Bulletin of the Menninger Clinic, 59* (4): 460–471.

Neri, C. (1991). *Campo: tre possibili impieghi e linee disviluppo dell'idea, in ambito psicoanalitico e psichiatrico*. Paper presented at the Meeting "I confini dell'individuo e del gruppo", Florence.

Neri, C. (1995). *Gruppo*. Rome: Borla.

Norton, K. (1992). A culture of enquiry—its preservation or loss. *Therapeutic Communities, 13*: 3–25.

Obholzer, A., & Roberts, V. G. (1994) (Eds.). *The Unconscious at Work*. London: Routledge.

Orgel, S. (1990). The future of psychoanalysis. *Psychoanalytic Quarterly, 59*: 511–515.

Pailthorpe, G. (1932). *Studies in the Psychology of Delinquency*. London: HMSO.

Pankow, G. (1976). Das Körperbild in der hysterischen Psychose. *Zeitschrift für Klinische Psychiatrie und Psychotherapie, 24*: 223–250.

Pao, P. N. (1979). *Schizophrenic Disorders*. New York: International Universities Press.

Paumelle, Ph. (1970). L'apport psychanalytique à la pratique psychiatrique de secteur. *Information Psychiatrique, 46* (10): 917–925.

Petrella, F. (1978). *Proceedings of the Meeting "Psicoanalisi e Istituzioni"*. Florence: Le Monnier.

Piaget, J., & Inhelder, B. (1966). *La Psychologie de L'Enfant*. Paris: PUF.

Pynoos, R. S., Steinberg, A. M., & Wraith, R. (1995). A developmental model of childhood traumatic stress. In: D. Cichetti & D. J. Cohen (Eds.), *Developmental Psychopathology, Vol. 2: Risk, Disorder and Adaptation* (pp. 72–95). New York: Wiley.

Racamier, P. C. (1970). *Le psychanalyste sans divan*. Paris: Payot.

Racamier, P. C. (1978). *Un foyer de cure psychothérapique. Réflexions à partir d'une experience de vingt années*. Milan: Cortina, 1998.

Racamier, P.C. (1992). *Le génie des origines. Psychanalyse et psychoses*. Paris: Payot.

Rascovsky, A., & Rascovsky, M. (1968). On the genesis of acting out and psychopathic behaviour in Sophocles' Oedipus. *International Journal of Psycho-Analysis, 49*: 390–395.

Rice, A. K. (1965). *Führung und Gruppe*. Stuttgart: Klett.

Rice, A. K. (1976). Individual, group and intergroup processes. In: F. J. Miller (Ed.), *Task and Organization*. London: Wiley.

Rinsley, D. B. (1974). *Treatment of the Severely Disturbed Adolescent*. New York: Jason Aronson.

Rosen, I. (1979) (Ed.). *Sexual Deviation* (second edition). Oxford: Oxford University Press.

Rosenbluth, M., & Silver, D. (1992). The in-patient treatment of borderline personality disorder. In: D. R. Silver & M. Madison (Eds.), *Handbook of Borderline Disorders* (pp. 509–532). Madison, CT: International Universities Press.

Rosenfeld, H. A. (1971). Contribution to the psychopathology of psychotic states. In: E. Bott Spillius (Ed.), *Melanie Klein Today, Vol. 1* (pp. 117–137). London: Routledge, 1988.

Roussillon, R. (1978). L'Institution-environnement. *Bulletin de psychologie clinique* (Lyon), 2.

Roussillon, R. (1995). *Logiques et archéologiques du cadre psychanalytique*. Paris: PUF.

Sandler, J. (1967). Trauma, strain, and development. In: S. S. Furst (Ed.), *Psychic Trauma* (pp. 154–174). New York: Basic Books.

Sandler, J. (1976). Gegenübertragung und Bereitschaft zur Rollenübernahme. *Psyche, 30*: 297–305

Sandler, J., Kennedy, H., & Tyson, R. L. (1980). *The Technique of Child Psychoanalysis: Discussions with Anna Freud*. Cambridge, MA: Harvard University Press.

Sassolas, M. (1987). Comment s'articulent, dans une structure intermédiaire, dynamique institutionelle et dynamique individuelle? *Revue Médicale de la Suisse Romande, 107*.

Scheeringa, M. S., Zeanah, C. H., Drell, M. J., & Larrieu, J. A. (1995). Two approaches to the diagnosis of post-traumatic stress disorder in infancy and early childhood. *Journal of American Academy of Child and Adolescent Psychiatry, 34* (2): 191–200.

Schilder, P. (1935). *The Image and Appearance of the Human Body* (Psyche Monographs 4). London: Kegan, Trench, Trubner. [Reprinted New York: International Universities Press, 1970.]

Schur, M. (1975). *La mort dans la vie de Freud*. Paris: Gallimard.

Searles, H. (1959). Integration and differentation in schizophrenia: an over-all view. In: *Collected Papers on Schizophrenia and Related Subjects* (pp. 317–348). London: Hogarth Press, 1965. [Reprinted London: Karnac Books, 1986.]

Searles, H. (1965). *Collected Papers on Schizophrenia and Related Subjects*. London: Hogarth Press. [Reprinted London: Karnac Books, 1986.]

Simmel, E. (1928). Die psychoanalytische Behandlung in der Klinik. *Internazionale Zeitschrift für Psychoanalyse 14*: 352–370.

Sinason, V. (1989). The psycho-linguistics of discrimination. In: B. Richards (Ed.), *Crises of the Self: Further Essays on Psychoanalysis and Politics*. London: Free Association Books.

Sinason, V. (Ed.) (1994). *Treating Survivors of Satanist Abuse*. London: Routledge.

Sinason, V. (1996). From abused to abuser. In: C. Cordess & M. Cox (Eds.), *Forensic Psychotherapy, Vol. 2: Mainly Practice* (pp. 371–383). London: Jessica Kingsley.

Somnier, F., Vesti, P., Kastrup, M., & Genefke, I. K. (1992). Psychosocial consequences of torture: current knowledge and evidence. In: M. Basoglu (Ed.), *Torture and Its Consequences* (pp. 136–148). Glasgow: Cambridge University Press.

Stanton, A., & Schwartz, M. (1954). *The Mental Hospital*. New York: Basic Books.

Steiner, J. (1993). *Psychic Retreats*. London: Routledge.

Stern, D. (1986). *The Interpersonal World of the Infant*. New York: Basic Books. [Reprinted London: Karnac Books, 1998.]

Stewart, H. (1961). Jocasta's crimes. *International Journal of Psycho-Analysis, 42* (2): 424–430.

Streeck, U. (1991). Klinische Psychotherapie als Fokalbehandlung. *Zeitschrift für psychosomatische Medizin, 37*: 3–13 .

Terr, L. C. (1991). Childhood traumas: an outline and overview. *American Journal of Psychiatry, 148* (1): 10–20.

Thomas, W. J. (1966). *Person und Sozialverhalten. Soziologische Texte, Vol. 26.* Neuwied: Luchterhand.

Tischler, L. (1987). Nurse/therapist supervision. In: R. Kennedy, A. Heymans, & L. Tischler (Eds.), *The Family as In-Patient: Families and Adolescents at the Cassel Hospital* (pp. 95–107). London: Free Association Books.

Treurniet, N. (1996). Über eine Ethik der psychoanalytischen Technik. *Psyche, 50*: 1–31.

Trimborn, W. (1994). Analytiker und Rahmen als Garanten des therapeutischen Prozesses. *Psychotherapeut, 39*: 94–103.

Tucker, L., Bauer, S. F., Wagner, S., Harlam, D., & Sher, I. (1992). Specialized extended hospital treatment for borderline patients. *Bulletin of the Menninger Clinic, 56*: 465–478.

Tustin, F. (1986). *Autistic Barriers in Neurotic Patients.* London: Karnac Books.

United Nations (1959). *Declaration of the Rights of the Child.* New York (20 November).

United Nations (1984). *Convention against Torture and Other Cruel, Inhuman or Degrading Treatment and Punishment.* New York (10 December).

United Nations (1997). *Multilateral Treaties Deposited with the Secretary-General* (ST/LEG/SER.E). New York (March 25).

Vandereycken, W. P. G. (1992). A large-scale longitudinal follow-up study of patients with eating disorders; methodological issues and preliminary results. In: W. D. Herzog, H.-C., & W. Vandereycken (Eds.), *The Course of Eating Disorders* (pp. 182–197). Berlin: Springer.

Vansina-Cobbaert, M. J. (1996). Pour le meilleur et pour le pire: le lien entre l'individu et le groupe. *Revue Belge de Psychanalyse, 29*: 33–46.

Vermote, R. (1995). Réalité psychique et formes. *Revue Belge de Psychoanalyse, 27*: 39–53.

Vermote, R. (1996). Een setting voor de behandeling van persoonlijkheidsstoornissen. *Tijdschrift voor Cliëntgerichte Psychotherapie, 34* (3): 39–48.

Vermote, R. (1997). Helende factoren in de behandeling van pre-oedipale stoornissen. In: M. Hebbrecht (Ed.), *Bouwen aan een Basis* (pp. 20–33). St.-Truiden: Sancta Maria.

Vigorelli, M. (Ed.) (1994). *Istituzione tra inerzia e cambiamento*. Turin: Bollati Boringhieri.

Welldon, E. (1988). *Mother, Madonna, Whore. The idealisation and denigration of motherhood*. London: Free Association Books.

Werbart, A. (1995). The future of psychotherapeutic environments: learning from experience at a Swedish therapeutic Community. *Psychoanalytic Psychotherapy, 9* (3): 296–287.

Wexler, M. (1971). Schizophrenia: conflict and deficiency. *Psychoanalytic Quarterly, 40*: 83–89.

Wilson, J. P., & Lindy, J. D. (1994). Empathic strain and countertransference. In: J. P. Wilson & J. D. Lindy (Eds.), *Countertransference in the Treatment of PTSD* (pp. 5–30). New York: Guilford.

Winnicott, D. W. (1945). Primitive emotional development. In: *Through Paediatrics to Psychoanalysis* (pp. 145–156). London: Tavistock Publications, 1958. [Reprinted London: Karnac Books, 1992.]

Winnicott, D. W. (1952). Psychoses and child care. In: *Through Paediatrics to Psychoanalysis* (pp. 219–228). London: Tavistock Publications, 1958. [Reprinted London: Karnac Books, 1992.]

Winnicott, D. W. (1958). *Collected Papers: Through Paediatrics to Psychoanalysis*. London: Tavistock Publications. [Reprinted London: Karnac Books, 1992.]

Winnicott, D. W. (1960). The theory of the parent–infant relationship. In: *The Maturational Processes and the Facilitating Environment* (pp. 37–55). London: Hogarth Press. [Reprinted London: Karnac Books, 1990.]

Winnicott, D. W. (1963). Dependence in infant care, in child care and in the psychoanalytic setting. In: *The Maturational Processes and the Facilitating Environment* (pp. 249-259). London: Hogarth Press. [Reprinted London: Karnac Books, 1990.]

Winnicott, D. W. (1965). *The Maturational Processes and the Facilitating Environment*. London: Hogarth Press. [Reprinted London: Karnac Books, 1990.]

Winnicott, D. W. (1987). *Playing and Reality*. London: Tavistock.

Winnicott, D. W. (1989). *Psychoanalytic explorations*. London: Karnac Books.

Winship, G. (1995). Nursing and psychoanalysis—uneasy alliances? *Psychoanalytic Psychotherapy, 9* (3): 289–299.

Yehuda, R., Kahana, B., Schmeidler, J., Southwick, S. M., Wilson, S., & Giller, E. L. (1995). Impact of cumulative lifetime trauma and recent stress on current post-traumatic stress disorder symptoms in holocaust survivors. *American Journal of Psychiatry, 148* (1): 10–20.
Zapparoli, G. C., Arrigoni-Scortecci, M., Balestri, L., Borgi, L., et al. (1988). *La psichiatria oggi*. Turin: Bollati Boringhieri.

INDEX